Educational Freedom and the Case for Government Aid
to Students in Independent Schools

Educational Freedom and the Case for Government Aid to Students in Independent Schools

EDITED BY

Daniel D. McGarry
PROFESSOR OF HISTORY,
SAINT LOUIS UNIVERSITY

and

Leo Ward, C.S.C.
PROFESSOR OF PHILOSOPHY,
UNIVERSITY OF NOTRE DAME

THE BRUCE PUBLISHING COMPANY
MILWAUKEE

Library of Congress Catalog Card Number: 65-28207

© 1966 THE BRUCE PUBLISHING COMPANY
MADE IN THE UNITED STATES OF AMERICA

Introduction

The present work is the collaborative enterprise of fifteen contributors. The writers are of varying faiths and viewpoints, but they are agreed that students in independent schools should not be excluded from sharing in educational tax funds. They feel that the greatest strength of their position lies in the wisdom and justice of their cause, and the good will of their fellow citizens.

One result of mechanization, technological inventions, population increases, and international competition has been to promote socialization in some fields. Education is an area of American life that has become rapidly socialized. Until recent times most education was provided on a private and family basis. But within the past century and a half this has radically changed. Today most education is subsidized by government and its financing is considered a community responsibility.

Public financing of education is based on the principle that education is vital to the community. It has been promoted by the fact that most families find it impossible to come up with adequate savings to meet the formidable costs of first-rate education when such are due, and find it easier to pay for these gradually, over the years, throughout their entire tax-paying span, with the government as collector, trustee, and administrator. While this development has been beneficial, it has given rise to a problem. How can we become increasingly socialized, and yet retain our personal liberties and preserve educational private enterprise?

Fortunately, we can find an answer in the way other democracies have solved the problem. This is to permit enough state subsidization of independent education to allow its continued existence. Because it is considered a public benefit, education in state schools is paid for by the public. Is similar education provided in independent schools any less a public benefit? And, as such, is it not entitled to some public subsidization and encouragement?

Various aspects of this problem are studied in the present work. We first establish the historical background and philosophical bases for our position (Chapters 1–3). We see how independent schools have played a pioneering part in the history of American education, to which they have made many valuable contributions; and we also see how our failure to allow aid to independent education resulted partly from conditions prevalent when our public system of education was launched. We are reminded that our free and pluralist democratic society requires free and pluralist education. And we make an inquiry into the respective rights and roles of parents, state, and church in education.

We then obtain international perspective, and see how this problem is handled in some eighty-five other countries (Chapters 4–6). We note that in communist countries all independent education is stifled and only state schools are permitted. We observe that in most democratic countries, on the contrary, direct as well as indirect public aid is given to independent education. We examine in greater detail the systems in the Dutch Netherlands, England, Scotland, Wales, Northern Ireland, France, and Israel. We also compare Czechoslovakia under three distinct regimes: Democratic, Nazi, and Communist.

The advantages, to the common good, of aid to independent education are next presented (Chapters 7–8). The general contributions of independent education are discussed; then the economic advantages of providing public aid to independent education are presented.

The "practicability" of aid is the topic of our fourth section (Chapters 9–11). The objection that such aid would be unconstitutional is first answered with reference to our federal constitution, and is then taken up with respect to our state constitutions. After which, various other objections against aid are discussed.

In conclusion, two participants give a firsthand account of a spontaneous, "grass-roots," parents' rights movement in favor of aid to independent schools that originated in 1959 and has rapidly spread across the nation (Chapter 13). And a professional bibliographer provides a select list of readings from the large number of publications stimulated by this problem (Chapter 14).

If the present work does anything to clarify an important issue, if it helps to prevent the demise of independent education, and if it makes our fellow citizens, legislators, and judges more familiar with some of the considerations involved, the contributors will regard their efforts as well spent.

Contents

Educational Freedom and the Case for Government Aid
to Students in Independent Schools

CHAPTER I

Historical Background for Freedom in American Education

Professor William W. Brickman*

The concept of freedom is basic to education in modern democracies. One speaks of freedom of the teacher, freedom of the child, academic freedom, and freedom to read. A free society and a free world imply a free educational system and process. A totalitarian, fascist, or communist way of life presupposes a very limited type of freedom within a framework of maximum control. In such a closed society, freedom in education may consist of ability to say or do inconsequential things. By way of contrast, in a democratic society the significance of the individual and of the group is balanced for the mutual benefit of all, and the individual has the widest possible scope for developing himself, as long as he does not infringe upon the rights of others.

The history of freedom in education in the United States is linked with that of the private or independent school, which may be defined as "an educational institution, free from political control, which selects its own aims, staff, curriculum, and pupils."[1] This category comprises both secular and religious independent schools.

INDEPENDENT SCHOOLS IN COLONIAL TIMES

We find the independent school at the very beginning of our colonial history. The leading authority on the subject, Professor Robert Francis Seybolt, has called attention to the existence of private schools in Boston even before the establishment of the famous Boston Latin

---

* Professor of Educational History and Comparative Education, Graduate School of Education, University of Pennsylvania; editor: *School and Society.*

[1] William W. Brickman, "The Historical Background of the Independent School in the United States," in *The Role of the Independent School in American Democracy* (Milwaukee: Marquette University Press, 1956), p. 63.

1

School in 1635. Seybolt says, "Private teachers appeared as early as 1630, or shortly after the town was settled."[2] Later in the century more private schools were made available to those who, for one reason or other, did not attend the town schools. One interesting feature of some of the private schools was that they anticipated contemporary coeducation.

Independent schools did pioneering work in education in the colonies. According to one writer, the Collegiate School, founded in 1638 in New Amsterdam, is "the oldest existing private secondary school in the country."[3] Since the records do not reveal any appropriation prior to 1643 by the Boston authorities for any school,[4] it is even possible to regard the private school as the prototype of secondary education in America. Another early independent secondary school was the Roxbury Latin School, founded at West Roxbury, Massachusetts, in 1645, controlled by a board of trustees, and financed, in the main, by private funds and special contributions well into the nineteenth century.[5] The founding document of the Roxbury School specified that the inhabitants took the initiative "to erect a Free schoole," because they were convinced that for "their religious care of posteritie" it was necessary to provide for the education of their children in "literature" in order "to fitt them for publicke service both in Church and Commonwealth in succeeding ages."[6]

The student of colonial educational history will often find it difficult to determine whether a given school was public or private or both. The "Agreement" of the Roxbury Latin School may have spoken of a "free" school, but it is clear that the support and control were private rather than public. On the other hand, such independent schools had the aim of preparing young people for "publicke service" both in the Church and in society. This is an early example of the concept of a private school acting in the service of all the people.

Historians have pointed out the difficulty of classifying the famous

---

[2] Robert F. Seybolt, *The Private Schools of Colonial Boston* (Cambridge: Harvard University Press, 1935), p. 3.

[3] Ernest B. Chamberlain, *Our Independent Schools: The Private School in American Education* (New York: American Book Company, 1944), p. 44.

[4] "Boston Town Records," 1877, p. 82, as cited in Newton Edwards and Herman G. Richey, *The School in the American Social Order*, 2 ed. (Boston: Houghton Mifflin, 1963), pp. 55–56.

[5] Paul Monroe, *Founding of the American Public School System* (New York: Macmillan, 1940), p. 148.

[6] Quoted in Richard W. Hale, Jr., *Tercentenary History of the Roxbury Latin School, 1645–1945* (Cambridge: Riverside, 1946), p. 2.

Boston Latin School, or those in Ipswich, Salem, Dorchester, Dedham, and elsewhere, as public or private.[7] Professor Bailyn has emphasized that "the modern concept of public education, the very idea of a clean line of separation between 'private' and 'public,' was unknown before the end of the eighteenth century."[8] Harvard College, founded in 1636, received financial aid from both public and private sources, but developed as an independent institution. Among other private secondary schools important in the early development of American education were the Hopkins Grammar School of New Haven (1660) and the William Penn Charter School of Philadelphia (1689).

During the eighteenth century, independent schools grew in number, type, and influence. There was a rapid transformation of society and institutions, with new emphases on industry, commerce, philosophy, and political theory. As a result, people looked for new educational content which would be correlated with the demands of the century. For example, a modern kind of vocational training was desired, and this need was fulfilled by private schools. Interestingly, these schools taught more than vocational subject matter; their course of study also included general subjects. In the words of Seybolt, the private vocational schools were "the most popular of all schools of secondary grade throughout the eighteenth century."[9] There was freedom to learn what anyone wanted and needed for his own development.

The very independence of the private schools made it possible for them to be more flexible and to offer a greater variety of subject matter, such as might rarely be taught in a town school. Professor Seybolt, who has examined carefully the colonial press, cites advertisements of schools which promised to teach many subjects. Thus, in 1709, Owen Harris' private school in Boston offered astronomy, geometry, navigation, surveying, and trigonometry. Isaac Greenwood, author of *Arithmetick, Vulgar and Decimal* and the first Hollis Professor of Mathematics at Harvard College, taught algebra and conic sections in 1727, and mechanics, optics, and astronomy in 1738–1739. Nathan Prince opened a private school in Boston in 1742, with courses

---

[7] E.g., I. L. Kandel, *History of Secondary Education* (Boston: Houghton Mifflin, 1930), pp. 112–113.

[8] Bernard Bailyn, *Education in the Forming of American Society* (Chapel Hill: University of North Carolina Press, 1960), p. 11. See also pp. 107–109.

[9] Robert F. Seybolt, *Source Studies in American Colonial Education: The Private School*, Bulletin No. 28, Bureau of Educational Research, College of Education, University of Illinois (Urbana: The University of Illinois, 1925), p. 53.

in mathematical subjects, geography, fortifications, and gunnery.

The growing cosmopolitan complexion of the colonies, as well as the rising interest in overseas and foreign trade, was no doubt responsible, in part at least, for the number of languages taught. Latin, Greek, and Hebrew were offered as a matter of course. Other languages in which one could obtain instruction in private schools were French, "for the children of the late seventeenth century emigrés,"[10] Portuguese, Italian, and even Celtic. One school, operated by Michael C. Knoll in New York City, could boast in 1750 of teaching French, Greek, Hebrew, Latin, and philosophy.[11]

From the standpoint of a land of democratic opportunity, the independent schools were ideal institutions. "Many youths, who wanted to engage in one or another of the business enterprises of the day, or who desired to cultivate a certain refinement of taste, found it necessary to turn away from the town schools and seek a more practical education elsewhere. The need for a type of education that was more functional was met by the private teacher."[12]

Another area of contribution by independent education was the evening school, the early beginnings of which were around the middle of the seventeenth century. The breadth of the offerings may be discerned in the following courses available in private evening schools before 1750: astronomy, bookkeeping, ethics, French, geography, German, Greek, Hebrew, history, Latin, logic, mathematics, metaphysics, natural philosophy, rhetoric, and surveying.[13]

Many young people in the eighteenth century enrolled in evening schools because they had to work during the day and could not, therefore, attend publicly supported schools. The availability of the private evening school furnished such persons freedom of opportunity to better their position without regard to their socioeconomic origins.

To protect the public, schoolmasters were required to obtain permission to practice their art. Thus, all teachers in grammar schools were required by the Massachusetts Legislature in 1701 to "be approved by the ministers of the town, and the ministers of the two next adjacent towns, or any two of them, by certificate under their

[10] Seybolt, *Source Studies in American Colonial Education: The Private School, op. cit.,* p. 10.
[11] *New York Gazette,* August 6, 13, 1750, as cited *ibid.,* p. 13.
[12] Edwards and Richey, *op. cit.,* p. 108.
[13] Robert F. Seybolt, *The Evening School in Colonial America,* Bulletin No. 24, Bureau of Educational Research, College of Education, University of Illinois (Urbana: The University of Illinois, 1925), p. 32.

hands."[14] A decade later the legislature ordered that "no person shall or may presume to set up or keep a school for the teaching and instructing of children or youth in reading, writing, or any other science, but such as are of sober and good conversation, and have the allowance and approbation of the selectmen of the town in which any such school is to be kept; grammar-school masters to have approbation as the law in such case already provides."[15] These laws made no distinction between public and private teachers.

The demands of the later eighteenth century were also partly met by the "academy" movement.[16] This new type of colonial education was independent, even though Cubberley labors to identify the academies as "semi-public" and "semi-private."[17] The academy was in a position to offer instruction in any subject for which students could be found. The extent of the possibilities might be inferred from Benjamin Franklin's educational proposals, published two years before the opening of his academy in 1751 in Philadelphia, in which the "most useful and most ornamental studies"[18] were to be taught. Franklin's Academy and Charitable School, financed by private and public funds, was the precursor of the University of Pennsylvania.[19]

Other early academies of note were the Governor Dummer Academy, South Byfield, Massachusetts (1761), Phillips Andover (1778), Phillips Exeter (1783), and the Deerfield Academy (1797). Of interest to students of the history of education was the founding in 1785 of the Zion-Parnassus Academy, near Salisbury, North Carolina, by the Reverend Samuel Eusebius McCorkle.[20] Besides combining religious with classical studies, McCorkle, who was also one of the founding fathers of the University of North Carolina, added teacher training

[14] "Acts and Resolves of the Province of Massachusetts Bay," I. 470, as cited in Seybolt, *The Private Schools of Colonial Boston, op. cit.*, pp. 91–92.

[15] "Acts and Resolves of the Province of Massachusetts Bay," I. 681–682, as cited in *ibid.*, p. 91.

[16] See Edgar W. Knight, *The Academy Movement in the South* (Chapel Hill: School of Education, University of North Carolina, 1918); George F. Miller, *The Academy System of the State of New York* (Albany: University of the State of New York, 1922); Harriet W. Marr, *The Old New England Academies Founded before 1826* (New York: Comet Press, 1959).

[17] Ellwood P. Cubberley, *Public Education in the United States*, rev. ed. (Boston: Houghton Mifflin, 1934), pp. 112, 245.

[18] Benjamin Franklin, *Proposals Relating to the Education of Youth in Pennsylvania*, reprint edition (Philadelphia: University of Pennsylvania Press, 1931), p. 11.

[19] Saul Sack, *History of Higher Education in Pennsylvania*, Vol. I (Harrisburg: Pennsylvania Historical and Museum Commission, 1963), pp. 264–269.

[20] J. F. Hurley and J. G. Eagan, *The Prophet of Zion-Parnassus: Samuel Eusebius McCorkle* (Richmond, Va.: The Authors, 1934).

to his course of study, thus becoming a pioneer in teacher education in the United States.

RELIGION IN EDUCATION IN COLONIAL TIMES

Religion was considered an essential element in education in colonial times. Most of the early colonial communities had "established" churches, and their schools were "church related" as well as "public." These schools naturally inculcated the religion and morals ascendant in their practically homogeneous society, and public authorities openly declared the religious as well as secular purposes of their schools. A law passed by the General Court of Massachusetts in 1647 required towns to provide instruction, elementary and grammatical, in order to defeat the efforts of "that ould deluder Satan to keep men from the knowledge of ye Scriptures." The religion inculcated in the community schools was generally a Protestant brand of Christianity, such as Calvinism in New Amsterdam and most of the New England states, Anglicanism in New York and many of the southern colonies, and Quakerism in Pennsylvania.[21]

Even where denominational uniformity was absent, the vast majority of the population were Protestant Christians. Thus their religious wants in education could be partly satisfied by avoiding controversial points, stressing agreement on the value of the Bible and the errors of Romish Papism, and using readings from a Protestant version of the Bible, along with scriptural prayers, and popular Protestant Christian hymns.

On the other hand, minority groups, such as Catholics, Jews, Lutherans, and Christian Reformed, frequently conducted their own schools wherever possible. At Newtown, Maryland, a Catholic elementary school was established by about 1640, and a secondary school by about 1677.[22] In the 1680's, the Jesuits opened a school in New York City. Minhat Areb, the first Jewish parochial school in New York City, was opened in 1731, providing instruction in religion, Hebrew, and (by 1755) Spanish, as well as the elementary "three R's."[23] By 1750, all but one of the Lutheran congregations in Pennsylvania had parochial

---

[21] Thomas Woody, *Early Quaker Education in Pennsylvania* (New York: Teachers College, Columbia University, 1920).

[22] James A. Burns, *The Catholic School System in the United States* (New York: Benziger, 1908), p. 92. An excellent history of Catholic education in this country is James A. Burns and Bernard J. Kohlbrenner, *A History of Catholic Education in the United States* (New York: Benziger, 1937).

[23] Alexander M. Dushkin, *Jewish Education in New York City* (New York: Bureau of Jewish Education, 1918), pp. 40, 73.

schools, and by 1800 the number of Lutheran schools in the country approached 200. Similarly the Christian Reformed Churches by 1800 had no less than 188 schools.

Catholics made schools a regular part of their missionary establishments, as well as a common annex to their permanent parishes. Education was promoted from the beginning in Spanish and French colonies in North America. The earliest school in the present United States is said to have been a Catholic classical school opened in 1606 at St. Augustine, Florida. In the missionary field, several Catholic schools were already in existence in the New Mexico territory in 1630, according to a report made that year. Missionary work among the Indians in Texas, begun in 1689, proceeded along similar lines. The same was true of missions in Spanish (Upper) California, established a century later. Besides the mission schools for the Indians, schools for the children of Spanish soldiers and settlers were opened in San Antonio, Texas, in 1789, and in San José, California, in 1795.

Similar schools were opened in French Catholic territories. In 1722, when New Orleans had no more than 300 inhabitants, a school was conducted there by a Capuchin Father. And in 1727, ten Ursuline Sisters arrived in New Orleans and set up a school, thus becoming the first professional women teachers on our soil. By 1788, there were six schools in New Orleans. Meanwhile Catholic schools were established in the tiny French settlements of St. Louis (by 1774) and Vincennes, Indiana (by 1786). In Maine, there was a Capuchin school for Indians by 1640.

In the English colonies along the Atlantic seaboard, as early as 1767, Catholics established enduring schools such as that connected with St. Mary's Church in Philadelphia, which became a "prototype" for the parochial school system in the United States.

THE CONSTITUTION AND FREEDOM
OF EDUCATION

At the time our Constitution was adopted, religion was definitely included in the pattern of American society and education. Thus the Northwest Ordinance of 1787 proclaimed that "Religion, morality, and knowledge, being necessary to good government and the happiness of mankind, schools and the means of education shall forever be encouraged." Similar sentiments, in more or less identical language, were expressed in several early state constitutions and laws. Legislation provided for grants of public tracts of land not only for education but also "perpetually for the purposes of religion," and it was obvious that people were willing to support a program of education *with* religion.

Although the United States Constitution has little to say about religion, what it does say is concerned with *freedom* of religion. The part of the First Amendment that says "Congress shall make no law respecting an establishment of religion" has been interpreted by some as setting up "a wall of separation between church and state." But the following part that adds "or prohibiting the free exercise thereof" has not been sufficiently explicated with reference to religious education. The opinion that the idea of rigid separation to the extent of exclusion permeated the fabric of American public opinion at the time of the founding of our country is obviously erroneous. Thus, for example, Governor Samuel Adams, on January 16, 1794, recommended to the legislature of Massachusetts that it establish "such modes of education as tend to inculcate in the minds of youth the feelings and habits of piety, religion, and morality. . . ."[24]

INDEPENDENT SCHOOLS IN THE NINETEENTH CENTURY

Independent schools continued to make important contributions in the nineteenth century. Private initiative brought about the establishment of the Free School Society (1805 ff.) in New York City. This organization helped to provide for instruction in "charity schools" from 1806 to 1853, when, under the name of the Public School Society, it turned over its schools to the Board of Education of New York City. The change of name from "Free" to "Public" in 1826 did not modify the private nature of the Society, which at the conclusion of its existence had provided 1200 teachers for the education of over 600,000 children in 115 schools.[25] Here, again, private activity promoted the public welfare and acted as a stimulus to the development of the public school. In Philadelphia, in 1827, the Society for the Promotion of Public Schools undertook a similar program. Children in other cities, such as Baltimore, Providence, and Washington, were also

---

[24] Quoted in Elizabeth B. Cowley, *Free Learning* (Boston: Bruce Humphreys, 1941), p. 28.

[25] William O. Bourne, *History of the Public School Society of the City of New York* (New York: Wood, 1869).

aided by the emergence of private philanthropic groups which organized and maintained schools.

The "monitorial" system of instruction, introduced by Joseph Lancaster into the United States in 1806, which made possible the teaching of up to 1000 children in a single classroom through the use of pupil-assistants, was used in the schools of the Free School Society in New York City and elsewhere.[26]

Private initiative was also instrumental in fostering teacher training. Mention has already been made of the work of Samuel Eusebius McCorkle. The Reverend Samuel Read Hall, author of the first native textbook on teaching, opened a private normal school in 1823 at Concord, Vermont. Four years later James Gordon Carter, an educational leader and scholar, established one at Lancaster, Massachusetts. These served as precedents and examples for the organization of public normal schools (1839 ff.).

In the field of adult education the most influential type of instruction was carried on by the "Lyceum." The first organization of this kind was set up on 1826 by Josiah Holbrook in Millbury, Massachusetts. A circular issued by Holbrook proclaimed that the American Lyceum was designed "for the improvement of its members in useful knowledge, and the advancement of popular education, by introducing uniformity and improvements in common schools, by becoming auxiliary to a board of education."[27] The significance of this voluntary body for the advancement of public education in America was pointed up in 1864 by Henry Barnard, when he stated that no organization "created so great and beneficent results as the American Lyceum."[28]

Independent schools were likewise pioneers in "modern," "progressive" education. A gymnasium was one of the features of the Round Hill School, founded at Northhampton, Massachusetts, in 1823 by George Bancroft, the historian, and Joseph Green Cogswell, the bibliographical scholar, who said, "We are deeply impressed with the necessity of uniting physical and moral education."[29] The pedagogical ideas and practices of Johann Heinrich Pestalozzi were propagated by A.

---

[26] John F. Reigart, *The Lancasterian System of Instruction in the Schools of New York City* (New York: Teachers College, Columbia University, 1916).

[27] Quoted in Cecil B. Hayes, *The American Lyceum: Its History and Contribution to Education.* Bulletin 12, 1932, U. S. Office of Education (Washington, D. C.: U. S. Government Printing Office, 1932), p. 3.

[28] Henry Barnard, *American Journal of Education*, XIV (1864), 535.

[29] Joseph Cogswell and George Bancroft, *Some Account of the School for the Liberal Education of Boys Established on Round Hill* (Northhampton, 1826).

Bronson Alcott in his school at Chesire, Connecticut (1825) and in his Temple School at Boston (1834–1839). Toward the end of the century, the Laboratory School established by John Dewey at the University of Chicago in 1896 was a progenitor of many of the experimental schools of the twentieth century. This was "a first-rate school run by a first-rate staff . . . (with) ample evidence that most of the children learned and learned well."[30]

The kindergarten movement represents another effort by private individuals to pioneer in educational work. Beginning with the German-speaking kindergarten inaugurated in 1856 by Mrs. Carl Schurz in Watertown, Wisconsin, the movement grew under the additional leadership of Miss Caroline L. Frankenburg (Columbus, Ohio, 1858) and Miss Elizabeth Palmer Peabody (Boston, 1860). Mrs. Matilde Kriege opened a private training school for kindergarten teachers in 1868 in Boston, while Miss Marie Boelte did likewise in 1872 in New York City. The first public kindergarten does not appear until 1873, when Miss Susan Blow, a disciple of Miss Boelte, was invited by William Torrey Harris, superintendent of schools in St. Louis, to inaugurate the system there.[31]

The private schools of Mrs. Emma Hart Willard in Connecticut and Vermont, and particularly her Troy Female Seminary, founded in 1821, which emphasized classical studies and teacher training, made a notable contribution to the advancement of the education of girls and women. In a similar way, Miss Mary Lyon, who founded Mt. Holyoke Seminary in 1837, promoted the idea of depth in female education.[32]

Finally, there is a variety of private educational pioneering which took place during the century and which can only be mentioned most briefly: the experiment by Miss Prudence Crandall with biracial education in her school at Canterbury, Connecticut, 1833–1838; the first school for blind children opened by John Fisher in 1832 in Boston; the first school for deaf-mute children organized in 1817 in Hartford;

---

[30] Lawrence A. Cremin, *The Transformation of the School: Progressivism in American Education, 1876–1957* (New York: Knopf, 1961), pp. 141, 142.

[31] Nina C. Vandewalker, *The Kindergarten in American Education* (New York: Macmillan, 1908).

[32] Thomas Woody, *A History of Women's Education in the United States,* 2 vols. (New York: Science Press, 1929).

and the successful experiment by the Monson, Massachusetts, Academy at midcentury with the education of young students from China.[33]

RELIGION IN EDUCATION IN THE
NINETEENTH CENTURY

Many public schools in the nineteenth century continued to inculcate religion, with views and principles, prayers and practices of the Protestant Christian variety. Readings from the Protestant version of the Bible were common, as were Protestant prayers and hymns. Observance of holy days accepted by Protestants was practiced, and presentations of history that reinforced the Protestant outlook prevailed. Protestant teachers were also generally preferred.

Protestantism in the public schools was strongest in rural and less cosmopolitan communities. In many larger cities, because of a bewildering variety of sects, and in accordance with a contemporary trend of "enlightenment," particular creeds and organized religions were often contemned in favor of neutralism, secularism, humanism, pragmatism, skepticism, deism, or even atheism. Meanwhile religious denominations that agreed neither with the tenuous amount of Protestant Christianity offered in some public schools, nor with the total neglect of religion in others, continued to operate and to found schools.

Although schools on all levels were conducted by religious groups, the greatest unanimity, as well as the greatest diversity of sponsorship, was found in higher learning. Most denominations were intent upon establishing colleges and universities, to serve partly as nurseries for religious leaders, and partly as preservers of the faith of their members who were becoming more educated.

Thus church-affiliated colleges multiplied, and long accounted for the greater part of higher education in this country. Practically all of our early colleges and universities established in colonial times were church-connected: Harvard was Puritan; William and Mary, Anglican; Yale, Congregational; Princeton, Presbyterian; King's College (now Columbia), Anglican; Brown, Baptist; Rutgers, Reformed Dutch; Dartmouth, Congregational. Similar institutions multiplied throughout the country in the nineteenth century.

Although a very small minority, Catholics[34] founded thirty-eight

---

[33] Yung Wing, *My Life in China and America* (New York: Holt, 1909).
[34] For Catholic education in the nineteenth century, see James A. Burns and Bernard J. Kohlbrenner, *op. cit.*

colleges for men between 1789 and 1850, together with numerous academies for women. Among the colleges for men, thirty still survive. The earliest was Georgetown College in Washington, D. C., founded in 1789. Examples of others were Spring Hill College in Alabama and St. Louis University, the first university west of the Mississippi.

The principle was gradually established that each Catholic parish should, if possible, have a school. Various teaching orders of women and men came to this country from Europe to staff Catholic educational institutions, while several native orders of Sisters arose to meet local needs. The First Catholic Provincial Council, held at Baltimore in 1829, declared: "We judge it absolutely necessary that schools be established, in which the young may be taught the principles of faith and morality, while being instructed in letters."

During the early decades of the nineteenth century, the idea was fairly widespread that education was almost entirely a concern of parents. But toward the middle of the century, the impression grew that education was mainly, even solely, a concern of the state. One reason urged was the need for "Americanizing" the families of immigrants. Such parents were often deemed incapable of directing the education of their children, even as working partners of the state.

Meanwhile, the public schools, now catering to more diverse elements, were obliged to become less concerned with religion and more secularized, especially in the large cities. Meanwhile, too, various influences contributed to a surge of prejudices against Catholics, who were immigrating to the country in increasing numbers. Catholics were often regarded as indigent, benighted undesirables, and designated, along with Jews and Negroes, as interlopers, weakening American society. Such sentiments led to the formation of various extreme groups which stressed "native Americanism" as opposed to "foreign" influences. Among such were the Native American Party, organized in New York in 1835; the so-called Know Nothing movement, organized in New York in 1852; the American Protective Association, formed in Clinton, Iowa, in 1887; and later the second Ku Klux Klan, which began in Georgia in 1915.*

---

* The first Ku Klux Klan, which was concerned primarily with preserving as much of the old order as possible during Reconstruction days in the South, originated as a social club at Pulaski, Tennessee, in the fall of 1865. It was disbanded by 1877. The second Ku Klux Klan, which was antiforeign, anti-Catholic, and anti-Jewish, was founded at Atlanta, Georgia, by William Joseph Simmons in 1915.

In early New York city and state, needy denominational schools received public support along with fully public schools. As early as 1795, the Common School Fund of New York State provided for public funds to denominational charity schools: Protestant, Catholic, and Jewish. In 1796, this arrangement was extended, and in 1801 the New York State Legislature divided the School Fund of New York City among its various religious denominations. Until 1824, these schools shared in public educational funds.

But new attitudes and movements, coupled with the fear of public school educational leaders that dividing the tax money would weaken their position, combined to cause first the city of New York and finally the New York State Legislature to withdraw subsidization from all but fully public schools. Efforts of Bishop John Hughes of New York to obtain a "fair share" of tax funds for Catholic schools failed in the 1840's. One of the results of this struggle was an adverse state constitutional amendment designed to cut off Catholic and other denominational schools from participating in public educational funds. At a time when public opinion throughout the country was unfavorable to Catholics, New York's decision was imitated in other states, and the New York pattern became general throughout the country, even to the extent of being written into several state constitutions.

Besides the New York plan of public subsidization of denominational schools, other local plans of public support were temporarily put into effect elsewhere, as at Lowell, Massachusetts, from 1831 to 1852; Poughkeepsie, New York, from 1873 to 1898; and Faribault and Stillwater, Minnesota, from 1891 to 1893. But these isolated examples lacked widespread roots or the support of state legislation, and did not endure.

One reason for the failure of such plans was a general despair of obtaining public funds. Another was political apathy. Another was a comparable abundance of private funds and liberal bequests, in a day when public taxes were minimal and educational expenses low, and at a time when the economy was expanding. Catholics in particular were able to operate their schools on small budgets because of the donated services of religious orders. And many Catholic bishops feared excessive state control in case their schools were to share in public funds.

After losing his bid for public support in New York City, Bishop John Hughes resigned himself to having Catholics rely on their own devices to support their schools, and adopted the maxim: "Let parochial schools be established and maintained everywhere; the days have come, and the place, in which the school is more necessary than the church."

This view was given official sanction by the Third Plenary Catholic Council of Baltimore (1884), which said: "Near each Church, where it does not exist, a parochial school is to be erected within two years from the promulgation of this Council, and is to be maintained *in perpetuum*, unless the bishop, on account of grave difficulties, judges that a postponement be allowed." This decree was the culmination of a growing tradition. The statement of the First Provincial Council of Baltimore (1829) has been quoted. The First Plenary Council of Baltimore (1852) declared: "We exhort the bishops, and in view of the very grave evils which usually result from the defective education of youth, we beseech them through the bowels of the mercy of God, to see that schools be established in connection with all the churches of their diocese. . . ." The Second Plenary Council of Baltimore (1866) urged: "in every diocese, schools — each close to the church — should be erected, in which the Catholic youth may be instructed in letters and the noble arts as well as in religion and sound morals."

Besides devoting one fourth of its decrees to education, the Third Plenary Council of Baltimore (1884) declared: "we not only exhort Catholic parents with paternal love, but we also command them with all the authority in our power, to procure for their beloved offspring, given to them by God, reborn in Christ in baptism, and destined for heaven, a truly Christian and Catholic education. . . ."

Despite difficulties and financial hardships, Catholic schools continued to multiply. Initially led by their bishops, Catholic parents came to see the great value of their schools in the upbringing of their children, and to be enthusiastic in their support and defense. On the elementary level, for example, in 1883 there were 2491 Catholic parochial schools in the United States; by 1933 this number had increased to 7462; by 1960 to 10,501. Schools of some other denominations likewise multiplied.

CONSTITUTIONAL QUESTIONS IN THE NINETEENTH CENTURY

The great educational statesman, Horace Mann, in one of his annual reports as secretary of the Board of Education of Massachusetts, said: "Children are not educated for themselves alone, nor for their parents alone; but also for the State, for the country and the world."[35] This viewpoint was influential in the theory underlying the Massachusetts Law of 1852, the first legislation in the United States requiring school attendance on a compulsory basis. There can be no doubt of the significance of this legislation for Massachusetts and as a precedent for other states.

The law of 1852 stated that "every person who shall have any child under his control, between the ages of eight and fourteen years, shall send such child to some public school within the town or city in which he resides, during at least twelve weeks."[36] Section 4, however, provided that if a person's child "has been otherwise furnished with the means of education for a like period of time, or has already acquired those branches of learning which are taught in common schools . . . then such person shall be held not to have violated the provisions of this act."[37]

An indirect result of the law of 1852, together with the Massachusetts law of 1855 which required compulsory Bible reading every day in the public schools in the state, was that it "made religion in the schools compulsory in the sense in which it had not been before, but this could be avoided by attending private schools."[38] This would be a solution for parents with financial means; but those who could not afford private school fees were compelled by law to have their children absorb religious doctrines to which they were opposed.

When we keep in mind the First Amendment, it appears that the rights of some citizens to freedom of religion were violated. By the nature of the population and the political leadership, children who were not Protestant would be exposed to alien teachings.

It is significant that "after 1855 the public schools, including elementary, high, and normal schools, soon dropped all religious content except the daily Bible reading and devotional exercises, for which there was strong local support, with the addition of moral instruction

[35] Horace Mann, *Eighth Annual Report of the Secretary of the Board of Education* (Boston, 1844), as quoted in Edgar W. Knight, *Readings in Educational Administration* (New York: Holt, 1953), p. 209.

[36] *Ibid.*, p. 229.

[37] *Ibid.*, p. 230.

[38] Sherman M. Smith, *The Relation of the State to Religious Education in Massachusetts* (Syracuse: Syracuse University Book Store, 1926), p. 319.

based on Christianity, but not taught as religion."[39] Still, the public schools of Massachusetts remained Protestant in atmosphere and in content.

The situation in Massachusetts was in line with what was taking place all over the country. The people of Massachusetts were trying to do two contradictory things at one and the same time: to prohibit public support to religious schools, and to safeguard the teachings of Christianity in the public schools — all in the name of a "wall of separation" between church and state.

In 1853, the Catholics of Detroit petitioned the state legislature for a portion of the public school fund to be allotted to their schools. They argued that, "notwithstanding the Constitution guarantees liberty of conscience to every citizen of the State, yet our Public School laws compel us to violate our conscience, or deprive us unjustly of our share of the Public School Funds, and also impose on us taxes for the support of schools, which, as a matter of conscience, we cannot allow our children to attend."[40] The petitioners declared that: "schools can be free only when the business of school teaching be placed on the same legal footing as the other learned professions, when all may teach who will, their success depending, as in other cases, on their fitness for their profession, and the satisfaction that they may render to the public; that in all cases the parent be left free to choose the teacher to whom he will entrust the education of his child."[41]

Decades later in Wisconsin, a well-known case involving the protest by Catholic parents that their child was compelled to listen to King James Bible readings in a public school was settled by the Wisconsin Supreme Court in 1890 through a writ of mandamus preventing the teaching of the Bible. According to the court, compulsory Bible reading, "although unaccompanied by any comment on the part of the teacher, is 'instruction,'"[42] and hence unconstitutional. Moreover, pupils who had to attend public schools on account of parental poverty, would be attending a place of worship, also unconstitutionally, if Bible readings were allowed.

[39] *Ibid.*, p. 320.

[40] "Report of the Superintendent of Public Instruction for Michigan, 1853," as quoted in Knight, *Readings in Educational Administration*, p. 413.

[41] *Ibid.*

[42] *State ex rel. Weiss et al.* v. *District School Board of Edgerton*, 76 Wis. 177 (1890), as quoted in Mark de Wolfe Howe, compiler, *Cases on Church and State in the United States* (Cambridge: Harvard University Press, 1952), p. 332.

In other instances, Jewish and Protestant groups likewise raised their voices against such compulsion.[43] In the words of two Protestant scholars, "Religious instruction in the public schools, whether it consists of reading the Bible, singing hymns, or offering prayer, is, in respect to the taxpayer, a coerced support of religion. Such instruction, especially if it is compulsory, is incompatible with the principles of religious liberty and freedom of conscience."[44]

THE TWENTIETH CENTURY AND INDEPENDENT SCHOOLS

For the twentieth century it is impossible to do more than sketch highlights in the development of the private school. The movements relating to the country day school, the junior college, technical education, remedial reading, foreign languages, and the like received much aid from independent institutions. Progressive schools, such as the Francis W. Parker School, which existed for more than three decades after its foundation in 1901 in Chicago, had an impact on both public and private education. Among other noteworthy "progressive" institutions were the City and Country, Dalton, Ethical Culture, Hessian Hills, Lincoln, and Walden Schools.

The private school in the twentieth century "functions as a center of religious education, a college-preparatory institution, a junior military academy, a substitute for home in the case of children coming from broken homes, and a locale for experimental techniques in education. It teaches individuals, both the brilliant and the slow; it welcomes pupils without means and offers special opportunities; it prepares for vocations and semiprofessions; and it remakes character. Basically, the independent school in the twentieth century aims for culture, religion, leadership, scholarship, and character. Such aims and functions bear witness to the meaning of the independent school for the country's culture and welfare."[45]

The rapid growth of religious schools within the independent school movement has been a phenomenon of the twentieth century. To some extent this might be attributed to the revival of religious concern at various times during the century. Other reasons include over-

[43] Anson Phelps Stokes, *Church and State in the United States,* Vol. II (New York: Harper, 1950), pp. 568–571.

[44] Alvin W. Johnson and Frank H. Yost, *Separation of Church and State in the United States* (Minneapolis: University of Minnesota Press, 1948), p. 72.

[45] Brickman, *op. cit.,* p. 75.

crowding and occasional shortcomings in public schools, as well as parental displeasure at the growing secularist atmosphere and amoral tone of the public school.

Between 1937 and 1952, Protestant day-school enrollment rose by 60 percent.[46] In one denomination, the Christian Reformed (Calvinist), the increase in the number of day-school pupils was about 120 percent from 1918 to 1949.[47] Catholic high school registration went up by 259.8 percent between 1920 and 1947.[48] The percentage of church-related secondary schools to the total number of nonpublic secondary schools rose from 47.8 in 1899–1900 to 80.3 in 1932–1933, and to 82.1 in 1940–1941, but fell somewhat to 80.5 in 1960–1961.[49] The registration in Jewish day schools increased from 9000 in 1944 to over 35,000 in 1956 and to more than 52,000 in 1964.[50]

Supporting the growth and development of denominational schools was the famous Oregon decision by the United States Supreme Court in 1925, which upheld parental freedom in education. Another important factor was the decision by Roman Catholic bishops at the Third Plenary Council in 1884 at Baltimore to establish a parochial school in every parish and to require Catholic parents to enroll their children in these schools. But according to a Catholic scholar, the remarkable rise in registration in the Catholic school system resulted "more from the private convictions of thousands of individuals than from the coercive force of law."[51] Canon 1379 of the *Code of Canon Law*, which went into effect in 1918, required bishops to establish elementary or secondary schools where needed. Whatever the reasons, there is ample evidence that there has been a "renaissance" of religious schools in the twentieth century, and that these now constitute a significant segment of the total educational effort in the United States.

[46] *Information Service*, National Council of the Churches of Christ in America, May 3, 1952.

[47] *Christian School Annual* (Grand Rapids, Mich.: National Union of Christian Schools, 1949), p. 53.

[48] Sister Mary Janet, *Catholic Secondary Education: A National Survey* (Washington, D. C.: National Catholic Welfare Conference, 1949), pp. 11–13.

[49] Diane B. Gertler, *Statistics of Nonpublic Secondary Schools, 1960–1961: Type of School, Enrollment, and Staff*, Circular No. 707, U. S. Office of Education (Washington, D. C.: U. S. Government Printing Office, 1963), pp. 4 and 14.

[50] Joseph Kaminetsky, "The Hebrew Day School Movement," in *School and Society*, Vol. 82, October 1, 1955.

[51] Gerard S. Sloyan, "Roman Catholic Religious Education," in Marvin J. Taylor, editor, *Religious Education: A Comprehensive Survey* (New York: Abingdon Press, 1960), p. 402.

THE CONSTITUTIONAL ISSUE IN THE
TWENTIETH CENTURY

We will now glance at certain constitutional and legal aspects of educational freedom in the United States in the twentieth century. The decision by the United States Supreme Court in the case of *Reuben Quick Bear* v. *Leupp* in 1908 was relevant to the question of educational freedom. Some Sioux Indians, opposing the use of federal money for Catholic schools on their reservation in South Dakota, claimed a violation by the Commissioner of Indian Affairs of the appropriation law of 1897, according to which the "settled policy" of the Government was "to hereafter make no appropriation whatever for education in any sectarian school." The ruling of the Supreme Court was that "we cannot concede the proposition that Indians cannot be allowed to use their own money to educate their own children in the schools of their own choice because the government is necessarily undenominational. . . ."[52]

The story of educational freedom in the courts was characterized by alternate gains and losses. In 1921, the Georgia Supreme Court ruled that a city law providing for the compulsory reading of the King James Bible and for compulsory prayer did not infringe upon the religious freedom of Catholic and Jewish pupils in the public schools.[53] The United States Supreme Court, in the case of *Meyer* v. *Nebraska* (1923), declared that a state law forbidding instruction in German interfered with parental freedom to educate children. Invalidating the Nebraska law, passed in 1919 as a reaction to the war, prohibiting the teaching of any subject in elementary school in any language other than English, the Court emphasized that "it is the natural duty of the parent to give his children education suitable to their station in life."[54] The Court went on to explain: "the legislature has attempted materially to interfere with the calling of modern language teachers, with the opportunities of pupils to acquire knowledge, and with the power of parents to control the education of their young."[55]

---

[52] *Reuben Quick Bear* v. *Leupp*, 210 U.S. 50 (1908), as quoted in Clark Spurlock, *Education and the Supreme Court* (Urbana: University of Illinois Press, 1955), p. 75.
[53] *Wilkerson* v. *City of Rome*, 152 Ga. 763 (1921).
[54] *Meyer* v. *Nebraska*, 262 U.S. 390 (1923), as quoted in John J. McGrath, editor, *Church and State in American Law: Cases and Materials* (Milwaukee: Bruce, 1962), p. 74.
[55] *Ibid.*

An even more dramatic instance of the sustaining of parental authority and educational freedom by the United States Supreme Court was the Oregon or *Pierce* v. *Society of Sisters* case (1925), in which the Court held unanimously that a state law forcing parents to enroll their children in public schools exclusively was contrary to the Constitution. In an oft-quoted passage, the Court asserted that: "the fundamental theory of liberty upon which all Governments in this Union repose excludes any general power of the State to standardize its children by forcing them to accept instruction from public teachers only. The child is not the mere creature of the State; those who nurture him and direct his destiny have the right, coupled with the high duty, to recognize and prepare him for additional obligations."[56]

Another instance of protection of freedom in education by the United States Supreme Court was the decision in *Farrington* v. *Tokushige* (1927) which declared invalid a territorial law in Hawaii for the control of church-related schools in which instruction was given in the Chinese, Japanese, and Korean languages. This law was unconstitutional, said the Court, because "it would deprive parents of fair opportunity to procure for their children instruction which they think important. . . ."[57]

In 1930, the United States Supreme Court by a unanimous decision in *Cochran* v. *Louisiana* upheld a decision by the Supreme Court of Louisiana permitting the use of state-owned textbooks by pupils attending parochial schools, because "the school children and the state alone are the beneficiaries."[58]

Relevant to the idea of freedom in education was the opportunity for needy students, including those studying at denominational colleges and universities, to be paid with public funds for work projects carried out under the direction of the National Youth Administration, established in 1935.

The principle of equal treatment of public and nonpublic school pupils was also recognized by the G.I. *Bill of Rights* of 1944 and the *National School Lunch Act* of 1946. The federal government seemed to be slowly gaining momentum in broadening the educational opportunities of all its citizens. But it began to hesitate. The *National De-*

---

[56] *Pierce et al.* v. *Society of Sisters*, 268 U.S. 510 (1925), *ibid.*, p. 80.

[57] *Farrington* v. *Tokushige*, 273 U.S. 284 (1927), as quoted in Spurlock, *op. cit.*, p. 174.

[58] *Cochran* v. *Louisiana State Board of Education*, 281 U.S. 370 (1930), as quoted in McGrath, *op. cit.*, p. 102.

fense Education Act of 1958 made grants to public schools, but only loans to parochial schools for the improvement of instruction in mathematics, modern foreign languages, and the sciences. Partial remission of loans as well as other advantages were conceded only to teachers in public schools. However, most of these inequities were later corrected. Independent and state institutions, except for junior colleges, were treated alike in the *Higher Education Facilities Act* of 1963, as well as in other federal legislation.

In 1947, the Supreme Court, by a five to four decision in the *Everson* case, declared that New Jersey's provision of bus transportation was constitutional. The majority opinion, as expressed by Mr. Justice Black, stated that the New Jersey law permitting public transportation for parochial school pupils did not constitute "the slightest breach" of the wall of separation between church and state. "We cannot say that the First Amendment prohibits New Jersey from spending tax-raised funds to pay the bus fares of parochial school pupils as part of a general program under which it pays the fares of pupils attending public and other schools."[59] This decision gave recognition to the principle that pupils in nonpublic schools can be included in programs of "general welfare" for children.

Although the Supreme Court's *McCollum* decision (1948)[60] prohibited "released time" for religious instruction by various denominations *on* school property during school hours in the school district of Champaign, Illinois, its decision in the *Zorach* case (1952) allowed "dismissed time" for the religious instruction of public school children *off* the school grounds.[61]

In 1963 the United States Supreme Court invalidated compulsory Bible reading and the recital of the Lord's Prayer in the public schools of Abington, Pennsylvania, and Baltimore, Maryland. Writing the majority opinion in this case, Mr. Justice Clark stressed that the government was neutral in regard to religion, and that the free exercise clause of the First Amendment "recognizes the value of religious training, teaching and observance, and, more particularly, the right of every person to freely choose his own course with reference thereto, free of any compulsion from the state. This the free exercise clause guarantees. . . . [It also] withdraws from legislative power, State and Federal, the

[59] *Everson* v. *Board of Education*, 330 U.S. 1 (1947), as quoted in McGrath, *op. cit.*, p. 122.
[60] *McCollum* v. *Board of Education*, 333 U.S. 203 (1948).
[61] *Zorach* v. *Clauson*, 343 U.S. 306 (1952).

exertion of any restraint on the freedom of religion. The purpose is to secure religious liberty in the individual by prohibiting any invasions thereof by civil authority. Hence it is necessary in a free exercise case for one to show the coercive effect of the enactment as it operates against him in the practice of his religion."[62]

RÉSUMÉ

The history of education in the United States demonstrates that both public and nonpublic schools have aided the development of the country in proportion as they were not under any unreasonable compulsion. Academic freedom for the teacher and pupil has tended to disseminate knowledge, broaden attitudes, and promote cooperation. The freedom granted to private schools, secular and religious, from colonial times to the present, has promoted progress and has been instrumental in the establishment of pluralism in education, whereby private schools parallel public ones. This pluralism has enriched American culture and life, and has served to avert a monolithic educational structure. Not only do independent schools have an established place in American life, they often do what public schools cannot do, as in the case of providing religious instruction. They are free to experiment, and they preserve freedom, competition, and flexibility in education. Their experimentation may, as it has in the past, help to guide our public institutions.

To ensure the maintenance of the plural system of American education, it is necessary to make certain that private schools keep open their doors. Parents and children who are devoted to religious values or have special wants or desires should have the freedom to choose the kind of education they prefer, and to follow their conscience without undue fiscal penalization. The elimination of the private religious schools on account of financial crises, brought about in part by growing socialization and increased educational taxation, may coerce parents to enroll their children in public schools, where they may be exposed to the absence of moral-spiritual values or to values they cannot accept. This we must avoid in the interests of freedom and progress.

---

[62] *School District of Abington Township, Pennsylvania, et al.* v. *Edward Lewis Schempp et al.*, 374 U.S. 203 (1963).

CHAPTER II

Pluralism in Education in a Free Society

Leo R. Ward, C.S.C.*

"One society subsisting amid multiple pluralisms" — this is the difficult idea to which America is committed in education, as in every social area. It is expressed in the motto *E pluribus unum;*[1] and today the idea and ideal have, with us in America, to go far beyond the meaning and intent of that classical formula. In practice, pluralism means a respect for differences with, at the same time, a constant regard for the common good. In education, pluralism means that we allow, enjoy, and even promote freedom in the sources and methods of education, and freedom, within responsible limits, in the subject matter taught, and in the philosophies and theologies underlying the content. But pluralism also means that we hold, or must learn to hold, that if private and public education do not work together for the common good — and as a rule at present they do not — this is very unfortunate.

Thomas Jefferson asked, "Why subject [men] to coercion?" And he answered, "To produce uniformity. But is uniformity of opinion desirable? No more than of face or stature." We want freedom to think differently and therefore to educate differently, and yet at the same time we want to work together in the field of education with all men of good will for the nation's common good. In everyday practice, those are the two indispensable sides of the pluralist idea and ideal in education: *E pluribus unum* — sometimes diverse philosophies and theologies with these giving rise to different types of schools, and nevertheless all working for the good of the child and the nation.

---

* Leo R. Ward, C.S.C., is Professor of Philosophy at the University of Notre Dame, Notre Dame, Indiana.
[1] "From many, one."

If there is one obvious characteristic of education in America, it is that we have had a great diversity and heterogeneity in education. This is the case today and it has been so throughout our history. At first, and for a long time, the majority of both our schools and our colleges were nonstate and nonpublic, and the people setting up our schools and colleges were primarily motivated by Christian faith. The result was that, though education often was tax-supported, the early educational institutions in America were not only independent but church-related.

In this connection, take the statement of Leonard Koos in regard to the private and the public high school: "After all, the history of American secondary education, even though it reaches back to the period of earliest colonization, is not a long one. Moreover, the history of genuinely public secondary education is much shorter. Although the Latin grammar school, the first of the secondary schools, had some public connections, it was not in a strict sense public." And the academy was much less public, so that it was not until the 1880's that the public high school "eclipsed the private secondary school numerically and proportionately."[2]

Even today, the independent colleges and universities, often church-related, outnumber the state-related ones. But over the past one hundred years we have also established many state colleges and universities, and, more for financial than academic reasons, the total number of students in these has lately grown faster and will continue to grow faster than that in independent colleges and universities.

We must recognize that from the outset a private-public diversity has been and is the order of the day in American education.

Besides, we inevitably have various levels of education, and these add a minor note of diversity. But the major continuing fact is that of public schools and independent schools on all levels. Many schools of various types and levels — that is the given situation. Yet all educators, whatever the type or level of their schools, are as if divinely called to work together as the national educational body. As educators and as citizens, we must insist on the duty of educators in private and public schools to work together in education. Why is it their duty? Simply because the *unum* or "one" is essential if *E pluribus unum* is to make sense in our national educational life. That is why we will insist on this point, commonly neglected today in both theory and practice. All schools, each

---

[2] Leonard V. Koos, *Private and Public Secondary Education* (Chicago: University of Chicago Press, 1931), p. 2.

severally and all together, are to serve the good of the child and therefore the good of the citizen, and also and concurrently the public or common good. Serving the good of the child and the nation — human persons, both individually and collectively — is what the school is called to do, and with us this is rightly a pluralistic service.

Here then we have at once three important factors to keep in mind: the pluralistic *fact* in education, the pluralistic *problem,* and the implied *law* stemming from the principle of *E pluribus unum.* The *fact* is the given variety of types and levels, and this is the given situation with which educational leaders are always confronted. The *problem* is to learn how to work together for the common educational good as well as for the good of children and youths and adults entrusted *pro tem* to the schools. The *law* — and let us not compromise on this law — is that all educators are to work together and to work for the common national educational good.

To say so much is simple — every school, every level, and every type is at work within its own precincts, each encouraged and enabled to work with a notable freedom, and yet each busy learning how to work with all others for the common educational good. This is easy to say. In practice, however, it has proved to be far from simple, and we feel obliged to insist that, though it is being done, it is far from being fully or satisfactorily done, and that most teachers and even many superintendents of private and of public schools are unaware that this pluralistic working is a mandate at all. Some will even resent mentioning it as such.

This failure to see and actually to accept the theory and practice of pluralism is one of the greatest weaknesses in American education.

WHAT IS PLURALISM?

It is therefore necessary to say what we mean in general by pluralism, and how educational theory and practice may be expected to fit into the overall pluralistic picture, especially in the United States.

Here are the relevant definitions of "pluralism" given by Webster:

1: the quality or state of being plural . . . 4a: a state or condition of society in which members of diverse ethnic, racial, religious, or social groups maintain an autonomous participation in and development of their traditional culture within the confines of a common civilization. b: a concept, doctrine, or policy proposing or advocating this state.

We are not proposing or advocating a doctrine or policy, but accepting and describing it. For that reason, we may proceed with the "state or condition" of society in which any of various groups — in our country, one must say Jews or Catholics or Protestants or secularists — has its own philosophy and theology, its own way of seeing man and the world, and to some extent its own pattern of conduct, and yet (we presume) does consciously or unconsciously work with the other groups, not under duress, but gladly, to achieve one common good and one common civilization. That is difficult to do because each of those groups has, to a certain extent, kept itself shut up in its own defensive ghetto. Of course, each group may, to some degree, have its own theory of man and nature and God, and this theory may only more or less coincide with those of the other groups. And yet the group, possessed and dominated by a desire for community, has (let us again presume) the practical wisdom and good sense to work with the other more or less divergent groups at the common national task. There is a common national work to be done by each working freely and independently, and by all freely working together.

The whole community of the nation, as well as many a smaller community will need to be organized on a pluralistic basis. This is because what we may call the "ideological complexion" of the community is almost sure to be "pluralistic": the philosophies are diverse, and so are the theologies, and this simply means that the various groups are in considerable disagreement as to what man is, what man's relation to nature is, what his relation to God is, and what the highest good is, as well as how and where it is attainable. These are basic human problems, and in replying to them men and groups are to be left free. Pluralism, says John Courtney Murray, arises "from the coexistence within the political community of groups who hold divergent views with regard to ultimate questions concerning the nature and destiny of man."[3] Here the reference is to the pluralistic fact, and not to any doctrine or policy defending or advocating the fact.

Consider a statement by another scholar of distinction who eulogizes "this process" of pluralism as he sees it in our country. In *Cultural Pluralism and the American Idea*, Horace Kallen says: "This process is an orchestration of diverse utterances of diversities — regional, local, religious, esthetic, industrial, sporting and political — each developing

[3] John Courtney Murray, "The Problem of Pluralism in America," *Thought*, XXIX (Summer, 1954), p. 165.

freely and characteristically in its own enclave, and somehow so inter-twined with the others as to suggest, even to symbolize, the dynamic of the whole. Each is a cultural reservoir whence flows its own singular-ity of expression to unite in the concrete intercultural total which is the culture of America."[4]

No doubt Dr. Kallen was a bit rhetorical, but we think his next observation, made in regard to the *inter* in intercultural, goes to the core of the ideal of pluralism. The *inter*, he says, postulates the parity of the different elements and "their free and friendly communication with one another as both cooperators and competitors."

Let us summarize and sharpen the meaning of pluralism in this way: on the one hand, we have groups with their own several traditions, each with its own philosophy and theology — secular, Christian, or Jewish — and perfectly free, so far as public policy and practice are concerned, to live by its own traditions and philosophy and theology. That is one side of the picture. The other side, just as important, is that each group has to work with other groups, i.e., is morally not free *not* to work for the common good along with groups whose tradi-tions and habits and philosophies and theologies may be notably different from its own.

On the one hand we have the freedom of groups, we may even say "the sacred freedom" of groups. On the other hand we have the com-mitment of each group to work with others for the common good. "Each group" — what do those words mean? In our country, the words refer especially to each of the four "religions," as we must now call them (since the Supreme Court has called "secular humanism" a "religion"). The four are Jewish, Catholic, Protestant, and secular.[5]

Each group must be allowed to be free. But each group must work with each other group and with all groups for the common good. Accordingly the problem, which is far from simple, is to respect all proper and nontreasonable diversity, while advancing all defensible unity. We say "nontreasonable," since to attempt to work with any group which aims to destroy our freedoms or our existence, is out of the question.

Believing Jews see God and man, and therefore educational processes and content, somewhat differently than do Catholics or Protestants or

----
[4] Horace Kallen, *Cultural Pluralism and the American Idea* (Philadelphia: Uni-versity of Pennsylvania Press, 1956), p. 98.
[5] "Secularism" or "secular humanism" limits its views and values to this world and to man in his present life.

secularists. One group sees "ABC" to be the proper understanding of a given situation, educational or other, whereas another group may see "ABX" or AXY" to be the answer. What a group holds to be correct theory is sure to affect how it views matters of public policy and practice. Take the instances of birth control, or the nature of authority, or the concept of evolution, or fornication, or the use of alcohol. What a group concludes about such a question is most likely a deduction from what it thinks about the nature of man and his origin and destiny and his relation to God. In any event, there is no use or justice in trying to pressure a group into thinking in lockstep with all other groups.

The freedom side is only one side of pluralism. The other side is the public-good side. Jews for instance may freely understand and believe as Jews. Also in many matters they may be well justified in working for Jews, but they would rarely be justified in anything like countering, much less in neglecting, the good of the whole people. Jews are too important a segment in the nation for them to become simply exclusive and ghettoized in seeking good. To the other groups, Jews must speak almost in the language of Ruth: "Your good will be my good." So too, of course, for Catholics, and Protestants, and secularists.

Once upon a time, it might conceivably have been meet and just for Protestants in America to work merely for the good of Protestants. But that day is buried in history. Today we live in a "pluralist" society. Professor Littell is mild in regard to the time factor when he says: "Only within our own time has America begun to shift from a mono-chromatic Protestant mentality to a conscious tri-faith pluralism." The fact of an "established" church, says Littell, has long ago gone over the dam, but he feels sure the monistic and therefore antipluralist mentality is still affecting some of the more backward and static Protestant churchmen, and is hurting at once their churches and the common good. His interesting work asks those fellow Protestants of his to surrender the now dead idea of a state church and to join in the general pluralist conception of American society.[6]

The pluralist situation is a two-sided phenomenon which may be expressed by saying that members of a group are to be free to see and to go their own way as long as their doing so is attuned to the general

---

[6] Franklin H. Littell, *From State Church to Pluralism* (Garden City: Doubleday Anchor Original, 1962), pp. 15, 104, 147.

social good, or at least is not against that good. The group's members, we repeat, might be Jews, Protestants, or secularists. Neither in their theory nor in practice will men ever overemphasize either side, the freedom side or the common-good side, if they are careful to respect both sides.

Take the statements of two experts on this duality. Eric Voegelin speaks of this "rich diversification of socially entrenched and violently vociferous opinion." What could be finer than this, as long as it is balanced by a strong affirmation of what Jacques Maritain has happily called "the same set of convictions concerning action" for the public good?

"LET SLEEPING DOGS LIE"

Pluralism means diversity and freedom. Or to turn the terms around: where men have freedom to be different and freedom of belief and of understanding and "seeing the world," there is sure to be pluralism. The "Freedoms" include freedom in education, above all freedom of choice as to the content and ultimate ends of education. Sometimes, nevertheless, those suffering from want of effective freedom in education are told, or tell themselves, that they ought to be thankful that they have as much freedom as they do. Why not let "good enough (or bad enough) alone"? Why not "let sleeping dogs lie"? Are not religious beliefs and freedom and education well respected in the United States? Where has religion ever been freer? Living in such a favorable climate, why not mark time? Why not honor the pluralist principle by doing nothing and keeping a discreet silence? Thus, "why stir up a hornets' nest" by suggesting aid to students in church-related schools? Church-related colleges and universities are being aided by federal legislation such as that passed in 1963, and quite likely they will in time be aided by our states along with public higher education. Why not let the matter rest at that? Why not grant the assumption that there is an essential constitutional difference between a high school senior and a college freshman?

The implied argument is that because peoples and faiths have suffered more injustice in other times and places, therefore citizens wanting their rights in schooling — or voting or housing or work — should be content and happy that they now suffer less. Must progress stop when it has gone only part of the way?

IS FREEDOM DIVISIVE?

Because pluralism means effective unity within assured freedom and diversity, it is difficult to achieve and maintain in education or anywhere else. In the exercise of freedom, some go different routes than others, and that is why the diversity or freedom side of pluralism naturally gives rise to the problem of "divisiveness" and the charge of "fragmentation." To those whose bent is to bring all things to a monolithic dead-level, it is a scandal to find groups, or even to think of groups, with their own beliefs about man and nature and God and their interrelations, and consequently about how people are to educate and to judge conduct and to live. Some are as if born "levelers," and some, perhaps feeling that their own way is "the American way," seem to be offended when their neighbors exercise the freedom to be different. We must therefore inquire whether private schools, church-related or others, are "divisive" and, in case they are, whether such an effect should be regarded as a deadly peril. It will be convenient to consider the subject under four heads.

First, we are fortunate in having a considerable and rather convincing study of the effects of private schooling on citizenship. This is the study made by Peter and Alice Rossi, who said they found no evidence that persons educated in Catholic parochial schools are less community-minded than Catholics or others educated in public schools. The Rossi study is important; it brought together data from several social-science studies, among them studies made in New England by the Harvard University Graduate School of Education and a study which covered most of Florida; and from the combined studies, the Rossis' conclusions are surprising because they are contrary to popular opinion; at any rate, the conclusions are of interest on the "divisive" and other issues. Here are those conclusions:

> . . . we could find no evidence that parochial schools tend to alienate individual Catholics from their communities. Parochial school Catholics are as involved in community affairs as anyone else of comparable occupational position. Furthermore, the choice of parochial-school education is apparently not so much a rejection of the public schools as a choice of something qualitatively different. It would appear that an improvement in the public schools would not materially affect their attractiveness to Catholics, for the greater pull of Catholic schools is based on religious qualities which the public schools have deliberately avoided. . . . We have been unable to find that parochial-school Catholics are very different from other Catholics.[7]

---

[7] Peter and Alice Rossi, *Daedalus*, XC (Spring, 1961), pp. 323–324.

Of course, this feature of "the greater pull" residing in religious qualities is not peculiar to Catholic schools; it is characteristic also, and quite naturally, of Lutheran schools, for instance, and Christian Reform schools and Mennonite schools and Jewish day schools.

The conclusion from social science would seem therefore to be strongly against the popular notion that private schools are lethally divisive, and against the perhaps somewhat rash assertion of Dr. James B. Conant that the greater the proportion of our youth attending independent schools, the greater the danger to democratic unity; and against his sudden, and we would say irresponsible, declaration in 1952 against all private high schools as (so he said) "divisive." Dr. Conant has by no means been consistent in opposing pluralism and freedom in education, but it was perhaps unfortunate — for him as well as for freedoms and pluralist unity — that he came out so vigorously against them.[8] Just as irresponsible and un-American have been the assertions of many others. Take merely two out of many assertions. First, it is said to be unwise to establish a "separate school system" "because that would lead to divisiveness."[9] Second, the "virus" of separate religious schools is said to be "the most debilitating and destructive factor in the American way of life" and to be an import and "not in the American tradition."[10]

We take such assertions to be a rejection of pluralism and freedom. At the same time, they show little knowledge of American history, and appear to be based more on feeling and *parti pris* or preconceived opinion than on careful study.

A second concrete way to consider the issue of divisiveness is to ask what their private education has done for many well-known Americans. Did it make them anticommunity and anti-American? Take the case of such men as George Washington, Thomas Jefferson, Theodore Roosevelt, Franklin D. Roosevelt, or John F. Kennedy. If we may make the assumption that persons are in part the products of schools, we may at least suggest that these patriots were products of private schools, since such were the only schools they ever attended. Would these men have been better Americans and better patriots if they had, instead, attended public schools? And would we want *all* Americans brought up,

[8] Dr. Conant's 1952 speech was published in *Vital Speeches,* and was reported, along with the ensuing lively discussion, by Benjamin Fine in the *New York Times.*
[9] William J. Sanders, "Spiritual Values and Public and Religious Education," in *The Public Schools and Spiritual Values,* ed. by John S. Brubaker (New York: Harper, 1944), p. 101.
[10] Maurice J. Thomas, *Phi Delta Kappan* (June, 1959).

from kindergarten through college and graduate school, in public schools — in what Professor Littell calls a "monochromatic" fashion? As lovers of freedom, should we perhaps even scold those who, so it seems, want to have all Americans pressured out of freedom of choice in education and pressured into a monolithic educational system? Should the freedom side of pluralism in education be abrogated?

We must say that for us history and tradition and "the American way" — to use an abused phrase — and freedom and our actual pluralism point definitely in another direction.

Our third observation grants what should be granted. It says that of course private schools, church-related and other, are divisive. In this respect they are like public schools. If we are to have private and public schools, each type must be divisive. What does our assertion mean? Three quite simple things: first, that the children in private schools are not in public schools — and vice versa: the children in public schools are not in private schools; second, that children in private schools are introduced to — they are there to be introduced to — some areas of knowledge not available to children in public schools, hence the gap and the divisive effect, not only of the private schools but of the public schools; and, third, it means that in either the private or the public school the children may, as the result of evil teaching at school or at home or at church, come to think that they alone are the good people, the elect, the top-ranking Americans, or even, beyond others, the children of God.

That is why we have to conclude that private schools are divisive and that public schools also are divisive. Pluralism is divisive, as is nature. One individual is not another individual, one group not another. To be divisive is the choice we make when we declare for freedoms and for living in a pluralist society. We could reduce that danger and eliminate it. The dictator's society or totalitarian communism is not in great danger of the divisive effect which freedom entails.

By this time we can readily see the two weaknesses of the "divisive" allegation. In the first place, it fails to observe the actual overall social situation, which is pluralistic. In the second place, it rests on a misunderstanding of freedom and is not only a refusal to allow and encourage freedom but a refusal to accept the ordinary effects of freedom. The divisive allegation, when taken seriously, rests on so bad a theory — that of totalitarian dictatorship — and is so unrealistic in fact that we were somewhat disappointed to see it repeated.[11]

A fourth realistic way to consider the challenge of "divisive" is in terms of the social stratification in the ordinary parish. From a social and status point of view, the children in a parish school are likely to be remarkably mixed. As a rule, a parish school is socially more heterogeneous than many a public school. In many instances, the parish cuts across social levels and usually does not do anything like "zoning": we all kneel at the same altar. The result is that many a parish school contains children from the perhaps somewhat elite side of the parish and at the same time children from the middle classes and from the poorer and even the slum side. In that way, so far from being divisive, it may well be more unitive and democratic than the average public school in the same city.

Leo Pfeffer has expressed in a simple way the point we are now making. He has said that social stratification more commonly occurs in the public school than in the parochial school:

> The intentional or *de facto* zoning which divides neighborhoods into upper class and lower class, Negro and white, Puerto Rican and native in the East, Mexican and native in the Southwest, results in public schools that are largely homogeneous in economic, social and ethnic groupings. Such homogeneity, if not completely absent in parochial schools, is far less prominent. If the children in parochial schools are all of one religion, they are more likely to be of different social, economic, racial and ethnic origins.[12]

To close this section on "the divisive question," we must again insist that freedom is divisive. This is true of freedom of choice in education and of every freedom a man or group can practice. And incidentally, this is why the situation of pluralism with its accompanying problems occurs in society. It is because persons and groups have and exercise freedom of thought, of beliefs, of association, of action. That, of course, is the freedom half of the pluralist situation, and, by itself, this freedom half, essential and basic to democracy, is divisive, and in the nature of the case it must raise problems. In short, there is no simple and easy way for the pluralist strands in society to be anything but themselves, and in practice the result will be that Jews really are in important ways

---

[11] As in *Public Funds for Parochial Schools? A Resource Document* (New York: National Council of Churches, 1963).

[12] Leo Pfeffer, *Creeds in Competition, A Creative Force in American Culture* (New York: Harper, 1958), p. 81.

divided from and separate from Catholics, and Protestants from Jews, and believers from Secularists. Democracy allows and encourages freedoms, and, though people can freely work together, their very freedom can be divisive.

The other half of the pluralist whole is the unitive half. Men and groups in education and every social enterprise must bend their efforts to some common and unifying goals of good. But left to itself, freedom could scarcely be said to be a unitive factor. That is not the way freedom primarily works. As Bishop Wright has said, for anyone to speak up on any debatable issue is "to divide the community." Such is one of the normal effects of freedom — of freedom to have our families, our own houses, our own beliefs and worship groups, our own schools and education.

In the democratic society, it is taken for granted that no person or group is to be challenged or penalized for exercising normal and constitutional freedoms. The Oregon decision of 1925 made the no doubt somewhat superfluous official statement that persons and groups may establish and operate their own schools. But if at the same time they are to be perpetually challenged and harassed and penalized in the attempt to exercise this freedom of choice in education, the freedom itself is brought into question, and it becomes almost a dubious asset to persons and groups. In its own nature, freedom is an open kind of thing and is the chief ingredient in the open society. But if freedom is crowded and punished, the society will be closed and freedom will be only half itself.

The late Canon Bernard Iddings Bell asked whether our mere "allowing" of private schools is not, in some instances, after all a kind of coercion. Canon Bell's reasoning was as follows: "If only public schools are state-supported, if to send children to a school not state-run is possible only at a cost beyond the means of ordinary parents, then the usual parent is in effect coerced to accept the public school even against his conscience. Where then is the liberty guaranteed by the Constitution?" The Canon concluded that this important liberty is, at present, almost impossible for the poor and reserved for the wealthy.

DE FACTO EDUCATIONAL PLURALISM

In his *Philosophy of Education*, Philip H. Phenix of Columbia University frequently mentions American pluralist society, and then outlines how the educator in particular is committed to pluralism. In general, he says that we everywhere encounter the fact of plurality: a plurality of religions, of scientific inquiries, of patterns of livelihood, and many diversified groups in a society at once diversified and unified. Furthermore, since we believe in rights and freedoms for persons and their groupings, one of our chief duties — says Phenix — must always be "encouraging diversity within unity."[13]

That is the overall setting, and within it occurs American educational pluralism. Dr. Phenix says that the educator is accordingly committed to pluralism: goals in education are many, situations are different, any two men are different, many and varied truths are given, and in various situations we have to invoke a multiplicity of rules. And because it is obvious to all that there are many ways of believing and of acting, the resulting minimum demanded of the educator is "tolerance and generosity toward those who differ" from him.[14]

Beginning with such a general statement of what we must do, our task in theory and practice is to make it more and more particular. Who, after all, is to do the cooperating so that diversity within unity will be the result? We would not say that every parent or every primary teacher is bound to see and consciously to work to promote at once the diversity side and the unity side of American education, even on the local level, and to promote the two sides working together. But every leading educator — every "educator" — and everyone purporting to develop a philosophy of education should see the two sides and consciously work to promote their working together. A *de facto* pluralism in American education may not be left to chance, merely left to "grow" like Topsy and to "work itself out." To be a real "educator," a person has some responsibilities imposed on him by society, and the society we have and prefer in the United States is a pluralist one. This society demands of the educator that he learn how to work toward unity in diversity, and diversity in unity; that he learn how to promote the total social good achievable through diversified education.

For one thing, the real educator will have to be a dualist in regard to the two types of education, private and public. The man unable to appreciate either the private or the public type is certainly not an American educational statesman. So too the Foundations; if they would see only one type, they would be halfhearted in their efforts to aid American education.

---

[13] Philip H. Phenix, *Philosophy of Education* (New York: Henry Holt, 1958), pp. 82, 219, 224–225.   [14] *Ibid.*, pp. 519–521.

Many others also are bound to aid in promoting pluralism in education. The clergy, for instance, and journalists and legislators can and often do have some passable understanding of the fact that ours has been and is now and is most likely to remain a pluralist educational system within a pluralist society.

In the volume already cited, Dr. Littell frequently says that many Protestant clergymen are, at best, only beginning to learn that ours is a *de facto* pluralist society. If this alleged lag is the case, we must also accept the fact that the same kind of misfortune befalls laymen and clergymen of other faiths. It is not merely Protestants who are retrograde in accepting pluralism.

Demanding freedom of choice in education, freedom for types of schools, for styles of teaching, and for modes of inquiry and selection of materials, allowing freedom of thought and philosophies and beliefs and theologies — all of this is one of the two necessary components of pluralism in education. The other component is the working together of all educators, at least in the persons of their leaders, and all types of schools for the good of every child and the general social good.

It is especially leaders such as teachers and administrators and top-flight educational specialists and philosophers as well as the several educational associations who must cooperate in achieving the overall educational good.

SHOULD WE "DELETE" PRIVATE SCHOOLS?

We have long ago reached the state where public schools are indispensable. The same holds for any mature democracy since, because of its very nature, democracy must aim to educate all. What we sometimes perhaps scarcely notice is that private schools in America are also indispensable. To get along without one type or the other, private or public, is possible and no doubt advisable in some villages or rural districts. It can scarcely be now thought possible in any large city, and it is in large cities where the bulk of our population is being progressively massed.

Each type of school, private and public, is indispensable to the idea of education in America. That idea is based on freedom, and is essentially a pluralist idea. Yet no matter how odd the fact, many of us still refuse to accept this in education. Thus, in his careful study of the Connecticut school bus case, Theodore Powell reports one man as saying his church council wanted all children to have a "truly American education in the one public elementary school system."[15] At least that man, along with his church council, was appealing to a monolithic principle quite at variance with American traditions and with current reality. So, unwittingly, was the American Federation of Teachers in a 1947 Resolution wherein they referred to:

> . . . the basic principle that the interests of the democratic society are best served where children of all component groups are enrolled in a common public school.

Pressuring parents to send their children to public schools, and *only* to public schools, is against the traditions of our people. It is a mistake, no matter how the pressuring is done. It is against the Constitution, too, as this was interpreted in the Oregon or *Pierce* case (1925), and the decision in that famous case was as if echoed when the Supreme Court said in *Prince* v. *Massachusetts* (1944): "It is cardinal with us that the custody, care, and nurture of the child reside first in the parents, whose primary function and freedom include preparation for obligations the State can neither supply nor hinder."

Our thesis in this section is that we should not, by any means, direct or indirect, delete freedom and pluralism in education. This is to say we may not delete private or public schools. We may not impose a particular philosophy such as "the State commandeers all"; "all in the State, nothing outside the State," to use Mussolini's formula. Through the Supreme Court or otherwise, we may not require all schools to be public, and public schools to be secularized. (These are hard sentences passed by the Court on itself, since the Court has said that secularism is a religion, and that we may not teach Jewish or Christian religion or any religion in public schools, and yet, so some would contend, the Court has secularized these same schools.) Professor Ulich of Harvard has said that we may not impose any philosophy of education as *the* American philosophy. This, he says, is because "we live today, especially in this country, in a 'pluralistic' society with many layers of opinion." In our nation, he continues, no one philosophy may expect sovereignty in education: not a Christian philosophy, nor a utilitarian one, nor the tyranny of science, to use his words, nor again what he calls a dogmatic educational pragmatism and experimentalism.[16]

---

[15] Theodore Powell, *The School Bus Case* (Middletown, Conn.: Wesleyan University Press, 1960), pp. 184–185.

[16] Robert Ulich, *Philosophy of Education* (New York: American Book Company), 1961), pp. 49–50.

In a word, a monolithic philosophy of education will no more do than a monolothic all-private or all-public type of school and education. In theory and practice, the monolithic will .do — and *has* to do — in a dictatorship, but is out of place in a democratic, pluralist society.

HOW TO ACT PLURALISTICALLY

Basically we have two types of schools and of education, and once these two types are granted, our love of freedom will find ways for the two to live and work together. Today the two types of schools and of education are too far apart. Let us begin with the negative, with the things they must not do, or, better, must no longer do.

Generally the leaders themselves, and again the teachers, in the two types know too little about each other. In that condition, each acts as if the other did not exist. They are mutually exclusive at both the national and the local levels, and this is most evident in the primary and secondary schools. An evil genius could hardly think up a more unnatural, repressed, and unhealthy situation. Take this remarkable instance. Officials of the Department of Health, Education, and Welfare (HEW) have frequently dodged, as far as possible, the problems of the private primary and secondary schools, and HEW officials have been embarrassed when they have had to consider those problems. This was evident in the "Memorandum on the Impact of the First Amendment to the Constitution upon Federal Aid to Education,"[17] which was authored by the then secretary of Health, Education, and Welfare and the then attorney general. All of which suggests that some highly placed national officials find it hard to go along with American educational pluralism.

Also refusing to accept this pluralism is the National Educational Association when, as notoriously has happened, this body has declared for public education only.[18] On retiring from the office of National Commissioner of Education, Dr. Sterling McMurrin said that the NEA "is not interested in higher education, is cool to the private schools, and is pathologically opposed to the parochial schools."

Some churchmen return the compliment by making strong statements

---

[17] "Memorandum on the Impact of the First Amendment to the Constitution upon Federal Aid to Education," Senate Doc. No. 29, 87th Congress, 1st Session, 7 (1961). See also Joseph F. Costanzo, "Ribicoff on Federal Aid to Education," *Thought*, 25 (Winter, 1961), pp. 485–536.

[18] See "NEA Pressure Group," *Catholic School Journal*, LXII (November, 1962), p. 4; "NEA and All American Youth: opposition to Federal Aid to Church Related Schools," *ibid.*, LXII (September, 1962), p. 7; and "NEA Outmoded?" *Commonweal*, LXVII (November 2, 1962), pp. 140–141.

against public schools. Thus to an attitude of being mutually exclusive these churchmen and associations and the HEW add an attitude of conflict and opposition. Both of these attitudes seem to be far from what is required by pluralist education in a pluralist society.

The way of mere "tolerance" is hardly better. Our highly pluralist society requires the positive cooperation of diverse groups, and pluralism in education also demands this cooperation. A bare "tolerance" of public and private schools for each other, a policy of live and let live, is inadequate. A mere mutual "bearing with one another," whether in the family or the community or in education, is a kind of standing insult. It is little better than totally disregarding one another, and this is just a little better than fighting one another.

Conflict and opposition will not do, nor will a mutually exclusive stance, nor even a bare tolerance. What we need and must work for is some kind of cocreative *thinking* with and for each other, as well as a cooperative *working* with and for each other.

CHAPTER III

Rights and Roles of Parents, Church, and State in Education

Professor John F. Britt[*]

The current crisis of the West is a crisis of education. Charles Malik in showing the need for reinstating the values of the West,[1] Christopher Dawson in advocating a study of Christian culture as a unifying force,[2] and Alphonse Genua in holding that our present crisis is one of education[3] are representative of present-day thinkers who demand that we raise the level of our debate about the schools to that of our civilization and culture.

God and nature have given parents the right and duty to develop their children to full maturity. Unable to fulfill this duty unaided, parents use the agencies of society to assist them as authorized delegates. Chief among such agencies are the church and the state. Nonetheless, both the church and the state have other bases for their rights and duties in education. The church is commissioned to teach and to nourish the souls of men. The state is required not only to encourage and protect the rights and duties of the church and the family, and foster their fulfillment, but also to provide the forms of education necessary for political, military, and other citizenship requirements. From these rights and duties flow many roles and functions, which are to be performed both within and outside of the classroom.

In education, these three — parents, state, and church — have mutual

---

[*] Dr. John F. Britt is Assistant Professor of Education at Duquesne University, Pittsburgh, Pennsylvania.

[1] Charles Malik, *Man in the Struggle for Peace* (New York: Harper and Row, 1963).

[2] Christopher Dawson, *The Crisis of Western Education* (New York: Sheed and Ward, 1961).

[3] Alphonse Genua, "Education: Purposes, Rights and Duties," *Report*, I (September, 1963), p. 23.

and reciprocal functions. And it is here that tension between them often arises. The state, in pursuing the common good, can demand compulsory education and tax its subjects for the provision of schools so as to bring citizens to a sufficient maturity for the ordering of society. The state can institute its own schools. The church can provide schools both on its own and in accord with the needs and wishes of parents. Private parties may also conduct schools. But neither the church nor private parties can impose taxes or distribute government revenues.

Notwithstanding, parents retain the continuing primary responsibility for the development of their children. Because of differences in attitudes and values, in the disciplines which make up the curriculum, and in the ultimate end and unifying force in the hierarchy of academic disciplines, the state has the responsibility to assist the initiative of the citizens in setting up and continuing schools that fulfill the dictates of the parents' consciences and preferences. Other countries have worked out means of fulfilling the rights of parents and children; there is hope that, with the issue clearly presented, all parents in the United States will demand a solution which will "take fully into account our basic truths about education, about freedom and the dignity of the human person, and the true purposes of life."[4]

RIGHTS IN EDUCATION

It may be assumed that men of good will desire the fulfillment of the rights of all and expect to be able to find acceptable solutions to their mutual problems. Such men recognize that finding and living a solution to problems which have been buried in prejudice and fear will mean a sacrifice on the part of all. Hence the necessity of a sacrificial open-mindedness toward the issue.

Recalling that our crisis is not merely one of the schools, but of education itself, let us define education as the adequate personal development of the individual in every aspect of human life — economic, cultural, familial, political, recreational, religious, and social — brought about within and by the learner through the direction of one who has learned. The personal development is adequate when the individual becomes able to direct others, as in the case of parents, or is able to continue his own perfection in accord with the demands made by his duties in life. These issues can be brought into focus by viewing the person as the subject of education, the school as but one

[4] *Ibid.*

of the agencies by which the person is educated. Yet only education within the school is formal education.

Beyond their responsibility for the necessary physical development of the child, the parents, the church, and the state have an intellectual function of passing on to the person those aspects of culture and civilization which he must possess in order to live as a man, as a social being, and as a sharer in the common good. Since life is something which depends not only upon knowledge but also upon feelings, these agencies must assist the person in forming attitudes, habits, and values upon which he can wisely decide and act.

How can the rights and roles of parents, church, and state be reconciled in the development of the individual in his personal and social life? The answer begins with the basis of the rights of each agency. Although church and state have distinct yet complementary rights, the child, who is the subject of education, and the parents, who have the primary responsibility toward the education of the child, must be seen as members of the church and members of the state, and as pursuing their fullest possible personal and social perfection.

What is the purpose for which the child is being educated? Prior to the child's birth, his parents have agreed to his existence. In marriage, they have decided that they so accept each other that they desire to continue themselves into the future. They know themselves so completely that they have agreed to act so that they will be reproduced. The child born to them is like to them. In a way, the child *is* the father and the mother, but in many ways, the child is not like the father and the mother. What newborn can walk or love? Though the parents are proud of their offspring, they understand that only years of physical, intellectual, and moral development can make the child really like to them. He is not yet fully their "image" in those positive attributes which make them most human. In fact, only when the child can bring forth other children and care for them and support them and educate them, can he be said to be fully like to his parents. This means that parents have the duty to care for and educate the child until the child can care for and educate his children. Parents have a continuing responsibility for the total personal development of the child until the child achieves maturity.

If parents see the need for the child to be like to them, they can also see the necessity of parents having the freedom to control the education of their children in harmony with their consciences and preferences.

The argument of this chapter is mainly rooted in the origin-image argument. We must move slowly to see exactly what the origin, nature, and destiny of man are or may be, and the implications of these for parents, church, and state. Reason as well as Genesis tells of our origin: "In the beginning God created heaven and earth." Then He brought forth Adam and Eve. In Adam and Eve, mankind originated from God, and was given dominion over creation and the mission to to perfect and continue itself.

An important question arises from recognizing that God gave man the power to act as an "image maker": to what extent should an image be a replica of oneself? The child obviously should be like the parents in the latter's positive good traits, but not in their negative shortcomings. This is a progressive feature of each new generation. And the child is to be like the family in those positive characteristics which distinguish his family from all other families, yet he is to be distinct from all the members of his family. The child is bound to the family by ties of blood and loyalty, and the parents have a responsibility, in accord with his uniqueness, to loose those bonds. Only a free, mature person will actually be a full image of the parents. Likewise the child must come to the point where his reverence and respect for his parents reaches a new level of perfection at the time when he no longer owes them obedience. The image of the parents becomes most like his parents at the very time that he is most independent of them: at the time that he is most himself. This means that the parents have a continuing responsibility for the total personal development of the child until he achieves maturity.

Yet what parents do not realize that the task is beyond themselves? Whatever their personal qualifications, they realize that the step-by-step advance of each child requires constant care and skill, and that the demands of our present society are such that no parents could fulfill the total education of their children.

While retaining the primary responsibility for the total personal development of the child, parents have a right to the aid of society in fulfilling this responsibility. Just as no duty can justly be imposed without a corresponding right to fulfill it, so the duty of the parents in the education of their children gives them the right to expect and demand cooperation from both church and state.

Upon what basis do parents make their demands of the church? Analogously to the parents, the church bears children of God as parents bear children of Adam. With this function of origin, the church takes on the obligation and the right to educate its spiritual children. As the parents continue themselves in their children, so the church continues itself in its children. Only to the degree that a person has become like to God has he approached his maturity within the church. Then only is the child actually an image of its Maker. The rights of the church in education come from the birth of the person into the life of God. This life demands religious and moral excellence, and along with this obligation comes the duty of the church to nourish.

The fact that the parents are to make the child like to themselves and the church is to make the child like to God does not raise a conflict nor lessen the responsibility of the parents. For the parents bring the child into the world and contract a total responsibility, embracing even the relationship of the child with God. Here arises the control the parents have even over the religious education which the child is obtaining.

But on what basis do parents make a demand of the state? Obviously the child is born into the family. Through the family he is born into the church and into the state. Just as the child remains the responsibility of the parents despite his membership in the church, so he remains the responsibility of the parents despite his membership in the state, a membership which has come about through the parents' participation in the state. The state obtains its rights, or better, its duties to its citizens in a different way than does the church. The state's rights and duties come from the principle of the common good. While parents and church are obliged to make the child like to themselves and to God, the state is obliged to assist the parents and the church in this undertaking by ordering the relations of all of its citizens in the public areas of their lives so that each can most fully complete his obligations and exercise his rights.

NATURAL RIGHTS

The rise of science during the past one hundred years initially encouraged disparagement of the idea of natural human rights. Nevertheless today men the world over are returning to acceptance of the natural law view. The shock of two world wars, the horrors resulting from the military applications of scientific and technological progress, and the desperate struggle with Communism have caused many to reconsider our foundations. The age of anxiety has been searching for an anchor — for a reality which will stabilize persons and society.

Thomas Jefferson and those who wrote our *Declaration of Independence* and the *Bill of Rights* had such in the security flowing from their conviction that the universe is based upon a natural law providing for a harmony and an order in human affairs analogous to the laws governing purely physical matters.

The symbol of our reacceptance of the natural law and the rights of man is the United Nations. Conceding the need for strengthening the UN, we can study its *Declaration of Human Rights* and increase our faith in the times. Thus it is held that all nations are equal, and that all men have personal dignity. The United Nations *Declaration of Human Rights* reads: "Article 16 (3). The family is the natural and fundamental group unit of society and is entitled to protection by society and the State" and "Article 26 (3). Parents have a prior right to choose the kind of education that shall be given their children."

In our *Declaration of Independence*, we also see acceptance of the natural law. Thus the *Declaration of Independence* says: "We hold these truths to be self-evident; that all men are created equal, that they are endowed by their Creator with certain unalienable rights, that among these are life, liberty, and the pursuit of happiness. That to secure these rights, governments are instituted. . . ." Their possession is inalienable. The end is the total personal development of the human person.

Since all men are created equal, the Founding Fathers desired that all would find equal assistance under the law in the exercise of their rights. It was the Founders' conviction that men have joined in political society and restricted the exercise of their rights in a limited degree only in order that they may receive the cooperation and assistance of government to fulfill more perfectly all of their rights. The *Declaration* concludes with this pledge: "And for the support of this declaration, with a firm reliance on the protection of divine providence, we pledge to each other our lives, our fortunes, and our sacred honor." This pledge was based on the confidence that their government would maintain and encourage conditions under which they might use their rights.

The natural right of parents in education has been affirmed in other sources. The Supreme Court has explicitly declared that this right is guaranteed by the Constitution of the United States. In the *Pierce* or Oregon case (1925), the Supreme Court said: "The fundamental theory of liberty upon which all governments in this Union repose excludes any general power of the state to standardize its children by forcing them to accept instruction from public teachers only. The child is not the mere creature of the state; those who nurture him and direct his destiny have the right, coupled with the high duty, to recognize and prepare him for additional obligations."

This principle was also invoked in the earlier *Meyer v. Nebraska* case (1923), wherein the Supreme Court declared unconstitutional a law of Nebraska which would have made it a crime for any teacher to teach any subject in an elementary school in any language other than English, and said, "Evidently the legislature has attempted materially to interfere with the calling of modern language teachers, with the opportunities of pupils to acquire knowledge, and with the power of parents to control the education of their young."

Religious leaders have repeatedly insisted on the prior right of parents to control the education of their children. In his encyclical, *On Christian Education of Youth* (1929), Pope Pius XI contributed much to clarify the knotty problem of the relative roles of parents, churches, states, and schools in education. Pius XI said: "Education is essentially a social and not a mere individual activity. Now there are three necessary societies, distinct from one another and yet harmoniously combined by God, into which man is born: two, namely the family and civil society, belong to the natural order; the third, the Church, to the supernatural order. . . . Consequently education, which is concerned with man as a whole, individually and socially, in the order of nature and in the order of grace, necessarily belongs to these three societies, in due proportion, corresponding, according to the dispositions of Divine Providence, to the coordination of their respective ends." Relative to the prior right of parents to direct the education of their children, Pius explains: "God directly communicates to the family, in the natural order, fecundity, which is the principle of life, and hence also the principle of education for life, together with authority, which is the principle of order. . . . The family accordingly holds from the Creator the duty, and hence also the right, to educate its offspring. This is an inalienable right because it is associated with a strict obligation. It is a right anterior to any right of civil authority and the State, and it is inviolable by any power on earth."

ROLES IN EDUCATION

How can we reconcile interests of parents, church, and state in the control of education in the United States today? Parents have a continuing and total responsibility toward the education of their children, including the formal education which takes place largely within the classroom. The church has a continuing responsibility toward its members within the total responsibility of the parents. The state has a continuing responsibility to promote conditions conducive to the common good. Fulfillment of these responsibilities will bring achievement of the objectives of education, including the full development of students as persons.

We can all agree that the child must be educated toward acceptable physical, emotional, intellectual, economic, recreational, social, moral, religious, familial, political, and aesthetic objectives. Thus an adult must be prepared physically to care for his needs. For his own good and for that of those with whom he lives, he must be beyond childish emotional reactions. He must be able to secure an adequate income and use his money wisely. In voting, he must be able to understand the ways in which the needs of his community and the world can best be met. He must be able to use his leisure time for his personal development and revivification. His relations with others should be a source of joy both to himself and to his associates. The integrity of society depends upon his knowing and doing what is good, just, and honorable, which cannot be separated from his relationship with God. Nor can his love of his family and his communities and his own development be perfected without an awareness of this dependency. Political life finds its meaning in the person and in his rights in relation to the common good. We should not ignore the aesthetic appreciation of what is noble and uplifting; the personal commitment which distinguishes the man of character from the shiftless; the thirst for knowledge which is unquenchable; and the ability to sacrifice for the common good. The physical and intellectual objectives in the list fit into a pattern of instruction; the moral, the psychological, and the spiritual into a pattern of formation.

In each of these objectives, we see that the parents have an important role to play. By the time the child enters kindergarten, he has been started on them. While he is attending school he is also receiving training at home, and the attitude of the home is shaping his application at school. Where the attitudes toward objectives in home and school conflict, the usual cooperation is absent and the student becomes confused.

The church has a responsibility for the life of the child in his relationship with God, while parents retain an overall responsibility. The state has a responsibility toward the common good, and, therefore, must safeguard these two agencies' rights and promote and cooperate with them. Simultaneously, the parents have a set of duties including the duty to observe the compulsory law of the state regarding the education of their children. Both the church and the state know from experience that parents usually lack the means to carry out this responsibility alone, and hence each is willing to provide help in the form of the school. The purpose of the school in either case differs in this: the state is at once fulfilling its obligation toward the needs of the parents and the requirements of the common good, while the church is fulfilling its obligation toward the needs of the child for moral and religious life as well as the needs of the parents to educate their children. The meeting place of the church and state is the classroom. Each can use the classroom to reach its objectives.

On a different level from the limited objectives of the academic disciplines, the problem of conscience arises. Besides the intellectual and physical objectives of a school, there are attitudes and values which will permeate the handling of the subject matter and the extracurriculars. Some subjects which parents consider vital might be totally ignored. A school which is offering courses aimed at intellectual objectives can be ignoring objectives which the parents hold themselves most responsible to provide. On the other hand, a school which is achieving the intellectual objectives can meanwhile be achieving further objectives for the parents and their children. Thus a church-related school may be ordered to the child and to the objectives of the academic disciplines together with additional ends which permeate education, for example, in extracurriculars. While a state school is ordered to the child and to the specific objectives of the academic disciplines, its link with the political order too often restricts its scope to secular objectives. Many parents unable to meet the fees in church-related schools may be thus put in the position of sending their children to secular schools despite the contrary urgings of conscience.

In expanding on the relations of the roles of the church and the parents, we have also to some extent pointed up the role of the state in education. The state has other areas of responsibility beyond the first fifteen years of a child's formal schooling. Not only has the state a responsibility for advanced education in the university, but it must also carry on a large-scale adult education program. Public resources should be applied to the task of educating for structural changes in our economy, for international life, for political and military responsibilities, and for the worthwhile use of leisure.

How can the common good be promoted by the state in fulfilling the rights of parents in education, without aiding religion to the detriment of consciences of atheists, and without showing preference to particular religions? Parents have a right and duty to develop their children toward their own image. Because of their own inadequacy, they must depend upon schools. These can be under the aegis of the church or of the state or of private parties. But parents must be in control, in order to assure the objectives which they consider necessary for their children. Atheistic parents desire the same formal objectives which theistic parents desire, with the exception of the moral and the religious. To the extent that schools ignore God, the atheistic parent can obtain the total assistance sought from the state.

But what about the other parents? Their children have a right to a pursuit of truth, including a full complement of educational objectives. To the extent that moral and religious objectives are ignored, parents desiring such are faced with a forced choice. Either: (1) they must, at their own additional, "double" expense, send their children to schools in which they spend the most fruitful hours of study on all of the objectives, or (2) they can attempt to supplement the lack of the spiritual aspect of education in a minimal manner during the poorer instructional hours outside of school, or (3) they can use the shared-time plan where available and divide the children's time between church-related and state schools, thus obtaining part of their objectives in each. Although a majority of parents now accept the forced choice of supplementing objectives in a secondary manner outside of the formal classroom, a significant proportion of parents accept the forced choice of providing for total educational objectives at additional expense and fiscal penalization.

Frank Bowles, president of the College Entrance Examination Board, in a recent statement concerning educational change in Europe, emphasized the control parents can exert: "The movement which thus early acquired the name democratization and a formally stated philosophy in England and France actually developed simultaneously in every European country. It took the very direct form of a substantial enrollment increase in the primary and secondary schools. The increase was not traceable to a change in either the structure or the standards of education as offered in those schools. It was, rather, due to what appeared to be a widespread and spontaneous decision by parents of school children that their children should remain in school longer."[5]

The taxpayer already recognizes his obligation to the education of youth. Parents of state schoolchildren, and all other taxpayers, can be convinced that all children have a right to the type of education which they require, and constitutional and legislative means will be found. As the burden of the educational "enterprise" increases, fair means of protecting, encouraging, and assisting the independent, private, and church-related schools will be seen as necessary for the common good and there will be a "widespread and spontaneous decision by parents" to employ these means.

What justification is there for the state to encourage and assist independent schools for the common good? The mature adult, the result of a long-term educational effort, is able to act in the economic, educational, familial, political, recreational, religious, and social areas of life in accord with the education he has received. Where schools of all types were successful in achieving the objectives in regard to the person, mature citizens show this forth in all areas of life. But with the financial burden of education becoming heavier, the independent schools may be forced to decide between quantity and quality, or between mediocrity and excellence, in achieving the objectives which are taught in state schools. Therefore, it is not a question of promoting and encouraging religion as an establishment, but of promoting and encouraging a school as a means of achieving the objectives which are taught in both state and independent schools. Therefore, it is not a question of promoting and encouraging religion as an establishment, but of promoting and encouraging a school as a means of achieving the objectives of education demanded by the citizenry of the United States for the common good.

This need not mean total financial backing. Nor must it involve direct financing and control of independent schools by the state. Various alternatives are available. For instance, parents might decide upon the institution to which they freely choose to send their children for education, and be allowed a proportion of tax support for the education of those children. Or again school districts could make arrangements to provide for the pursuit of those objectives which

---

[5] "Education in the New Europe," *Daedalus*, XCII (Winter, 1963–1964), p. 378.

are most costly in state schools or through visiting teachers. There are further solutions.

Because education is compulsory and because the cost of education has increased so much, many citizens, who earlier had little sympathy for this matter of conscience on the part of something like a quarter of our children and their parents, now see that the issue must be faced.

SOME VITAL QUESTIONS

Each generation must re-examine and dedicate itself to living these basic truths in its own context. With respect to our problem, we may restrict ourselves to six vital, interrelated questions:

Question One: What do present world conditions imply for the educational policies of the United States?

To find the common good in education in the United States today, we must go beyond the view of our Founding Fathers, and consider the total present world situation. No longer can we restrict our preparation for life to a knowledge of those facts and skills adequate for homes and small communities. Each person finds himself interdependent upon all others across the nation and in all other nations. Furthermore, no single government can solve its economic, educational, familial, political, recreational, religious, and social problems entirely apart from other governments. Attempted solutions by one country or a small number of countries are inadequate. Only with the united wisdom and moral insights of at least a majority of free countries can the common good of mankind be achieved.

Only if we see the complexity of the new world our graduates will enter, can we accept the sacrifices and meet the demands of the education which our children require. Education can no longer be limited to those subjects which are relatively inexpensive. We must be willing to invest heavily in education if we are to be just to our children, and we must provide them with a complete education in the fullest possible sense.

Question Two: What about equality of educational opportunity?

What does equality of educational opportunity mean? Each person is to be educated in accord with his talents and merits, both because he is a person and because he is a member of society. As a person and a member of society, he has a general right; as a person and a member of a particular society, he has a specific right.

Three essays in the Winter, 1963–1964 issue of *Daedalus* contemplated the current European educational situation. Until 1955, economists, demographers, and sociologists agreed with educators that the traditional educational systems of the European nations were doing a fairly adequate job of passing on cultural values and preparing the young for life. But the structures of European society — its transportation, production, distribution, agriculture, and services — have so changed that the present new society cannot continue with educational systems built on the premise that education has a twofold purpose: to educate an elite to lead society, and to educate the masses to follow.

A spirit of democratization has united with the changes of the second industrial revolution to force schools to provide new curricula and new means of entrance and advance for a growing number of students. Only if each child is given the opportunity to develop to the full extent of his abilities and talents will the youth of today accept the claim of society that it is adequately preparing them for adulthood.

Question Three: What is the present relationship between state and parents in education in the U. S. A.?

In the United States, at present, toward the children whose parents accept the education obtainable in the state school, the state exhibits a warm concern; but toward the children whose parents cannot accept the education obtainable in the state school, the state exhibits a coolness: a policy of mere neutrality and toleration. In accord with the Supreme Court's decision in the *Pierce* case, the state recognizes the prior right of the parent toward the education of the child and the right of the parents, coupled with their duty, to provide more than the basic minimum education obtainable in state schools.

Generally speaking, parents are willing to pay taxes for the education of those who wish to use the state schools. But parents whose conscience demands that their children cannot be allowed to use the state school desire some means by which the commonly pooled tax funds can be distributed for the good of *all* children. This tension within the relationship is similar to the tension in the racial area of civil rights. In each case a large segment of the populace holds that an injustice of long standing is being continued because of exaggerated fears and prejudices. And in each case, hopes are high that true equality of educational opportunity will be achieved.

Question Four: What limitations, if any, on their rights have been accepted by parents whose consciences demand independent schools?

Granted that such a tension exists, we are led to ask: What limitations, if any, on the use of their rights have been accepted by those whose consciences demand an independent school system? Historically, in our country, the state has enjoyed the juridical right to found schools and demand taxes in support of these schools. Historically, too, those parents who have found that the objectives of education which they recognize as necessary for their children are not provided by state schools have been protected in continuing the tradition of independent schools, although it would probably be saying too much to pretend that they have in practice been encouraged to do so.

All can agree that each child has the right to an education which is equal to the education of any other child of like ability. The disagreement comes over content, and as to what constitutes an education. In the first part of this chapter we divided education into the formal education of the classroom, where the intellectual disciplines are taught, and the education of the school, where other objectives are also achieved. In the case of those elements which are ignored in public schools, namely, the inculcation of religious and spiritual truths, we obviously have a chief motivating factor for the vast majority of independent school systems. Since the state is not allowed to teach the discipline of religion, the parent who places this type of knowledge in the first place cannot in conscience send his child to the state school. For in it, not only does the child not learn what many parents consider to be the most important truths, but the absence of this discipline tends to subvert the hierarchy of the disciplines. The child is taught by indirection that the truth about God is insignificant or negligible because the state school ignores it.

In the case of extracurriculars, we must recall our earlier distinction between academic disciplines, which can be taught directly, and attitudes and values, which cannot be taught directly. Attitudes and values are emotional and voluntary ways of responding to truth, to good, and to beauty. Example and encouragement, based on a hierarchy of values which the teachers and the students respect, indirectly lead individual students to form a similar hierarchy of attitudes and values. Though some of this effect can be expected to take place within the classroom, the ordinary means is through activities which result from the total school situation, mainly in extracurricular activities. Here the students carry into action the affective impact of what they have learned.

To the extent that religion is not one of the disciplines of the state school, carry-over to the total school situation is practically impossible. In its place, enthusiasm for art, drama, sports, patriotic demonstrations, and the like are used to express the attitudinal impact of the student's scholastic endeavors. A second source of attitudes and values is the relationship between student and teacher outside of the classroom. Through personal counseling and advice, the teacher can imbue the child with examples and expectations to enable the child to structure his value system.

A special spirit pervades the total school situation where religion is not only seen as the central discipline, but as a unifying and integrating principle of the entire curricular and extracurricular offerings. Instead of lessening the reality and the content of any discipline, religion augments and perfects this knowledge within the child. Those parents who are forced to forego inclusion of religion in the day-to-day education of their children have accepted great limitations upon their rights in being compelled to accept a condition contrary to the promptings of their consciences.

Question Five: What limitations are imposed on the teacher in the state school?

To complete our analysis, we must consider the question: What is the position of the teacher in the state school? Ultimately the school is what the teachers make it. Their knowledge of their disciplines, their skill in teaching, and their moral probity are the essentials which constitute good schools. Nonetheless, the teacher who has the highest ideals and the truest respect for religion is necessarily restricted in what he or she can teach in a state school. He cannot teach the truths of religion. He can by his example guide the children toward his ideals, yet he cannot explain these ideals, which are rooted in his religion. His hands are tied so that he cannot show the children *why* he acts and thinks as he does. At most, he can talk about the institution of religion in a neutral manner: he cannot teach or inculcate the truths of religion. This restriction acts as a two-edged sword: one edge cuts the liberty of the teacher to teach; the other cuts the right of the child to truth. Outstanding teachers in the state schools will continue to show a high ideal of moral and religious dedication despite this restriction, and children will find some basis for attitudes and values in their example. But a question of conscience is: Can such a restriction upon teaching religion and religious attitudes and values be reconciled with the obligation to know, to love, and to serve God with our whole heart? While respecting the marvelous work of the teachers in state schools, many parents must answer in the negative.

Question Six: What problems must be solved if we are to face the issue?

The problems which this chapter has raised must be met in the spirit of the historic tradition of our people's monumental struggle for liberty, equality, justice, and peace. The main issue is the reconciliation of the rights of parents and children toward a twofold educational system, independent and state. The chief problems are to provide equality of educational opportunity for those who are conscience-bound not to send their children to state schools; to find a way by which parents who are taxpayers can fulfill their obligation to educate their own children in schools teaching and inculcating all the objectives they recognize as essential for full human development; to maintain respect for the consciences of those who do not believe that religion is a necessary educational objective; and to recognize the objectives of the various disciplines or sciences taught in all acceptable schools. We must accept the obligation of the state to promote and encourage the exercise of their rights by the church and parents, not for the purpose of supporting an establishment of religion, but for the purpose of preparing the young to meet their tasks and challenges in a structurally changing society. We must also accept the need for some limitation on the exercise of the rights of those parents who do not accept the state school as adequate for the development of their children. By means of these considerations, a valid solution, based upon mutual trust and respect, and in accordance with the respective rights and duties of parents, church, and state, is to be found. Calmly, charitably, and legally, we must and will solve the issue. As Alphonse Genua says: "In the current crisis we may well appear to be debating about schools, but the primary issue is education. Only those solutions will be satisfactory which take fully into account our basic truths about education, about freedom, and the dignity of the human person, and the true purposes of life."[6]

---

[6] *Report*, I (September, 1963), p. 23.

CHAPTER IV

International Panorama: World Survey of Aid to Independent Education

Professor Daniel D. McGarry*

In determining our public policy toward independent education, we should not overlook the experience of other countries. In this rapid survey of some eighty-five countries, certain generalizations emerge. Only rarely do democracies exclude all forms of religious instruction from the public schools and refuse public aid (direct as well as indirect) to independently controlled schools, including those that teach religion. Such exclusion and refusal are, however, the rule among communist and totalitarian countries.

PUBLIC AID TO INDEPENDENT EDUCATION: FORMS AND CONDITIONS

There are various ways in which democratic countries contribute to the financing of independent education, various conditions for public assistance, and various degrees of public supervision.

Aid given by governments to independent education is of two kinds: direct and indirect. Direct aid runs the spectrum from public provision of total operational expenses and construction costs, through varying percentages of one or both. Operational aid is the most usual. A common form of operational subsidy is full or partial payment of teachers' salaries; another consists in per-pupil grants to parental associations operating schools. Allowances are also made for various specific pur-

---

* Professor of History, St. Louis University; Acting Research Chairman, Citizens for Educational Freedom; editor: *Educational Freedom* (a periodical).

poses, such as certain types of instruction. Indirect aid takes such forms as tax exemptions, bus transportation, school lunches, medical and dental expenses, and the like. Usually both direct and indirect aid are given. Aid may be provided by national, state, and/or local governments.

CONDITIONS REQUIRED FOR AID

In countries that provide aid to independent education, various reasonable conditions for participation are usually laid down by the government. Such conditions are generally beneficial. They do not deprive parents and independent schools of essential freedoms. It is usually stipulated that religious and moral parts of the school program are to be free from state control. Secular aspects of the curriculum are, however, subject to such requirements as minimal qualifications for teachers, inclusion of certain subjects (such as the national language, history, and civics) in the course of studies, etc. In some cases the schools cannot charge fees, and in some minimal teachers' salaries must be paid.

COMMUNIST COUNTRIES

Independent education is not permitted in communist countries, wherein the state appropriates and standardizes minds in their formative years.

Communist Stalwarts. The communist giants, Russia (U.S.S.R.) and China (People's Republic of China) have both uprooted religion from public education and banned all private education. They have thus effectively eliminated religion from the educational process.

Communist Rumania, Bulgaria, Albania, Yugoslavia, and Cuba all follow the pattern established by Russia, whereby independent schools are totally suppressed, and religion is completely banned from the public schools.

Central European Communist Countries. In the recently communized Central European countries of Poland, Czechoslovakia, Hungary, and Eastern Germany, all independent schools have been suppressed in accordance with the communist pattern. But some minimal religious instruction has been allowed in public schools. For religion was so basic in the lives of the people and so strongly rooted in their education that its immediate eradication might foment dangerous discontent. It is evident, however, that this religious instruction is begrudgingly tolerated by the authorities.

DEMOCRATIC COUNTRIES

A contrast is provided by most democratic countries, which pursue a policy of free choice, tolerance, and "pluralism," encouraging various approaches in education as in other fields.

Most democratic countries follow a policy of religious toleration and neutrality, as well as one of separation of church and state. Where their people have a prevailing religion as well as strong religious convictions, democracies usually provide for religious instruction in public schools. At the same time they make participation voluntary, and allow aid to independent schools.

Democratic countries do not merely acknowledge the right of independent schools to exist, they also foster independent education. While providing free public education generously, they assist accredited independent schools to the degree that such schools need assistance.

Western European Democratic Countries. Practically all European democracies, where concepts of individual rights and personal freedoms, as well as strong religious convictions are deeply rooted, give substantial public aid to independent education. The only exception is Greece, which pleads poverty.

In the United Kingdom of England, Wales, Scotland, and Northern Ireland, optional religious instruction is provided in the public schools, and state assistance, ranging from about 60 to 100 percent of costs, is given to independent or "voluntary" schools.

Lutheranism, the religion of the vast majority, is taught in the public schools of the Scandinavian countries of Denmark, Sweden, and Norway, as well as Finland, although Catholics, Jews, and others may be excused. State subsidization is available for independent schools, such as those of Catholics and Jews, which may receive from 50 to 90 percent of their expenses from the government.

France: despite separation of church and state, and a period (1880's to 1940's) of government hostility to religious education and church-connected schools, France now permits religious instruction in public schools on a voluntary basis. It also subsidizes independent education, and voluntary schools conducted by "parental associations" are aided by the government.

In the German Federal Republic (West Germany) the prevailing religion in a region is usually taught in the public schools, except in the so-called "secular schools." Substantial public aid, most of which comes from the various *Länder* (states), is also given to independent schools.

In the Dutch Netherlands (Holland) public schools are of the secular type; but independent schools fulfilling government requirements are financed on the same basis as the public schools.

In Belgium, religious instruction is provided in state schools according to the prevailing faith, with voluntary participation while support is given by national and municipal governments to independent (including church-related) schools. The same is also true of Austria.

In Greece, religious instruction in the Eastern Orthodox Christian faith is provided in the public schools; but public authorities state that resources are too limited to allow direct aid to independent schools at present.

In Switzerland, religious instruction in the prevailing faith in each district is provided in public schools, while state-aid is given to independent church-related schools of recognized public utility.

In Ireland, public financing of education is effected by grants to denominational school systems, Catholic, Protestant, and Jewish. Participation in religious instruction is voluntary.

In Italy, Portugal, and Spain, religious instruction is provided in the public schools on a voluntary basis, and grants are made to independent schools. But, although the Portuguese Constitution guarantees such subsidization for independent education, it is only occasionally given in practice.

Democracies of English Descent: Larger States of Earlier Origin. Democracies of English descent include such larger states as the United States, Canada, Australia, New Zealand, and the Union of South Africa, as well as such smaller states as Trinidad and Tobago, British Honduras, Jamaica, and the Bahamas, which have only recently become self-governing.

Of five major democracies of English descent, four include religious instruction, usually interdenominational, in their public schools. Practice in the fifth, the United States, is intermediate and transitional from interdenominational religious instruction to strict secularism in public education.

Three of these five democracies now give direct aid to independent education; two give mainly indirect aid. Of the latter, New Zealand seems to be on the way to providing direct as well as indirect aid, which would leave the United States as the solitary exception.

Direct aid in some of these countries has been slow in coming because they emerged from colonial status at a time when the British government left the financing of education mainly to private enterprise. The mixed nature of their population has also made the provision of schools for children of different beliefs difficult, and attention has meanwhile been absorbed by the problem of providing massive public education for a rapidly expanding population.

In the United States of America, government aid to independent schools on elementary and secondary levels has been mainly indirect, and restricted to such help as tax exemptions, school lunches, and (occasionally) publicly provided student transportation and textbooks. Some relaxation of this policy is seen in the Federal Elementary and Secondary Education Act of 1965. More extensive and sometimes direct aid has been given on higher educational levels. Our policy on direct aid to students in independent schools on all levels is presently in a needed state of flux.

In Canada, in public schools religious instruction is provided at the end of the school day. In all except two provinces there is direct public aid for independent schools, and in five out of ten provinces, provinces with 75 percent of the population, schools conducted by "religious and ethnic minorities" are financed in the same way as state-operated schools.

In Australia, interdenominational religious instruction is offered in the public schools, except in Victoria, where denominational religious instruction is provided. Until recently, most aid to independent schools has been indirect. Now, however, some states make educational allowances to parents of children who attend independent schools, and the federal government has adopted a plan of direct aid to independent secondary schools for buildings and equipment.

The situation in New Zealand has been and is much as in Australia. Interdenominational religious exercises and instruction are provided in public elementary schools at the beginning of the day. Only indirect aid has been given to independent schools, except in special cases of need. But this indirect aid has been rather liberal, and has taken about a dozen forms, among which are bus transportation, food and milk, dental treatment, and both agricultural and manual instruction. New Zealand now shows signs of providing direct aid to independent education.

In the Union of South Africa, interdenominational religious instruction is provided in public schools, while private schools with religious instruction have received government grants.

Smaller States in the British Commonwealth of Nations, such as Trinidad and Tobago, British Honduras, Jamaica, and the Bahamas, which have only recently emerged from colonial status, are familiar with more modern British policies relative to state aid to education, and usually follow the British example of allowing aid to all recognized independent schools, including church-related ones.

Latin American Democracies. There is legally required separation of church and state in most Latin American countries and *de facto* separation in others. At the same time, religious instruction in the prevalent form of religion (Roman Catholicism) is provided in public schools on a voluntary basis, except in Mexico. In the majority of Latin American countries, public aid is also given to independent schools which meet government standards.

In Mexico, the government has been declared responsible by the Education Law (Article 4) to encourage private education: "independent education of all kinds is deemed to be in the public interest, and regulations shall establish to what extent the state is required to contribute and assist its expansion." As a result, "independent schools receive grants, subsidies, and an exchange of services from the states."[1]

In Guatemala, Honduras, and El Salvador, the general Latin American pattern prevails, so that Catholic religious instruction is provided in public schools on a voluntary basis, and state subsidies and grants are given to independent schools. The like is true of Haiti and the Dominican Republic.

South American Republics usually follow the Latin American policy of allowing optional religious instruction in public schools, and providing considerable government aid to independent schools. Among such countries are: Colombia, Venezuela, Ecuador, Bolivia, Peru, and the "ABC Countries": Argentina, Brazil, and Chile. Only occasionally, however, does Paraguay give direct public assistance to independent schools.

Near Eastern Democratic States. The small progressive Near Eastern democracies of Israel and Lebanon are Western in their approach.

Israel, to accommodate diverse views, has three types of publicly supported schools: (1) secular public schools, fully supported by the state; (2) religious public schools, also fully supported by the state; and (3) independent schools, which are mainly operated by minority religious groups, and receive a large public subvention.

Lebanon, whose population adheres to various religions, allows each

[1] UNESCO, *Financing of Education,* pp. 198–199.

group maximum freedom by granting state subsidies to independent educational establishments on all levels.

MOSLEM COUNTRIES

Most Near Eastern countries are relatively homogeneous in their adherence to the Moslem faith, and many of them accordingly include Moslem religious instruction in the curriculum of their public schools. This is the case in the United Arab Republic, Yeman, Saudi Arabia, Iraq, Jordan, Libya, Bahrein, Kuwait, Pakistan, Turkey, and elsewhere.

The governments of some Moslem countries, culturally homogenous and economically underdeveloped, provide support only for public schools. Such is the case in Afghanistan, where the population is almost exclusively Moslem, and the Islamic faith is included in public instruction. According to the UNESCO survey, "The education system of Afghanistan is centralized and entirely state run."[2]

However, while usually providing Moslem religious instruction in their public schools, more advanced Moslem countries, particularly those with non-Moslem minorities, allow government aid to independent schools. Among such countries are Egypt, Morocco, Jordan, Syria, Turkey, Iraq, Iran (Persia), and Pakistan.

FAR EASTERN COUNTRIES

Most noncommunist Far Eastern countries have achieved independence only recently. Most of them are underdeveloped and wrestling with numerous problems, and several of them have to carry on war to avoid being swallowed up by communist neighbors.

Many of these countries cannot be used as indicators of anything more than temporary adaptation to current needs. Omission of aid to independent schools in some is explained by the poverty of the country, or a weakness of popular religion, or a hostility to foreign ideologies.

In the Buddhist countries of Burma and Cambodia there is no religious instruction in the public schools, and no public assistance to independent education.

In Laos and Ceylon, also predominantly Buddhist, religious instruction is provided in many public or quasi-public schools. In Laos, the religion usually taught is Buddhism. There is some government aid to independent schools in Laos. In Ceylon, where some 2,500 independent schools were nationalized in 1960, the religion taught is that predominant

---

[2] *Ibid.*, p. 81.

in the particular district, so that religious schools have been allowed to retain something of their previous identity.

In South Vietnam and the Republic of Korea, where religious pluralism obtains, public authorities report that, because of the impoverished condition of their countries, no public aid is at present given to independent schools, but they indicate that they consider this situation temporary and extraordinary.

In the predominantly Buddhist country of Thailand, state grants-in-aid are given to independent schools.

The Philippines have been subject to both Spanish and American influences. Despite avowed separation of church and state, optional religious instruction is allowed in the public schools, and priests are allowed to teach in the school building. As of 1955, no direct public assistance was given to independent schools — a practice obviously a result of American influence.

Apart from the Philippines (where religious instruction is permitted in public schools), the larger Far Eastern noncommunist states provide government aid to independent schools. Included in this category are India, Indonesia, Japan, and the Republic of China.

Over 90 percent of the independent schools and their students in India are subsidized and "aided" by federal, state, and local governments. The Indian Constitution (Art. 15, Sec. 2) forbids financial discrimination against schools conducted by religious or linguistic minority groups.

Indonesia follows the Dutch pattern and has provided public grants up to 100 percent of the expenses of independent schools, which are accepted as a part of the public educational effort. The Moslem religion is taught (on an optional basis) in Indonesian public schools.

Although Japan has a constitutional separation of church and state, introduced in 1946, under American auspices, the Japanese government aids independent schools by a law passed as early as 1949, three years after its new constitution.

On the island of Taiwan (Republic of China), religion is not taught in the public schools, but aid is given to private schools, including those that teach religion.

EMERGING COUNTRIES OF AFRICA

Several emerging African nations are in a state of flux, and policies toward religion in education and public aid to independent schools have not yet been permanently determined. If such countries go communist, there will be no room for religion in public education or for independent schools. If they remain democratic, they may follow the examples of most Western democracies and allow state aid to independent schools, including Christian schools, that are doing a good educational job. Examples of African countries that are already doing this and publicly assisting independent education are Nigeria, Dahomey, and Ghana.

CONCLUSION

We have seen that in eleven communist countries, which represent one third of the world's population, independent education has been stifled. Only state schools are permitted and religious instruction is generally excluded from them.

On the other hand, most democratic countries allow religious instruction in their public schools, making participation a matter of choice. Out of some seventy-four noncommunist countries seen, about sixty allow religious instructions in public schools. About sixty-five provide direct public assistance for independent education, and practically all give indirect aid. In general, democratic countries aid independent education, and most countries give direct as well as indirect aid. Only a few limit their assistance to indirect aid, and even these make exceptions.

Several countries, particularly in Africa and Asia, are in an "emerging" status. With such countries, the example of older established democracies carries great weight. We must not make our decisions on the school question lightly, on the basis of provincial prejudices, or partial considerations. The future of freedom is in our hands.

CHAPTER V

Freedom and Equity in Dutch Education

Edwin H. Palmer*

The national system of education in The Netherlands has made a unique contribution to the solution of the problem of educational freedom. In essence this plan has been in effect since 1920, thus affording almost a half century of practical testing. This writer was acquainted with the system before having studied in The Netherlands, and he was thoroughly opposed to it, chiefly because he felt that it contradicted the principle of separation of church and state. But after four years of firsthand acquaintance with this plan, he became convinced that America can profit greatly by carefully analyzing both the present system and the years of dialogue that preceded it.

I. THE PAST

The history of the modern Dutch educational system is usually known as the *schoolstrijd*, the "school struggle." The *schoolstrijd* was essentially a struggle for freedom. It had two phases: (A) the struggle on the part of independent schools for the legal or constitutional freedom to exist; and (B) the struggle for the actual freedom to exercise this legal freedom. The parallel (C) struggle on the university level will also be discussed.

A. STRUGGLE FOR LEGAL FREEDOM

After the Reformation, Dutch public education was generally and thoroughly Calvinistic. Article 36 of the *Belgic Confession* — the con-

---

* Pastor, Grandville Avenue Christian Reformed Church, Grand Rapids, Michigan; former dean, Westminster Theological Seminary, Philadelphia, Pennsylvania.

65

fession of the dominating Calvinistic, Reformed churches — delineated the duty of the state in general and its operating of the schools in particular. That article stated that the state's task was to "remove and prevent all idolatry and false worship, that the kingdom of antichrist may be thus destroyed and the kingdom of Christ promoted."

In the eighteenth and nineteenth centuries, the philosophy of the Enlightenment gradually supplanted the philosophy of Calvinism in the schools. Rationalism, deism, and naturalism came to be the order of the day. To be sure, the Reformed faith had left its mark upon the people, so that some teachers still continued teaching in its spirit. Even Article 22 of the Educational Law of 1806 specified that the schoolchildren should be developed in "all social and Christian virtues." Yet, according to the next article, the distinctive doctrines of the different churches could not be taught. School classes were to be opened with "a short and appropriate Christian prayer in a reverent fashion." Yet the Christianity offered had lost its vitality and character because it had been purged of the specific and concrete in order not to offend anybody.

The transition in the Dutch schools from Calvinism to a vague inter-denominational religion that outwardly had some Christian trappings may be compared to the similar transition in American public schools during the same period. Originally, our nation's schools were positively Christian and had a distinctively Protestant character, but gradually they lost that distinctiveness in the interest of a lowest-common-denominator philosophy that would mollify various Protestants, Roman Catholics, or Jews. Just as the American Roman Catholics opposed Bible reading in the American state schools in the past century, chiefly because the Authorized Version was used, so also the Dutch Roman Catholics opposed the Bible in their state schools. Furthermore in 1830 a royal degree forbade the use of any books in class that would be offensive to religious groups. Twelve years later another royal degree allowed any cleric to request any teacher in the governmental schools to furnish a list of all the books that were used in his class. If the cleric found any books that were objectionable from a religious standpoint, then an appeal was made to the supervisor, who had the authority to remove them. As a result of these various forces, the Dutch school soon became a school without the Bible. Some even charged that it was anti-Christian.

This change from Calvinism to humanism aroused an increasing dissatisfaction with the state schools and made many desirous of establishing schools where their children could be educated in the same philosophy of life as they received at home and in church. Here were the seeds of the *schoolstrijd:* the desire for schools that reflected the families' religious convictions and the lack of freedom to have them.

The first laws that regulated all the schools of the country (1801, 1803, 1806) technically allowed independent schools. There were many in existence in 1800. But the freedom to establish new schools was so greatly restricted that few independent schools were established in the first half of the nineteenth century. Permission had to be granted by the local governments. Sometimes, however, when the authorities realized that the requests for new schools arose out of a dissatisfaction with the "neutral" state schools, they refused permission. Other requests were granted only after much delay. This lack of school freedom was one reason many Dutch came to Michigan and Iowa in 1846 and the following years.

Gradually, complete freedom to establish independent schools became a reality. In 1842 a royal decree opened the way for appeals when local communities declined permission to establish schools. The most fundamental change came, however, six years later when the constitution was revised. The year 1848 was one of many European revolutions, and the knowledge of what was happening elsewhere led King William II to introduce constitutional changes that were finally adopted. Among them was a regulation that guaranteed the right to establish free schools, i.e., nongovernmental schools (free from government control). The government, of course, maintained its right to demand that the teachers be capable and of good moral character. This victory for freedom was the result of the collaboration of the Reformed (Protestant), Roman Catholic, and Liberal political parties.

The spirit of the revisors of the constitution is seen in the position of a member of the Reformed party, Van der Brugghen, who emphasized that the right to educate does not belong to the state but to the parents. The state's duty, he said, was only to see that there were good teachers. In the same line, Groen Van Prinsterer (also Reformed) had expressed himself earlier (1840) in Parliament: "Parents who, with or without sufficient ground, are convinced that the religious orientation of the teaching in a particular school is un-Christian, must not, either directly or indirectly, be hindered from giving their children the kind of education that they feel is necessary before God. Such coercion, I say it plainly, is intolerable and must cease. It is presumption that springs from the doctrine of the French Revolution which views the children as the property of the state."

The constitutional revision also provided that governmental education be provided everywhere in the country, and it codified the royal decrees of 1830 and 1842 so that the teaching in the state schools would be given "with respect for everyone's religious convictions."

Although the constitution gave freedom for the establishing of independent schools, hampering restrictions by the local governments still remained in effect until the new educational law of 1857. In 1849, for example, only two new Protestant schools came into being. Even Groen Van Prinsterer, the political leader, was able to establish a Christian (Protestant) school in 1849 only after having been denied the privilege for five years. But in December of 1849 the Liberal prime minister, Thorbecke, encouraged the school authorities to be more liberal in their handling of requests for new schools. As a result, some forty independent schools were established between 1849 and 1857. But it was the new educational law of 1857, the Van der Brugghen law, that gave in practice what 1848 gave in principle.

From that time on, the independent schools grew in great numbers. A prime reason for this growth was the "neutralization"[1] of the governmental schools. Between 1849 and 1857 a great struggle developed over the character of the state schools. Some (Groen) wanted a *facultatieve splitsing* of the state schools into at least three groupings: Protestant, Roman Catholic, and Jewish. This and other solutions were voted down in Parliament in favor of a "neutral" school in which the teachers were to "abstain from teaching, doing or permitting anything that was in conflict with the respect due to the religious ideas of others" (Article 23).

Yet the same article demanded that the children receive an "upbringing in all Christian and social virtues." For a few years this ambiguity created a conflict in practice, similar to the situation in American state schools. In spite of Supreme Court decisions which have ruled out religious indoctrination, teachers in certain American communities, especially predominantly Protestant or Roman Catholic ones, have openly taught religion in the classrooms. Sometimes it has been difficult to note differences in the instruction in the Christian and state

---

[1] "Neutralization" and "neutral" are put in quotes in this chapter because in many people's minds there is no such thing as "neutral" education. Even secularism is a religion. It relates studies to ultimate values, even if in a negative way.

schools. So also Holland still had a Christian heritage and conscience which it did not want to overthrow entirely in its state schools. It did not want to appear heathenish. Yet neither did it want to offend the religious sensibilities of the non-Christian. The absolute "neutrality" interpretation came to clarity in two decisions. One was in 1860, when a capable Jewish lawyer, A. de Pinto, protested the teaching of the Bible in the state schools. The other decision was in the following year, when a school inspector, Hofstede de Groot, was discharged because he advocated instruction in Bible stories, including the central facts of Christianity.[2]

Thus in fifty years Dutch education had changed from a "Christian" education to a secular education. The educational act of 1806 had required an instruction that would be "Christian," even if it had robbed the word of most of its significance. The law of 1857 was soon interpreted to mean that education was to be absolutely "neutral." It was this character of state education, coupled with the newly won right to establish freely schools of one's choice, that led to the great growth in independent schools, especially among the Reformed Protestants and Roman Catholics. The Union of Christian Schools — "the schools with the Bible" — had already been formed and was active. In 1868 the Roman Catholic bishops sent out a *Mandement* in which they roundly condemned the state schools and encouraged schools of their own faith. "What are we to think," they wrote, "of schools where the influence of the church and religion has been banished . . . ? Catholics may not approve such teaching. The teaching in the public neutral schools may never be viewed as anything else than a sad necessity."

B. Struggle for Actual Freedom

Now began the second phase of the *schoolstrijd*. The first phase centered on the right to legal existence, the second on the right to actual existence. The first concerned formal freedom; the second, material freedom. The first lasted fifty years; the second was to last seventy years.

There are three principal dates to remember in this moving, second phase of educational freedom: 1878, 1889, and 1920. The first date marked a defeat for freedom which, however, proved to be a catalytic force that eventually led to freedom. The background of the defeat began in 1871, when a report was made to Parliament concerning the effect which

---

[2] Note that America is approximately 100 years behind Holland's timetable. This is true both of the prohibition of Bible readings in governmental schools and of financial equalization.

the lack of proper education was having on the army. The prime minister, Kappeyne van de Coppello, correctly interpreted this to mean that Dutch educational standards had to be raised and that this could not be left to accident or the arbitrariness of some. Therefore, he sought to improve the quality of instruction in all elementary schools by introducing a bill in 1878 which, among other things, would limit the size of the classes to forty students and which would demand better training for teachers. The orthodox Protestants and Roman Catholics reacted strongly against this proposal, for they saw that whereas the government schools would have little difficulty meeting these new standards, since they were supported by tax money, such a bill would increase the already difficult financial burdens of their own schools. Some questioned the democracy of a school tax method whereby public money was given to schools to which some had conscientious objections, and was denied to their own schools, even though these schools met the demanded academic standards and even though their pupils also needed a good education for the army. They saw that the governmental schools were placed over against their own schools in a favorable competitive position through their own tax money. They reacted against this financial inequality.

In the midst of the 1878 debate, Abraham Kuyper — later, prime minister — came to the heart of the matter when he wrote in his paper, the *Standaard*, on July 23: "The whole school question is a question of poor and rich. If you are very rich, then, even if you have been blessed with twelve children, there is no school problem for you, either on the lower level of education or the higher. But, woe to you if you do not have that much money. Freedom to establish a school with the Bible — oh, yes, certainly you have that. The law is as liberal as can be. You certainly may have a school with God's Word — if you pay for the school. Listen well, now — after you have paid for your neighbor's school."

Such reasoning apparently made little impact upon the members of Parliament, for both houses decisively passed the Kappeyne bill.

But then the sleeping nation was aroused into an action that would not only affect the educational system but also the political life of the nation. Kuyper led a *Volkspetitionnement* by which an impressive 305,102 people (out of a population of four million) and 421 churches signed a petition requesting the king not to sign the bill. But he did, and the law went into effect.

These events proved to the Protestant and Roman Catholic political parties that Parliament did not truly represent the majority of the people. Only 11 percent of the male population over twenty-three years of age was eligible to vote for members of Parliament. The Protestant party, in particular, was thus to become a spokesman for the *kleine luyden,* the "common people." By taking a positive stand for greater emancipation of the voter and for freedom in education, Kuyper attracted many to his party. In fact, although the Protestant Anti-revolutionary party had been in existence for many years, 1878 may be considered as the birthday of the *organized* party. Furthermore, Kuyper's eyes were opened to the fact that since 164,000 Roman Catholics had signed the petition, it might be possible to form a coalition government with the Roman Catholic party. This was the coalition which eventually brought educational equality and freedom to Holland. Such cooperation was not easy for either party. Both held to strong convictions and unpleasant memories. Yet they realized that without compromising their religious beliefs or holding back their attack on the other's theology, there were certain areas in politics where it was necessary to work together. This policy continues to the present day.

In 1887 the Protestants and Roman Catholics were able to modify the constitution so that 26.8 percent of the male population over twenty-three years of age was able to vote. And in the following year, they succeeded in replacing the Liberal party's leadership and were now ready for a new educational law. Thus the 1878 defeat was basically a victory for freedom in education.

The second major date in the *schoolstrijd* for material freedom was *1889.* After the Protestants and Roman Catholics formed the coalition government in 1888, Prime Minister Makay introduced and secured the passage of an educational bill that partially revised the inequities of the ten-year-old Kappeyne law. This law of 1889 provided that the free schools should receive their proportional share of the national funds for the salaries of the teachers. The taxes were to be distributed according to the number of students in the schools.

The Makay law did not yet provide full equity for the free schools. Only a third of their total educational costs was supplied, and the new demands for better education wiped out much of this newly won aid. But the principle of equity was attained for the first time. The free schools were now put on a basis similar to that of governmental schools. The latter were no longer considered as sufficient for all the people.

The pluralism of religious convictions was respected. This was the beginning of the full realization of actual educational freedom. The principle had been won, but it would take another thirty years to reach full *financiële gelijkstelling* (financial equalization) between the free and the governmental schools.

The third important date to remember in the second phase of the *schoolstrijd* is *1920*. Between 1889 and 1920 there was a gradual financial emancipation process for the free schools. This evolution was crowned with what some consider to be the acme of justice, equality, and freedom in the world's educational systems.

We mention only the highlights in those thirty years. In 1901 a law granted the free elementary schools financial rights equal to those of the governmental schools in the building of schools. However, there still remained favoritism for the state in many financial areas, including the supplementation of the national funds for building costs by the local communities. Two years later pension laws treated the teachers of the free and state schools in equal fashion. In 1905, Parliament increased the outlays for both the salaries and the upkeep of all elementary schools. The year 1912 saw another increase in allotments for the operating expenses. Laws in 1905 and 1909 provided modest beginnings in the principle of financial equality for secondary schools.

By a royal decree of 1913, a "pacification committee" was appointed from all political parties in an attempt to end the *schoolstrijd* by modifying Article 192 of the Constitution. After three and a half years of debate, in which all the arguments pro and con of the previous years were brought forward again, Parliament overwhelmingly reached a "pacification" decision. The Lower House accepted the proposed constitutional change by a vote of 57 to 10, and the Upper House passed it unanimously.

Three years later, the constitutional principle of *financiële gelijkstelling* was embodied in the Elementary Educational Law of 1920, the lifework of the Minister of Education, Dr. de Visser. It was overwhelmingly accepted by a vote of 75 to 3 in the Lower House. Two of the three who voted against the bill were communists.

The significant features of the revised constitution and the Visser law are these:

1. In the 1915 constitution the adjective "public" was dropped in front of "education," so that Article 192 now read: "Education is the object of continual governmental care."

2. The governmental schools were to be the financial norm for the aiding of the free schools. This aid pertained to teachers' salaries, erection of buildings, and maintenance costs.

3. The government was given the right to investigate the academic and moral qualifications of all teachers and schools.

4. The freedom from governmental interference in matters of religiously oriented instruction, guaranteed in 1848, was preserved.

The *schoolstrijd* was now ended. The nation recognized that the free schools were as significant for education as the governmental ones, and, therefore, that all should receive equal financial treatment. Instead of distributing taxes to only one type of school, a type that many did not want because of religious convictions, the nation chose to give the taxes to all, regardless of their religious creed. In this way it did not use the taxing power of the nation to coerce parents to choose secularistic schools when secularism was contrary to their Jewish, Roman Catholic, or Protestant beliefs. The poor now had as much freedom of educational choice as the rich. Actual — and not only theoretical — equality and freedom had been won.

C. STRUGGLE FOR LEGAL AND ACTUAL FREEDOM ON THE
    UNIVERSITY LEVEL

Just as on the lower level of education there were two phases of the *schoolstrijd*, so also there were two phases on the university level: (1) the *strijd* (struggle) for a legal or constitutional freedom to exist; and (2) the *strijd* for an actual freedom to exist.

In the first part of the nineteenth century, the government had a monopoly on higher education, operating the nation's only universities: Leiden, Utrecht, and Groningen. These, including the divinity schools, were governed by a rationalistic, humanistic philosophy of life that only vaguely had affinities with Christianity. The right to establish free universities was written in the constitution at the same time that the legal freedom was granted to the elementary and secondary schools (1848). But without parliamentary laws to implement this right, the constitutional theory was an empty right.

The same arguments that were used in the *schoolstrijd* for freedom on the lower level of education were also used in connection with the higher level. Some were frankly against Christian education on any plane. Others followed the French Revolutionary idea that only the state had the right to run a university. But Parliament recognized that free choice in university education is also the right of parents and private organizations. Accordingly, a major victory for the legal freedom of higher education was won with the passage of the Heemskerk educational law of 1876. This law regulated the establishment of new private universities. Four years later (1880) the law was first utilized when Abraham Kuyper established a Calvinistic university in Amsterdam. Significantly, he called it the Free University, a name which symbolized the goal of the *schoolstrijd* on all levels. It was called "Free" because it was free from governmental interference. The professors were not restricted to teach only what would not offend a Roman Catholic, Jew, modernist, or humanist. Rather, they were free boldly to relate all their instruction to the Word of God as they interpreted it. Today there is a second free (with a small "f") university, a Roman Catholic one, established in Nijmegen in 1923. There are also some business and technical colleges or institutes.

Constitutional freedom having been won, there remained, nevertheless, two restrictions which deprived the free universities of a great portion of their actual freedom. First of all, the degrees of nongovernmental universities did not enjoy the status of *effectus civilis*. Students who graduated from the Free University were obliged to take exams under professors in a state university before they could be admitted to certain professions. Thus, although free universities could be established, the degrees were not of the same value, even though their instruction might have been superior to that of the governmental schools. Prime Minister Kuyper realized that this was a serious denial of freedom, not only for his own university, but also for any free university that might be established in the future. After a bill to rectify this inequity was defeated, Kuyper succeeded in holding new elections for Parliament, and the new Parliament passed the law in 1905. Thus he "refounded" the university on its silver anniversary.

The second restriction on actual freedom was financial. Although independent universities were permitted to be established, no financial aid was given to them at the beginning. This meant in effect that the wealth of the whole nation was poured into universities with a philosophy of life that was radically different from that of the majority of the nation. Freedom for all with favoritism toward one. In this way, it was reasoned, all independent universities would suffer great handicaps through the competition of tax-supported universities, and their actual freedom would suffer greatly. The parallel to this situation is seen in

America, where private universities, which used to have the majority of students, have now lost that majority to the governmental schools and are continually diminishing. Tax money to governmental schools has made it impossible for many private colleges to compete, thus forcing them out of existence and denying them their actual (not legal) freedom.

In Holland the responsibility of the government to treat all educational systems equally was seen in principle in Kuyper's educational act of 1905. As a token, Parliament allotted four thousand guilders to any qualified free university. This sum was insignificant in comparison with the millions which the state universities received, but the principle had been established.

For many years, however, there remained opposition to any increase in subsidy. But gradually the nation came to see that the independent universities performed an important, public, cultural function that the state universities could not fulfill for a great percentage of the people. It believed that governmental and independent universities should have equal opportunities for development. Accordingly, in 1948 almost the whole Parliament, including the socialists, voted a *financiële gelijkstelling* for all universities. The percentage of costs paid to the various independent universities varied somewhat, but in 1960 a law completely equalized these payments for the nation's four "free" universities: the Free University of Amsterdam, the Catholic University of Nijmegen, the Catholic Economic University of Tilburg, and the Economic University of Rotterdam (secular). The law authorized payment of 95 percent of the operating expenses and the capital outlays which had the approval of the Ministry of Education, Arts, and Sciences.

In these ways a great measure of actual freedom has been granted to nongovernmental universities.

II. THE PRESENT

How do the present laws in The Netherlands work out in a concrete situation? Suppose some parents of certain religious convictions are dissatisfied with the elementary education in the state schools — primarily because they feel that God is left out. These parents can form a school association. They then make a petition to the local government for aid in establishing a school according to their religious principles. If their town is under 50,000 in population, they will have to guarantee that there will be fifty children in school. If they are in a municipality of

50,000 to 100,000, the required number will be one hundred. If they are in a city of 100,000 or more, the minimum will be one hundred and twenty-five. If there are not enough children to form a new school, then the parents may send their children to a neighboring town where there is a school of their own choice. The government will pay for the transportation in this case.

Within thirty days, the municipal authorities must give an answer. If the answer is "yes," then the municipal authorities proceed to build a school. They pay for the entire cost of the buildings and furnishings. They will also pay for any additions, for the lighting, heating, cleaning, general upkeep of the building, and the means of education (books, maps, and the like). The school association has freedom to pick the kind of building that it wants, but the state school is the norm by which the financial aid is granted. In other words, this school association may not choose a luxurious building and expect the civil authorities to pay for it.

Each year the school board will have to draw up a budget for the cost of operating the school (apart from salaries), and this must be approved by the municipal authorities and by a national inspector of education. It will be judged by the cost in the state school, although it may go over that set amount if real need can be shown by the independent school. When approved, the town or city will pay it all.

To protect the town from "fly-by-night" schools, the school boards must put in escrow 15 percent of the cost of the building and furnishings. If, at the end of thirty years, the school is still in existence and still has the required number of pupils, then the money is returned with interest. If not, it is forfeited.

As far as salaries are concerned, the national government, rather than the local government, pays these entirely on the same pay scale as is operative in the governmental schools. It determines how many teachers were necessary for the student body the previous year. Then it gives the money to the school board, which in turn pays the teachers directly.

Thus the national and local governments pay equally to the free and governmental schools all the expenses which are necessary for a good education.

All of these privileges demand that the recipient schools fulfill certain conditions. In other words, the people are not going to allow any school — a dancing school or driver's school — to waste the money. What are these conditions? What means are there to determine if the conditions are fulfilled? Is the freedom of the schools lost after all?

To begin with the first question, the national government appoints inspectors for all schools. The ministry of education strives to appoint inspectors of the differing faiths in proportion to the faiths of the schools represented. These inspectors have free access at any time to any classroom. Their duty is to visit every teacher and pupil in their classrooms at least once a year. Among other things, they have the right to check the following matters:

1. The teacher-pupil ratio. Remember that the national government pays the salaries.

2. The teachers' general health and moral character.

3. The teachers' teaching certificates.

4. The overall plan of study and the content of these classes. Just as in America, they demand that certain subjects be taught.

5. The holding of at least 1,040 classes per year for each student.

If schools do not live up to these conditions, the inspector can report this to the Department of Education, and the financial aid will be terminated. This practically never occurs. These conditions are necessary in order to insure the proper academic and health standards in the schools and a wise use of the taxpayers' money.

But the desired and necessary freedom is still retained. Complete freedom remains in the following areas:

1. The appointment of the teachers, principals, and other personnel. This is left entirely in the hands of the local school boards.

2. The nature of the instruction, whether it will be oriented to the Calvinistic, Lutheran, Roman Catholic, Jewish, or so-called "neutral" faith. The inspectors may check on the quality of instruction, but not on the nature of the instruction. The inspectors may demand that so many hours of Dutch history be taught, or literature, or Dutch, but they may not interfere in the slightest with the religious orientation of these subjects, the philosophical presuppositions which govern this instruction.

3. The method of teaching. The method of education in the Dutch schools ranges from the classical type of instruction to the progressive type.

4. The pupils who are admitted. The state schools, for obvious reasons, are required to accept all children. But the free schools may set up their

own standards of acceptance and principals may dismiss children because of behavior.

Thus, there is complete freedom in the essential matters of education.

III. LESSONS FOR THE FUTURE

What lessons can be learned from the Dutch for the future of independent education in the United States?

1. *Equality works.* Hard historical facts demonstrate that it is possible to have financial equality for all schools without undesirable by-products, such as governmental interference in the schools.

2. *Equality and freedom go hand in hand.* Equality does not necessarily entail lack of freedom or government control. One of the greatest fears that Roman Catholics, Jews, and Protestants have with proposals for government aid is this fear of governmental interference. "He who pays the piper calls the tune," many say. Here three observations should be made:

a) The experience of Holland demonstrates that a system can be worked out whereby there is no government control. After the Makay law of 1889 had passed the Upper House of Parliament, a voters' organization called Marnix feared that this principle of financial equality would mean loss of freedom. They protested and appealed to the Lower House to defeat the proposed bill. Remarkably enough, just before the final victory in 1917 and 1920, a group of the Calvinistic Antirevolutionary Party also feared government interference. Repeatedly, the fear was expressed in the Dutch *schoolstrijd*. But Holland managed to work out a system which permitted both equality and freedom.

First of all, the nation rewrote the constitution so that the government may not interfere in the slightest with the religious orientation of any classes of the free schools. As was seen in the previous section, both the constitution (1917) and the law (1920) expressly spelled out the areas of freedom. Nothing more could be desired from this standpoint. The restrictions, such as on the teachers' academic qualifications, the number of school days per year, and health and safety measures in the school buildings, are what independent schools in America already have.

This writer can also vouch from personal experience that this freedom is real. Four years at the Free University convinced him that no professor there even thinks of tailoring his lectures in order to please the government. It was exactly this governmental interference in the state universities that caused the leaders to want a free university, and they are certainly not going to give up that freedom.

Dr. Maarten Rooy of the University of Amsterdam said in a published lecture at St. Michael's University, Toronto, on December 8, 1960: "In my opinion, which is that of a philosophical liberal, and opposed to certain tenets of denominational parties, the Dutch school system reflects to the highest degree respect for basic human freedom, particularly for freedom of thought and religion, as well as mutual respect amongst citizens in regard to each other's creeds and philosophies. The Dutch constitutional school system is an excellent instance of the implementation of what Jacques Maritain terms the 'democratic charter.' "

The *Christelijke Encyclopedie* (Kampen, 1958) in the article on "Inspectie Onderwijs" states: "The national inspectors visit the private schools, but they are not permitted to interfere with the principial[3] side of the instruction. The inspectors of the private school associations must do that."

From all sides — from an Amsterdam teacher of forty-five years of experience, a former government school inspector in Rotterdam, and the executive secretary of the Christian Union and School Council in The Hague[4] — the unanimous judgment of those who have been involved in the Dutch school systems is this: the parents are perfectly free in the choice of books, pupils, teachers, and principals. And the teachers have always been able to say what they thought was their Christian duty to say.

b) In America we should adopt a type of financial system that meets the American historical needs. I have no objection to the Dutch system at all. It works. But to calm American fears, I believe we should turn to and follow a system already in use in America. This is the aid-to-the-student rather than aid-to-the-school program, patterned on the G.I. Bill of Rights, the New York State Scholar Incentive Program for higher education, and similar programs in many other states. In these two specific cases, there has been no governmental interference at all with the private universities which these students attend.[5]

---

[3] A word translating the Dutch adjective *principieel*, which means pertaining to principles, i.e., one's moral, religious, or philosophical convictions, which govern one's conduct.

[4] These testimonies are in the form of personal correspondence with the author.

[5] In 1946 and 1947 more than 50 percent of the college students were receiving aid from the G.I. Bill of Rights.

c) Under the present American school system, there is already great governmental control of private education. In addition to regulating independent schools in numerous ways, the government, by collecting taxes from all and then distributing them only to the governmental schools, has effectively prevented many parents from establishing schools of their own choice and has prohibited the poor from attending them when they are established. This is government control by taxation.

3. *Equality is based upon parental rights.* Elsewhere I have called this principle the separation of family and state.[6] All through the Dutch *schoolstrijd* the chief pillar for equality was this principle of parental rights. It was argued from different sources that according to nature and the Bible the parents have the right to educate the children as they desire. It was a French Revolutionary concept that the children belonged to the state. But the protagonists of free schools stressed the rights of parents. Some parents may want to delegate their authority to teachers who are simply an extension of the home. Others may want to delegate their authority to the church. Still others may want to delegate their authority to the state. But the responsibility of choice rests primarily with the parents.

4. *Equality solves the problem of the relation of religion to education.* One of the best results of proposals of financial aid to *all* students, regardless of race, color, or creed, is that it solves the troublesome and ever-recurring problem of the relation of religion to education in governmental schools.

It is noteworthy that most western European democracies do not have this problem. As in the case of Holland, the reason can be found in their system of school taxation, a system which in one form or other does not financially penalize parents who choose a God-centered education. Holland has recognized the pluriformity of its people and has not attempted to superimpose a monolithic educational system on all, financially penalizing those who do not desire a secularistic education. But it grants all — regardless of their philosophy of education — equal financial aid. In one stroke, the problem vanished in Holland.

When a nation attempts to superimpose a single system of thought upon a pluralistic people, it is bound to fail. Some will have conscientious objections to whatever the Supreme Court decides concerning religion in the state schools. If the court rules God, Bible reading, and prayer unconstitutional in the classroom, it offends the religious sensibilities

---

[6] "Separation of Family and State," *Torch and Trumpet* (March, 1962).

of those who desire them in. If it retains them, it offends those who do not recognize God. If it allows school subjects to be interpreted in the light of the "religion of secularism,"[7] then it offends those who believe God should be related to all of life. But if it relates God to all of life, a choice must be made among the various concepts of God: the Jews', the Unitarians', the Roman Catholics', or the Baptists'. Whatever one it upholds, it offends the others. The obvious reason for the insuperable dilemma is that the government is favoring with billions of dollars one philosophy of education over others.

The only way for our government to extricate itself from its present difficulties is by frankly recognizing that America is a pluralistic nation, a people of many faiths, and then allowing parents complete freedom of educational choice without forfeiting their school taxes. Then God, the Bible, and positive religious instruction may be ejected from the state schools, and no one's conscience will be offended. For no financial favoritism will be shown to secularism as is presently the case, but all will have their proportionate share of school taxes to select the school of their own choice.

5. *Equality and freedom should also hold on the university level.* The Dutch recognized that the principles of financial equality which are valid for the first twelve years of a child's education are also valid for the succeeding years at the university. There is nothing sacrosanct in the number twelve.

In America the national and many state governments have essentially recognized this truth by granting scholarships to students at any academically accredited university. New York, for example, will grant a scholarship to any New York resident in any accredited New York college or university and not only to state ones. As a matter of fact, governmental aid of this nature may be the only way that free American colleges can survive and remain free.

Tuition assistance, such as that given through the G.I. Bill of Rights and the New York State Scholar Incentive Program, may be able to reverse the tragic trend of the decline of free colleges. The startling facts threatening our academic freedom are that, although in the beginning of our national history colleges were under private control, by 1900 only 62 percent of the American college and university students attended free colleges and universities. In 1950 the figure had

---

[7] Supreme Court Justice Potter Stewart's characterization of the state schools in his minority opinion in the 1963 Bible reading case.

dropped to 50 percent. In 1960 the percentage slid still further to 41 percent, and the bottom is not in sight. At present, through governmental financial favoring of one type of education, we are seeing the dramatic but silent and little-known transition from free education to government-controlled education. The Dutch system of governmental aid (on the American scene through scholarships) may point the way to true educational freedom in American universities.

Holland has also introduced a system that, with certain modifications, might well be emulated. Kuyper's 1905 educational act provided that chairs could be established at the state universities by differing religious groups. (Naturally, the state demands that the instruction be of university caliber.) In this way, the Roman Catholics and Calvinists, in particular, have been able to offer courses in state universities for credit, and the one-sided approach of "neutralism" or secularism has been modified. Because different viewpoints may thus be taught, the monopoly of the secularists is partially broken.

6. *Equality is worth possible inefficiency.* The charge of inefficiency that is familiar to American ears was made repeatedly in the Dutch situation. It was feared and is still asserted in some quarters that equality and freedom in education will greatly increase the cost of education because of the inefficiency of having two or three schools where one would suffice.

The Dutch answered this problem in two ways:

a) By recognizing a partial truth in the assertion, but also by recognizing that freedom is more important than efficiency and that conscience is dearer than money. Economics is an important factor, but it may not be the most decisive one. The problem is similar to that of a dictatorship versus a democracy. A dictatorship is much more efficient, but also much more enslaving. The Dutch saw that efficiency was not the only criterion by which the problem of schools should be solved.

b) By restricting the building of schools to groupings of certain size, such as a minimum of fifty children in towns of 50,000 or less, and by requiring 15 percent of the building costs to be put into escrow for thirty years. These two conditions have checked the mushrooming of schools for a handful of pupils.

7. *The asserted decline of the public schools should not be viewed emotionally.* An oft-made objection to the Dutch system is that it has resulted in a comparative decline of the public schools, and, therefore,

is undesirable. The facts in the situation are that the proportion of students attending the free and the state schools has been almost exactly reversed in the seventy years since the granting of the first subsidy. In 1890, 71 percent of the pupils in elementary schools went to the state schools and 29 percent to the free schools. In 1958 the percentages were 28 percent in state schools and 72 percent in free schools. The state school percentages decreased until 1950. Since that time they have remained steady, and apparently the situation has stabilized.

The first reply is that it all depends on what we mean by "public" schools. The free schools may be considered "public," since they serve the public and are controlled (in a broad sense) by the public.

If it is felt that it is wrong for state schools to decline in this fashion, the question must be asked: Is it democratic to impose on 70 percent of the Dutchmen a system of education that they obviously do not want? The people have rejected overwhelmingly the governmental schools and have exactly the kind of schools they desire.

As for America, it is emotionalism that states that the governmental schools will go out of existence if every student has his fair share of school taxes. Most Americans want exactly the type of secularistic education that the state schools now provide and, therefore, will continue to use these schools. The state schools will decline in proportion to the people who desire a God-centered education. But this is democracy at its best: allowing the people, in fulfillment of their parental rights, to choose the kind of education they desire without being penalized.

8. *The equality struggle needs new slogans.*

a) *"Free Schools."* The terms "public" and "private" are not precise characterizations of state schools and free schools. On the contrary, they create the false impression that only the state schools are performing a public function and that the "private" schools are not. But a careful analysis will reveal that the so-called "private" schools are public in the sense that they perform a public function — a function which, left undone, the state would have to perform. One seventh of the population is trained in these schools, and these citizens will make significant civic, cultural, religious, scientific, and economic contributions to society.

In a 1963 memorandum on *The Netherlands — Education,* The Netherlands Information Service (New York City) states this principle admirably, "Thus, the distinction between 'public' and 'private' schools in The Netherlands does not refer to Government schools on the one hand and privately sponsored schools on the other, but to 'non-religious' and 'religious' schools respectively. Both types are 'public' in the American sense of the term." That last sentence, astounding as it may seem to most American ears, means that the free schools serve the public welfare, prosperity, and need equally as well as do the state schools and, therefore, both are supported by public funds.

Thus the terms *private* and *public* could better be replaced by the terms *free* or *independent* and *state* or *governmental*.

b) *"Equalization."* The Dutch have repeatedly used the term *gelijkstelling*, "equalization." The concept is that the free schools should be put on a par with the state schools, that education belongs fundamentally in the hands of the parents, and that the government should not play favorites. The state should treat all schools equally, regardless of whether they are agnostic, Protestant, Jewish, or Seventh-Day Adventist. The terms *equality* and *equalization* would strike a familiar chord in most American ears and have a favorable aura about them.

9. *The struggle may last a long time.* It took the Dutch seventy years, 1848–1920, to attain equality in education; Americans should never become discouraged in their *schoolstrijd*. They should ask only one thing: Is it right or wrong? If wrong, we want nothing to do with it. But if right "principally,"[8] then we should not be discouraged by delays. We must, therefore, think out our position in principle.

If we are convinced that our goals are significant and founded in just principles, then we can tolerate delay without becoming discouraged. We must first see what is right and then work hard for it, even if it takes a long time. The Dutch example should warn us that we may possibly need to be "principially" strong for several years to come.

---

[8] See footnote 3, p. 79.

CHAPTER VI

Educational Freedom in England and Wales, Northern Ireland and Scotland, France, Democratic Czechoslovakia (to 1938), and Israel

R. F. Cunningham, London, England
Brother Edmond Drouin, F.I.C., Canton, Ohio,
and Rabbi Alexander Mittlemann, Montreal,
Canada

Government Aid to Schools Founded by Voluntary Bodies in England and Wales, Northern Ireland and Scotland

R. F. Cunningham*

This segment is concerned with public subsidization of independently conducted education in England and Wales, as well as Scotland and Northern Ireland, in what the English call "voluntary" schools. The term "voluntary" is here used rather than "private" or "independent," which are often employed to refer to such schools in other countries. In the United Kingdom, "private" or "independent" refers to schools which are fully fee-paying and almost completely independent financially of the state. "Voluntary" schools, in contrast, although mainly controlled by nonpublic authorities, are a recognized and subsidized part of the "public" system of education. The latter is thus a "dual" or two-sided system, to which the voluntary schools belong equally along with the county (or "state") schools, though their control is different.

---

* Mr. R. F. Cunningham is secretary of the Catholic Education Council, London, England.

THE STORY OF STATE AID TO VOLUNTARY
SCHOOLS IN ENGLAND AND WALES

It was not until 1833 that the state intervened in education in England and Wales. In that year, for the first time, the government made a financial contribution to the costs of education. It began with the modest sum of £ 20,000 (at current rates of exchange $56,000, though obviously at the prices of those days worth very much more). Until then, voluntary bodies, mainly religious in character, had borne the whole burden of providing education. After that date the financial contribution and the interest of the state in education grew, and this was reflected in the rising volume of the grants made to voluntary bodies conducting schools. With time, the task of providing an educational system grew to a scale beyond the resources of voluntary bodies assisted only by government grants, for the population increased, and with the Industrial Revolution, rose particularly in the cities where the influence of the voluntary religious bodies engaged in education was weaker.

The year 1870 saw the establishment of local school boards empowered to levy "rates" in aid of education (that is, property taxes). In 1902 the multitude of school boards was replaced by a smaller number of Local Education Authorities (LEA) which were general-purpose local government units. After 1944 the responsibility for education was further restricted to the present smaller number, all of them major authorities in legal status, that is, county councils or county boroughs, though they vary greatly in population from as little as 40,000 to over 4,000,000. These successive types of local authorities have been empowered to establish and conduct schools out of their own revenue from "rates," assisted by a grant from the central government, which in recent years has covered about 60 percent of their expenditure; and over the years they have become responsible for a wide variety of educational services. Their schools, now called "county" schools, amount to nearly 80 percent of all schools in the public sector, the remainder being "voluntary" schools.

The year 1870 thus marked the beginning of the change from the time when all schools were the result of voluntary initiative and depended very heavily on voluntary funds, though they were aided by state grants. After that date the county schools developed with the help of steadily increasing support from public funds, whether local or national. For a long time the financial position of voluntary schools continued to be extremely difficult, and the next 75 years were marked by intermittent violent controversy about church schools (for the voluntary schools were usually church schools).

At times the controversy was a major political and party issue, which threatened to topple governments. Its history is long and fascinating, but cannot be described here. One should note, however, that though at times secularist opinion played a substantial part, the main protagonists were always the different religious groups; on the one side, though in no sense generally allied, were the Church of England (with the biggest group of schools) and the Catholic Church, and on the other, the "Free Churches," embracing the mainstreams of "Non-Conformity": Methodists, Presbyterians, Congregationalists, and Baptists.

The "Free Church" opposition to church schools had several facets. It took its stand on the principle that schools should be nondenominational, but not that they should be secular; "Free Churchmen" looked to broadly Christian teaching given by teachers assumed to be Christian. One of their objections to the existence of denominational schools was that in many areas, for lack of an alternative school, Free Church children might be obliged to attend Church of England (Anglican) schools. Although this objection did not apply to Catholic schools, which usually catered exclusively to Catholics, they also maintained strong opposition to Catholic schools on general grounds.

Before proceeding to look at the system which grew out of the 1944 Act, it is worth noting some general characteristics of the English educational system. In the first place, the present system derives from a past of voluntary effort; and as it has developed, there has continued to be a strong system of independent education (that is, fee-paying schools "private" by choice), which in matters of educational practice and standards has on many occasions set the pace for the whole educational system. Second, the public system which developed was not a centralized state system, but a system run by local authorities under the general direction and control of the Ministry of Education, but less and less under its detailed control. Third, by tradition, schools and teachers retain very extensive freedom over the curriculum. Fourth, there has always been a strong sentiment in favor of parental freedom of choice, which is indeed an aspect of a strong sentiment in favor of personal and individual freedom.

All these factors, combined with the existence of a strong system of independent schools, have made for diversity in the English system (in this context England means England and Wales), and have eased the path of voluntary schools. It is also relevant that, in England, schools have not usually been seen as the instruments of social unification, so that the argument that a system of voluntary schools is "divisive" is rarely heard.

THE PRESENT SYSTEM IN ENGLAND AND WALES

Based on the Act of 1944 and its subsequent amendments, English schools may be grouped into three general classes, the first two of which account for the vast majority of pupils:

a) "Maintained" schools, which belong to the system of education financed by the state and local authorities;

b) "Independent" schools, which do not receive any direct support from the state or the local authorities, but are patronized by the wealthy;

c) "Direct-grant" schools, with partial support from the government.

Denominational schools are to be found in all categories.

The latter two classes do not concern us in the present discussion because of the more limited relations between these schools and the government. The maintained school system has two components: "county" schools and "voluntary" schools. "County" schools are those provided by and controlled by the Local Education Authorities under the Ministry of Education. "Voluntary schools" are schools started by voluntary bodies. The principal voluntary bodies in education in England and Wales are the Catholic Church, the Church of England (the Church of Wales in Wales), and the Jews.

In "voluntary" schools, the powers of the voluntary body over a school depend upon the particular status of the school. There are three kinds of status: aided, controlled, and special-agreement. Special-agreement status has only been available to a limited number of schools; and controlled status is very much the product of special conditions, so that it is not of wide interest.

THE POSITION OF AIDED VOLUNTARY SCHOOLS

We will accordingly limit our discussion to "aided" voluntary schools. Once a school becomes "aided," the local education authority is responsible for meeting all the costs of maintaining the school, except costs for repairs to the exterior. Repairs to the exterior are the responsibility of the "managers" or "governors,"[1] but the latter are helped by a grant of 75 percent of the cost from the Ministry of Education. For most practical purposes, therefore, the full cost of running the school is met by the local authority or the Ministry. This applies to all costs, e.g., teachers' salaries, books, heating, lighting, and cleaning. The salaries of teachers in "voluntary" schools are at the same rates as those of teachers in "county" schools.

Ownership of the school remains in the hands of the voluntary body responsible for it, and religious instruction is that of the denomination concerned. Two thirds of the managing or governing body of the school are appointed by the voluntary body, one third by the local authority. The managing or governing body controls the religious instruction which is given during school hours, and has power over the appointment of teachers, subject to a veto by the local education authority on grounds of educational unsuitability. The local authority has a similar power of veto over the dismissal of a teacher on the same grounds. Managers or governors may appeal to the Minister of Education against the use of this veto.

In practice the managers or governors of a denominational school are enabled to appoint teachers of beliefs acceptable to them, provided the candidates are suitably qualified in other respects. The academic and professional qualifications required would in general be the same as in county (i.e., purely state) schools.

In a secondary school, the governors control the secular instruction. In a primary school the control of the secular instruction is normally vested in the local authority. In practice, however, in England the control of the curriculum is very largely in the hands of the teachers (except to the extent that it is dictated by examinations) and, despite the difference in law between aided primary and secondary schools on this point, there is not in practice a discernible difference between the degree of freedom enjoyed by primary and secondary schools.

It should be emphasized that even in county schools the legal responsibility for the secular instruction rests with the local authority, not the central government. In aided secondary schools the choice of books, materials, etc., is in the hands of the governors, though the power is usually exercised for them by the teachers.

---

[1] In primary schools there is a "managing" body; in the secondary schools a "governing" body.

In aided primary schools, this power is theoretically in the hands of the local authority as a result of their legal control of the secular instruction, but in many cases the rules of management made for individual schools provide that it shall be in the hands of the managers. In practice, the choice is normally made by the teachers. In the unlikely event of a local authority trying to force unsuitable books on a denominational school, an appeal could be made to the Ministry of Education. There have, however, been no serious difficulties over this question.

The day-to-day control of the running of the school is in the hands of the managers/governors (or of the headmaster, depending on the points involved), and they also control the admission of pupils. This means for example that a Catholic school can give priority to Catholic pupils, though it is not allowed to refuse a non-Catholic who wishes to come, if there is a place free.

What is the extent of control by the state or the local authority?

Buildings in new schools must conform to the national standards applied to all schools within the "public" system, both county and voluntary. Older buildings will eventually have to be brought up to the same standard. The Ministry of Education controls the national building program, and the main priority since the war has been the building of extra schools for additional numbers of children. The rebuilding of old schools has therefore had to wait.

Teachers are normally expected to have the same qualifications as in other schools.

The schools are open to inspection by the Ministry's inspectors and the officials of the local authority. They have, however, no power to inspect religious instruction.

The Ministry has reserve powers which it may use in the case of serious and persistent failure to conform to adequate educational standards. But these would be used only after all other measures of exhortation and persuasion had first been employed.

The foregoing describes the position of "aided" schools once established. The following deals with the construction of voluntary schools.

AID FOR CONSTRUCTION COSTS

For building, grants are available, at the rate of 75 percent of the cost of building, in the following circumstances:

a) Rebuilding or modernization of a school, either on the same site or elsewhere. This applies also where there is a reorganization of school accommodations, e.g., where one new school replaces two old schools; a grant is then available for the building of roughly the same amount of accommodation as existed before.

b) Building of aided secondary schools to match aided primary schools which existed in 1959, so that children starting their school life in a denominational aided primary school may be enabled to complete it in a secondary school of the same denomination.

c) Building of schools for pupils whose families have moved as a result of housing developments from areas in which they could have attended aided primary schools of the same denomination. The grant here is in proportion to the number of pupils of this type attending the new school.

The principle behind the very complicated legislation on grants for building is that the voluntary bodies can have grants to rebuild, replace, and improve school accommodations they have previously possessed, and also to build secondary schools where they have already had primary schools (that is, to complete their existing system of education), but not to extend it to provide for greater numbers of children. They may build schools for the extra number of children, but without receiving a capital grant.

Two additional points deserve mention:

1. In all aided schools, whether built with or without a grant, the local authorities are responsible for providing the movable furniture and equipment.

2. In all aided schools, the local authorities are responsible for providing the accommodations for meals (cafeteria, lunchroom, etc.). Since this is quite a substantial part of a school, in any school where a 75 percent grant is paid for building, the voluntary bodies are in effect receiving the equivalent of nearly 80 percent of the total cost of the school.

FOUNDING OF NEW AIDED VOLUNTARY SCHOOLS

When can new aided voluntary schools be built?

Proposals for new aided schools require the approval of the Ministry of Education. The local authority has also to be consulted, and may submit objections to the Ministry. So long as there are sufficient pupils of the denomination concerned, the only major obstacle that arises generally is the refusal of the Ministry to agree to a new school for the reason that there are already enough schools in the area. This difficulty has not yet been encountered on a large scale; and because the total number of children in the country is increasing rapidly, it is not likely to become a general problem in the foreseeable future. In some cases, local authorities have been willing to sell or lease to voluntary bodies schools which are surplus to their requirements.

In a very few areas the local authorities are hostile to voluntary schools, and in these areas a number of voluntary schools owe their existence to the Ministry's having overruled the local authority.

NORTHERN IRELAND

So far this article has described the position in England and Wales. The position in Northern Ireland is not very different and consequently does not need special description.

SCOTLAND

In the remaining part of the United Kingdom, Scotland, the system is, however, basically different. As long ago as 1918, a permanent settlement was reached under which the Catholic and Episcopalian authorities agreed to sell their schools to the Local Educational Authorities (LEA), so that they became the property of the public authority, which thus became entirely responsible for their management and all the costs of upkeep, staffing, etc. The LEA's undertook to provide new schools for the children of the denominations concerned.

The appointment of teachers was also to be in the hands of the Local Educational Authority. But here came the essential safeguard which meant that in practice the schools remained as Catholic or Episcopalian as they had ever been. Teachers were required by the Act to "satisfy both the secular authority and the religious authority, the first as to qualifications, the second as to character and religious belief." The Act provides in addition that "an unpaid supervisor shall be appointed, who shall report to the education authority as to the efficiency of the religious instruction given in such school. The supervisor shall have right of entry at all times set apart for religious instruction and observance." In practice this supervisor is the local priest or minister.

Freedom of Education in France
Brother Edmond G. Drouin, F.I.C.*

The French Revolution of 1789 failed to establish a viable new order and left the schools in the hands of Napoleon, who used them as instruments of power.[1] During the first half of the nineteenth century, as France lived through a variety of political regimes, adjustments were gradually made to permit nonpublic initiative in education. The process was intricate.[2] Some measure of freedom of teaching was recognized by the *Guizot* Law (1833). Private initiative and church schools were allowed in elementary education under conditions of minimal control. But secondary schools were left in the hands of the state. The *Falloux* Law (1850), permitted nonpublic participation in secondary education, and some degree of liberty was later established in higher education by a law of 1875. Statutes of this nature usually recognized freedom of teaching as basic, prescribed conditions and minimal standards for its exercise, and specified that the clergy and members of religious orders were not to be deprived of this freedom.

In the latter part of the century, particularly during the decade from 1880 to 1890, a renewed spirit of "secularism" struck at church-related education, the most organized sector of nonpublic education. As a result of the work of Jules Ferry and his associates, the laws of 1882 and 1886 established sharp distinctions between public and private schools (*écoles libres*), and completely secularized public education.

Much of this legislative program reflected a legitimate desire to establish a national system of education. Unfortunately, the fairness which motivated earlier legislators was missing, and church-related institutions received unnecessarily hard treatment. "It was an interesting paradox that policies initiated by the state for the liberation of some

---

* Brother Edmond G. Drouin is Librarian at Walsh College, Canton, Ohio.

[1] Broad coverage of this problem is available in Louis Grimaud, *Histoire de la Liberté de l'Enseignement en France* (new edition: Paris; Grenoble: B. Arthaud, 1944–   ; 6 volumes published, 1944–1954; Vols. 3–5 published through Paris: Rousseau; Vol. 6, Paris: Apostolat de la Presse). This revised edition, the result of thirty years of study by a French lawyer, covers the Old Regime through the "July Monarchy." Material on the later part of the century must be studied in the first edition (Paris: Rousseau, 1898), 601 pages.

[2] Other aspects of the problem may be studied in Antonin Debidour, *Histoire des Rapports de l'Église et de l'État en France de 1789 à 1870* (Paris: Felix Alcan, 1898), 740 pages, and *L'Église Catholique et l'État Sous la Troisième République (1870–1906)* (Paris: Felix Alcan, 1906–1909), 2 vols.

(schools) should result in the repression of others. While the government continued to assert that it was granting 'freedom of education' to the private schools, it was apparent that it could not tolerate their equality with its own institutions."[3] This was discrimination.

For the successors of Ferry, extinction was to be the next objective. In one century, the attitude of the government had gone full cycle from the destructive spirit of the Revolution of 1789 through varying degrees of accommodation to the drastic "separatism" which prevailed at the dawn of the twentieth century as Émile Combes and Aristide Briand led a new war.[4]

Article 13 of the "Law of Associations" (1901), concerning the legal incorporation of associations, required religious orders to register and obtain formal approval in order to continue in existence. A subsequent law completed a plan of penal action. Applications were received and held. Then, through several sessions of the Chamber of Deputies (1903), they were systematically turned down. Expropriation was the reward for service. Combes was soon able to boast that his strategy had closed over 16,900 educational institutions. Action was completed by a law of 1904 which forbade teaching of any kind to members of religious orders (congréganistes).

In spite of such harshness, aid from local funds given in specie to needy children attending private schools was sanctioned. The principle was extended after World War I when the government helped to meet the cost of educating the children of dead or wounded soldiers and provided scholarships even for such children attending private schools. Priests retained the right to teach as individuals, and were sometimes hired in public institutions.

World War II helped to bring about a real change. The Pétain regime allowed religious orders to reorganize, and it extended subsidies to church-related institutions. A new era of cooperation dawned when peace was established.[5] The Marie law (1951) made government

[3] Evelyn Martha Acomb, The French Laïc Laws (1879–1889), The First Anti-Clerical Campaign of the Third French Republic (New York: Columbia University Press, 1941), p. 182. For additional information see Sister M. Justine Redmond, Laicism in the Schools of France (Washington, D. C.: The Catholic University of America, 1932).

[4] Louis Capéran, L'Invasion Laïque, de l'Avènement de Combes au Vote de la Séparation (Paris: Desclée de Brouwer, 1935), 474 pp.

[5] See William W. Brickman, "Church, State, and School in International Perspective," in William W. Brickman and Stanley Lehrer (eds.), Religion, Government, and Education (New York: Society for the Advancement of Education, 1961), pp.

scholarships available to private school students, and the *Barangé* law (1951) permitted disbursements on a *per capita basis* from the national treasury to associations of parents representing individual private schools. These funds were earmarked mostly to upgrade teachers' salaries. Private secondary agricultural schools were given special attention in the *Laurent* law of 1955 which extended subsidy through the Ministry of Agriculture. Such measures reflect a new recognition of the public purpose served by nonpublic education, an understanding of freedom of education as a basic right, and perhaps, at last, the beginning of a realization that a liberty exists not merely by the fact of its verbal expression in statutes or constitutional law, but rather by the existence of conditions making its exercise possible.

New experiments in cooperation have begun in France.[6] The *Debré* law of December 31, 1959, permits schools to sign contracts with the government. One form of agreement links the school, as a unit, with public authority, which finances its operation in return for some measure of control. Another relationship establishes a bond between the state and individual qualified teachers, who thus become salaried from the public treasury. Three years after the enactment of the law, schools which remain unbound by such engagements are to refer applications to adjustment committees (*comités de conciliation*) empowered to act on the continuance of disbursements provided by the earlier *Barangé* law.[7] Although the new experiment is limited in nature and many of its operations have been left undetermined, it seems that a more equitable basis of operation will finally lighten the economic burden of those who exercise their freedom of choice in education by utilizing nonpublic institutions.

The Example of Czechoslovakia and Israel
Rabbi Alexander Mittlemann*

Since this article is based mainly upon personal observations, I wish to start with some personal remarks. I would like to express my joy

---

167–173; Bernard Mégrine, *La Question Scolaire en France* (Paris: Presses Universitaires de France, 1960); Benigno Benabarre, *Public Funds for Private Schools in a Democracy, Theory and Practice in Fifty-one Countries* (Manila: Philippine Islands, 1958), pp. 200–209.

[6] Edmund G. Ryan, S.J., "France Supports Catholic Schools," *Catholic Educational Review*, LX (March, 1962), pp. 163–173, and *Études* (Paris, June, 1965), pp. 772–788.

[7] As this book goes to press, the original three-year term is being extended.

* Rabbi Alexander Mittlemann was born and educated in Czechoslovakia, and served between the years of 1936 and 1949 in the public and independent school

over the fact that I can freely describe and say what I have to say about my experiences and observations of educational problems in Czechoslovakia and Israel. This would be quite impossible were I now in my native country — Czechoslovakia. It is therefore delightful to live and write in these United States of America, where everybody may think freely and speak and write with equal freedom. A person who underwent both fascist oppression and communist regimentation knows how to appreciate such things.

CZECHOSLOVAKIA

DEMOCRATIC CZECHOSLOVAKIA (1919–1938)

Czechoslovakia, caught between the rival powers of Germany and Russia, is a small country, deeply rooted in religious ideals. Carved out of the remnants of the Austro-Hungarian Empire after World War I, the new country of Czechoslovakia had many problems. Democratization was the guiding principle of the republic's legislators. This led them to respect the rights of the various national minorities which lived in Czechoslovakia in considerable numbers. German, Hungarian, Polish, and Jewish nationals elected a number of deputies to the National Assembly corresponding to their proportion of the population. The same was true for regional, district, and local administrative bodies.

"The right of every individual to education is the same as his right to live," words of Thomas G. Masaryk, was the slogan of the Czechoslovak republic. The Germans, as well as the Hungarians and other minorities, had adequate educational facilities. The Germans, for instance, had a university and two institutes of technology, which were supported by the state, and, of course, the requisite number of the various intermediate and elementary schools.

---

system of that country as a teacher, principal, and superintendent of schools. His observations are of special value because he is comparing the prewar situation in Czechoslovakia under the classic Masaryk-Beneš democracy, the wartime interval under the fascist regime, and the postwar period under communist rule.

In 1949, Alexander Mittlemann emigrated to Israel, where he again had various experiences in the field of elementary, secondary, and higher education. He describes how the young state of Israel dealt with the problem of education in a heterogeneous society of various strata and backgrounds.

In 1958 the author arrived in the United States and, while working for his Ph.D. at the University of Pittsburgh, was engaged in teaching and administration. After similar occupation in Southern California, he became Educational Director of the United Torahs of Greater Montreal and a member of the faculty of Education at Macdonald College of McGill University, Montreal, Canada.

Schools were either state-, municipal-, or church-supported, and were accessible to everybody. Since all elementary schools were subsidized by the state, there was no tuition. Even secondary and higher schools had very low fees, and most of their students were exempt from such. Scholarships and cheap accommodations enabled poor students to continue their studies. Education was not an exclusive privilege of the wealthy.

Moreover, school authorities were anxious to reform and modernize methods of teaching. The educational systems of other countries were carefully studied, and suitable improvements carried out.

Many new school buildings were needed, partly because the education of Czech and Slovak children had not received due attention under the old Austro-Hungarian regime, and partly because there was a remarkable increase in school attendance under the new regime. In the first fourteen years of the republic's existence, about 1400 new primary schools were erected and over 2600 enlarged and modernized.[1] They had spacious and hygienic classrooms and halls, and well-equipped laboratories, science rooms, and gymnasiums. Two new universities and five other institutions of higher education were established. Education made great headway in the twenty years of independence. In the last years of Hungarian rule, there were only 429 elementary schools in which the Slovak language was used; under the republic the Slovaks had more than 3000 schools. No less striking was the progress of higher education. In Hungarian Slovakia there had been no Slovak secondary schools; under the republic they numbered 284. In addition, a Slovak university was established in Bratislava (Pressburg), the Slovakian capital. In the short period of Czechoslovakia's independence, the rising Slovak generation was intellectually well equipped for future responsibilities.

The Czechoslovakian state school system constituted about 40 percent of all institutions in the country. The remaining 60 percent were educational institutions of various types and systems: community schools and so-called "parochial" schools of various denominations. They all were called "public" schools if they reached the established minimum enrollment. And all schools of a "public" nature enjoyed state subsidies if they followed basic requirements of the Ministry of Education and Culture concerning hygiene, curriculum, and supervision.

According to a state law which dated back to 1867 and 1868, each

---

[1] Jan Cech and J. E. Mellon, *Czechoslovakia* (London: Drummond, 1944), p. 35.

school recognized and accredited by the state received about 90 percent of its teachers' salaries from the state. The patrons of the school
were obligated to pay only the remaining 10 percent and to maintain
the school building. For this maintenance, the law provided large
subsidies. Thus, only about 10 to 15 percent of the total budget
was the burden of the community, church, or synagogue which maintained the school.

What were the reasons for the positive financial attitude of the
Czechoslovak government to the nonstate schools? The concept of
European education was deeply rooted in the Judaeo-Christian understanding of the natural right and duty of parents to direct the education of their children according to their convictions, philosophy, and
beliefs. This partly originates in the biblical command which states
that it is the father's duty "to teach the children diligently and to
continue with instruction in knowledge and observance of the Torah."[2]
Until the appearance of the synagogue and formal schools, the family
was almost the only agency of education. It was thus that the high
esteem of the family's importance developed in pre-Christian Judaism.
As it is stated also in the New Testament, the synagogue was essentially a teaching institution.[3] So was the church throughout ancient
and medieval times, and so it was in our century in most European
countries. We should therefore not be surprised that prewar Czechoslovakia, under the classic democracy of Masaryk, had a very positive
attitude toward independent schools. With all its liberalism — and
probably just because of this liberalism — the state felt obligated to
pay the basic costs of this service in recognition of what the communities, churches, synagogues, and other nonprofit civic organizations
offered to the public in education. This notion, namely that every educational institution which was worthy of the name deserved the maximum financial support of the state because it performed a public
function, was deeply rooted in the minds of the people and the
government. No government in prewar Czechoslovakia ever questioned
this right of the independent nonstate schools.

What did the independent educational institutions offer the state
in return for the financial subsidy? They offered a well-rounded education for boys and girls from the nursery and kindergarten up to the
highest academic level. Every such school had its own educational

---

[2] Dt 6:4–9.
[3] See, e.g., Mk 1:21; and Lk 6:6.

philosophy and orientation, as well as its chosen textbooks and direction, but it had also the common core prescribed by the independent
school authorities and approved by the Ministry of Education and
Culture. This common core included such subjects as reading, writing,
arithmetic, geography, and history. The goal of every educational institution was the same: namely, to rear better people and a better
generation. The leaders of the state understood that all of these
schools were doing a good civic service. President Masaryk, himself
a deeply religious philosopher, often publicly praised the contribution
of the independent schools for democracy, humanity, and good citizenship. The simple yet significant contribution of independent schools
to the common good was that they stood as equal partners with the
state-school system in bringing up a new and better generation.

What were the motives that led many parents and leaders of nonstate schools to prefer these schools over the state schools? In studying
this question, one comes to the following conclusions:

Although the nonstate schools were not in competition with the
state schools, they were established and maintained to provide a
religious orientation and education which was not and could not be
provided adequately by the state school system, in spite of the fact
that the latter offered a voluntary course of two hours of religious
instruction per week. Patrons of the nonstate schools felt that the state
school could not fulfill the educational prescriptions of the Scriptures,
as in the sentences of the prophet Isaiah, who said: "All thy children
shall be taught of the Lord: and great shall be the peace of thy
children."[4] Sometimes overcrowded conditions in the state schools
were another reason for the establishment of new nonstate schools.
Furthermore, some of the state schools were greatly secularized and
had what many felt were harmful moral and spiritual influences.

NAZI CZECHOSLOVAKIA (1938–1945)

The independent school was considered a link which united home,
church, and state. A destruction of this link meant a destruction of
home and church; it also meant, unfortunately, destruction of the state.
In 1939, when the Nazis occupied Czechoslovakia, they first closed
hundreds of Jewish schools, then also the Christian schools. The fascist
regime of the puppet "sovereign" Slovak state[5] excluded children of

[4] Is 54:13.
[5] Hitler granted the eastern part of Czechoslovakia a kind of "sovereignity" under
his control during the years 1939–1945.

Jewish faith from any school higher than the elementary grades. Jewish schools first lost their state subsidy, and later they were shut down. The theological colleges were closed, among them the famous rabbinical school Yeshivah in Bratislava (Pressburg).

This was only the beginning. In 1942, as was happening all over Nazi Europe, the Jewish population of Czechoslovakia was sent to concentration camps and exterminated. More than 400 Jewish educators were killed, along with 300,000 of their co-religionists. A similar fate befell thousands of Christians who opposed the Fascists.

COMMUNIST CZECHOSLOVAKIA (1948)

After the war the communist regime continued and extended this destructive policy in education. All nonstate schools were closed and nationalized. Although the Education Act of April 21, 1948, Section 19, provided for religious instruction in the public schools under church supervision, with the Ministry of Education reserving the right of "supreme direction and supervision," it was clear that this was the end of religious education. The communists started with the school, and ended by taking away from people their human rights and privileges. The situation is tersely summarized in the UNESCO bulletin *Financing of Education,* where under "Czechoslovakia," in the section "Public Authorities' Contributions to Independent Schools," there is the simple statement: "There are no independent schools."

ISRAEL

The example of the relation of the state toward education in prewar democratic Czechoslovakia may be compared to that in the republic of Israel. This nation came into being on May 14, 1948; though small in size and population, it became a factor in world thought, a place of democracy, humanity, and progress in the Middle East.

The feature that strikes one first about education in Israel is its numerical expansion — sixfold, from about 100,000 students in 1948 to over 600,000 pupils in 1963. The continuous growth of school population, and the determination of the community to absorb every school-age child into school created numerous difficulties, but also registered spectacular achievements.

The state of Israel has established free and compulsory education for children of ages five to fourteen. This is the law for all schools: the state schools, the state-religious schools, and the independent schools, all of which are supervised by the Ministry of Education and Culture. All schools receive almost 100 percent of their payroll budget for their teachers and other personnel. This is true of the Arab as well as the Hebrew schools, and of schools of Jewish, Moslem, and Christian denominations.

The state of Israel drew upon the governmental religious and educational policies that had prevailed under the Turkish Empire and the British Mandate in Palestine, as well as upon the ancient traditions of the Bible and the Talmud. The declaration issued upon the establishment of the state of Israel proclaimed: "The State of Israel will foster the development of the country for the benefit of all inhabitants; it will be based on freedom, justice, and peace, as envisaged by the prophets of Israel; it will ensure complete equality of social and political rights to all its inhabitants, irrespective of religion, race, or sex; it will guarantee freedom of religion, conscience, language, education, and culture. . . ."

The State Education Law, passed in 1953, which instituted a national school system, established a unified, but not a single school system. For the common state school system is organized in two school forms — the state general school and the state religious school. The law thus recognized the coexistence of two approaches to education. The religious state school was defined by the law as "State education, with the distinction that its institutions are religious as to their way of life, curriculum, teachers, and inspectors." In addition there are "Non-Official Recognized Educational Institutions." In this category is the school system of the Independent Education of Agudat Israel, a system of religious schools, whose secular program is under the supervision of the state. This independent system receives a large public subvention in the form of financial grants. By 1963 the teachers of this Independent School System were practically paid in full by the state. The secular programs of public and Christian and Moslem schools are also supervised by the Ministry of Education and Culture, and likewise receive full financial support.

EPILOGUE

After comparing the educational scene in the United States with the examples of prewar democratic Czechoslovakia and the Republic of Israel, one may come to the following conclusions:

1. The so-called "nonpublic" schools are important and valuable ele-

ments in American education. They perform a vital public service by providing general as well as religious education to over seven million children. They are "public" schools, inasmuch as they perform public services and serve the public. They, therefore, deserve public support.

2. The variety of school systems in our pluralistic society is a sign of strength and democracy. Their destruction would be the beginning of the end of a free society. The example of Czechoslovakia, occupied now by the communists, should be a warning. There, as in other communist-controlled countries one political party introduced one monolithic, monopolistic school system and destroyed not only the other parties, but also the other schools, freedom, and democracy.

Within the framework of the constitution and laws, some way should be worked out to provide public support for the children of these schools to enable them to continue in their work, which assures diversity within unity. In so doing, the public, the several states, the local communities, and the federal government will contribute greatly to the welfare of education and the welfare of the whole country. Former Princeton University President Harold Dodds has said: "When it is no longer possible for a man to find a school for his children except within a universal-public school system, it will be too late to worry about freedom as we have known it, for it will be gone."

CHAPTER VII

Contributions of Independent Education

Professor J. Marion Snapper*

The case for independent schools in American society can be stated in many ways: legally, morally, historically, comparatively, to name a few. But abstract and theoretical arguments are not enough. The American mind is pragmatic when it comes to questions of public policy.

The pragmatic mind operates something like this: "All right, granted that in principle there is a strong and sufficient case made for the existence of independent schools in American society; granted further that you have made a sufficient case for the granting of government recognition in the form of financial support for such schools, I am still not satisfied that this is sound public policy. What evidence can you offer to show that *in practice* the consequences of this policy are and will be good for American society?"

This tough-minded pragmatism is in large part a product of the American experiment in voluntarism and pluralism. It is the American way of getting along in a society which is committed to a dynamic diversity. Sidney Hook describes it:

> The method of the empirical temper, of the democratic process, of cultural pluralism is open-minded but not tender-minded. It is a perpetual invitation to sit down in the face of differences and reason together, to consider the evidence, explore alternative proposals, assess the consequences, and let the decision rest.[1]

This chapter is a response to that invitation: to sit down in the face of differences and reason together, to consider the evidence in a scien-

* Professor of Education, Calvin College, Grand Rapids, Michigan.
[1] Sidney Hook, *Political Power and Personal Freedom* (New York: Collier Books, 1962), p. 38.

tific manner. Let us begin with the following hypothesis and see whether the facts bear it out.

The independent school performs for the state its secular purpose in requiring formal education for all children, and in the process of so doing makes positive contributions to the welfare of American society and to the democratic way of life.

CONTRIBUTIONS OF INDEPENDENT SCHOOLS TO THE NATIONAL EFFORT IN EDUCATION

The state requires every parent to see to it that his child receives a formal education. In this the state has a secular purpose in mind, namely, that no child shall grow up in ignorance, but that every child shall be prepared to take his place as an informed citizen, equipped to the extent which his natural talents allow to make his contribution to the general welfare of the state and the society in which he lives.

All elementary and secondary schools which are permitted to operate in the state are performing this public function for the state. And the state may be expected to restrain those schools which educate children in a manner inimical to the welfare of the state, as by teaching subversive doctrines or not meeting certain educational standards.

Thus independent schools are performing a public function for the state no less than the schools which are called public. They perform precisely the same secular purpose which the state has in mind when it requires a formal education for all its youth. This is their most obvious contribution, and it is made under the same legal and accreditation requirements which govern all of compulsory education. They are distinguished, however, in that they do not receive public support for the service which they perform.

One out of seven American citizens receiving formal education at the elementary and secondary levels today is receiving that education in an independent school. Fifteen percent of the young adults taking their places in society as soldiers, scientists, teachers, skilled laborers, have been prepared for that service by an education received in an independent school.

This contribution may also be measured in monetary terms. The National Education Association estimated that the nation would spend more than $21 billion to educate 41.7 million youngsters enrolled in the public schools in 1963–1964. Were it not for the independent schools those figures would have to be revised to read: $24.5 billion to educate 48.7 million youngsters. This represents an *annual* relief to the American taxpayer of approximately $3.5 billion.

Those who support the independent schools also pay their full share of the $21 billion cost of the public schools. Thus the independent school, with her supporters, is making a double investment in the future of America. Money spent for education is no longer considered consumption of wealth, but investment. Dr. Walter Heller, later to become chief economic adviser to President Kennedy, summarized the economic outlook for education in 1959. He pointed out, for instance, that in *Fortune* magazine's classification of the gross national product:

> *Fortune* is also including under investments several items that are generally investments in the nation's well-being or proficiency and hence its productivity, expenditures for education, *both public and private.*[2] [Italics mine.]

This contribution of the independent school may be recognized at the local level as well. In an issue of the *Pella* (Iowa) *Chronicle* (October 16, 1962), featuring the newly completed local Christian High School, the editor wrote:

> This business of developing good citizens and training tomorrow's leaders is a costly, but wise investment. Bringing this monumental task of educating our youth into focus at the present time is Pella's Christian School Society . . . a church-related group (however its schools are open to the public). . . . It is the opinion of this writer, although not associated with the Christian School Society, nor a subscriber to its educational-religious doctrine, that the Society's decision to seek financial aid from the entire community is a practical and reasonable approach. . . . One of our liberties in the United States is to educate our children according to our beliefs — in public, private, parochial, and church-related schools. We can foster this freedom, aid our friends and community by responding to the current appeals of the Christian School Society.

The perceptions of this editor are worthy of summary. First, he regards the local independent school as a public institution in that it both performs a public function and is open to the public. Second, he reasons that because this is so, the public ought to support the independent school. Third, he recognizes that the independent school is an expression of a basic human right, the right to educate our

---

[2] Walter W. Heller, "Economic Outlook for Education," *National Education Association Journal,* XLVIII (December, 1959), 48.

children according to our beliefs. And he recommends that we implement the *Pierce* decision of the United States Supreme Court which upheld the state's right to require all parents to educate their children and the parents' right to determine what kind of education they shall receive while meeting the state's secular purposes.

CONTRIBUTIONS TO THE ACADEMIC ASPECTS OF AMERICAN EDUCATION

The independent school makes important positive contributions to the welfare of American society and to the democratic way of life. Quantitatively, the independent school does contribute one seventh of the total national educational effort. The qualitative character of that contribution must also be assessed.

With respect to academic standards, there is probably just as wide a range of performance in the independent schools as there is in the public schools. Overall, there is no evidence to indicate that they are not doing as well as the public schools. The independent schools have generally set for themselves the same academic standards as public institutions. They seek and obtain accreditation from regional associations such as the North Central Association. They compete for the same scholarships and public recognitions of excellence, with at least equal success. They use the same standardized tests to determine how they are doing. Annually thousands of students transfer freely between public and independent schools. Their graduates are accepted into public and private institutions of higher learning where the requirements for admission are the same for all.

Operating alongside the public schools, independent schools have provided a competitive factor in the world of American education. Competition is quite universally accepted as being an integral part of the American way of life. Government itself has set curbs on the growth of big business. There is always stout resistance to proposals for the centralization of scientific research in one governmental agency. In the American economy we recognize the fact that monopoly does not produce the best commodities, and the same can be held true for education. "The public has no way of knowing how 'good' their schools are unless there are other schools against which to compare."[3]

Independent schools have aided American education by experiment-

---

[3] Dan Dodson, "Foreward: Democracy and Private Education," *Journal of Educational Sociology,* XXX (April, 1957), p. 338.

ing with different educational techniques and programs. John Dewey did much of his experimental work in an independent school. It was an independent school which first brought the kindergarten to the American scene. Parent-teacher associations were first made a prominent part of a school program in independent schools. According to one source:

> Practically every new movement in secondary education has begun in some private or semi-private institution, and only gradually been adopted by the public high school.[4]

We need not establish here which schools have made more innovations or contributions. We only wish to observe the value of cross-fertilization between competing institutions. They learn from each other. In a sense they are each other's consciences. A pluralistic system of education offers the likelihood that there will be available more responses to a rapidly changing environment.

CONTRIBUTIONS TO DEMOCRATIC SOCIAL IDEALS

More problematic to the pragmatic temper of the American mind is the area of education which involves certain important incidental learnings which take place in a school. It is not difficult to recognize the contributions which have thus far been described. But over the past fifty years there has been much expression of concern about some of the social and psychological consequences of independent school education. Underlying this concern is an awareness that one of America's ideals is always at stake, namely, the ideal of unity in diversity.

This concern is not a new one. The thirteen colonies were united on certain very fundamental principles and goals, but, at the same time, in their diversity they found it necessary to devise a series of compromises in order to bind themselves together politically. Those bonds were sorely tried in the early days of the Republic, and within a century they were nearly destroyed. It took a war to hold the nation together politically. We are still struggling with the social and economic consequences of the "War Between the States" and the issues which brought it about. Those events are part of America's ancestral memory.

Many Americans also have ancestral memories of the divisiveness

---

[4] Edward Hall, "Schools of Independence," *Teachers College Record* (March, 1961), pp. 74:436.

among religious groups which resulted in decades of war, bloodshed, hatred, and persecution in Europe. Many had come to these shores to escape those conditions. Whatever expectations are held for America, they include the hope that we shall not here duplicate the bloody and tragic divisiveness of earlier European history.

It is quite understandable, therefore, that during the past century there has been much concern expressed over the role of independent schools in American society. Many of them were begun by immigrant groups, employed a foreign tongue in earlier years, and gave other evidences of attempting to preserve the way of life which had been left behind in Europe. Other independent schools were looked upon as contributors to a class distinction in American society not unlike the European system with its Etons and Harrows. It ought not be surprising that such charges as "un-American," "divisive," "breeders of prejudice and hatred" have been made against independent schools. However, the pragmatic temper of America is not interested in charges made without substantiating evidence.

Social scientists have begun to study the effects of independent schooling on the above characteristics. A considerable body of research has been accumulated and more is yet to come. In a very good summary of the research, Joshua Fishman describes it as follows:

> The foregoing studies are sadly insufficient as a research program. . . . Nevertheless, these studies do serve as straws in the wind, and our confidence in them is bolstered by the consistent trend they show. The minority-group school is patently unable to rechannel the major strivings and the behavior of the child in relation to the "America-American-Americans" complex. Not only is the child's response to American values, goals, and opportunities beyond regulation or substantial modification by the school, but also this response is well established even before the child attends school.[5]

The major thrust of Fishman's conclusion can be restated: The independent school does not in fact pose a threat to the unity of American society. "The core of that society is white, Protestant, middle class, and it attracts all other particles to it. This is the culture into which immigrants are assimilated, and it forms the one accepted set of standards, expectations, and aspirations. . . ."[6]

It would seem that the time has come to lay to rest the assertion

---

[5] Joshua Fishman, "Childhood Education for Minority-Group Membership," *Daedalus*, XC (Spring, 1961), p. 343.
[6] *Ibid.*, p. 329.

that independent schools threaten the unity of American society. Harvard historian Henry Steele Commager, in reporting his analysis of the American high school in the mid-twentieth century, said:

> In the nineteenth and early twentieth century — up to 1914, in fact — when our schools were confronted with the children of immigrants and of freedmen having no knowledge of American history or institutions, and when the problem of creating a harmonious society out of heterogeneous racial and religious elements was a pressing one, the schools were properly required to, and did, take on large responsibilities here. That problem is no longer acute; indeed, we may question whether it still exists in any serious sense.[7]

Not only may we question whether the problem exists in any real sense; we may question whether or not our problem has not become quite the opposite of what it once was. Harold Hodgkinson, in a remarkably perceptive analysis, comments that:

> We can extoll the virtues of pluralism to our heart's content, but most recent analysis indicates that Americans are becoming much more alike in nearly all aspects of life. . . . If it is true that American culture is becoming increasingly monistic and less able to deal with deviant social norms, then we cannot rely on the advantages of pluralism in our dealings with other nations and in our internal affairs. If we are becoming a monistic society, we cannot expect to surpass other societies which are *avowedly* totalitarian and can exploit a single system of social norms to the fullest extent possible.[8]

Hodgkinson goes on to state that all indications point toward a continuing trend to homogenization and standardization in American society. And if this is indeed the case, then we should call for a reevaluation of our present institutions, which, conceived in a pluralistic setting, may no longer be fulfilling their function. We have a choice today. First, we may plan to "continue on the road toward a completely homogenized, monistic state," or, second, "we may return to a more open condition and encourage the development of divergent and vocal groups, resulting in a truly pluralistic society." To Hodgkinson the first alternative is totally unacceptable, "as it violates most of the assumptions of the American heritage." Of the second he says that it seems desirable, but "unrealistic in that it is difficult to see

---

[7] Henry Steele Commager, "A Historian Looks at the American High School," *The High School in a New Era* (Chicago: University of Chicago Press, 1958), p. 13.
[8] Harold Hodgkinson, *Education in Social and Cultural Perspectives* (Englewood Cliffs, N. J.: Prentice Hall, Inc., 1962), p. 128.

how the trend toward a monistic system could be arrested, how more diversity could be intentionally injected into the culture."[9]

Independent schools appear among the most obvious institutions which can be used intentionally to inject diversity into the culture. The children who attend them are found to be drawn to the core of our culture, and the philosophical and religious differences which characterize those schools are capable of contributing to diversity without threatening the basic unity of our society. But if independent schools are going to contribute to cultural diversity in a more effective way, then their status must be changed. Rather than being thought of and treated as somehow foreign to the "America-American-Americans" complex, they ought to be recognized as indigenous to the American commitment to a dynamic cultural pluralism.

Research confirms the assertion that independent schools teach democratic values. A study comparing the attitudes of independent school children with the attitudes of public school children shows that the independent school children exhibited as much interest in local politics as did children of the same religious faith who attended public schools. In this study, conducted at the Harvard Graduate School of Education, it was further found that 80 percent of the parochial school children expressed attachment to the community, while 79 percent of the public school children expressed such attachment. It was also found that 33 percent of the parochial school children showed interest in local politics, with the same percentage holding true for the public school children. The conclusions of the study included this:

> We could find no evidence that parochial schools tend to alienate individual Catholics from the communities. Parochial school Catholics were as involved in community affairs as anyone else of comparable occupational position.[10]

Sociologist Joseph H. Fichter conducted similar tests among elementary school children. He came to the conclusion that parochial school children learned the same democratic ideals that public school children did. For example, 91 percent of the parochial school children tested were tolerant of Negroes, while 87 percent of the public school children were; 94 percent of the parochial school children believed

---

[9] *Ibid.*

[10] Peter and Alice Rossi, "Background and Consequences of Parochial School Education," *Harvard Education Review*, XXVII (Summer, 1957), p. 195.

that all citizens should vote, while 91 percent of the public school children believed the same.[11]

One of the perplexing problems facing American public education is the increasing tendency for attendance lines to follow lines of social stratification. The neighborhood school serves a well-defined geographic area peopled by children of common socioeconomic status. When those lines tend to coincide with racial lines it is called *de facto* segregation, a segregation just as real as *de jure* segregation, but not supported by the sanctions of the law. Independent schools are not commonly peopled by students drawn from such tightly defined geographic areas. Consequently, in urban areas the students in the independent school are likely to be drawn from a wider range of social classes. The independent school studied by Fichter had a student population representative of a wide range of social classes. Despite this fact, he found that the independent school children showed considerably less awareness of class than was evidenced in an earlier study by Stendler of a New England public elementary school.[12]

It is not possible to cite or even summarize all of the evidence available from sociological studies which bear on the influence of the independent schools on the children who attend them. The above references are representative and adequate for the time being to demonstrate that the independent school, while performing for the state its secular purposes in requiring formal education for all children, makes positive contributions to the welfare of American society and to the democratic way of life. The independent school child is drawn to the core of American values, aspirations, and ideals. Prejudice, class consciousness, and intolerance are at least as effectively dealt with as in the public schools. At the same time the independent school offers promise of fostering a much needed diversity in a society which is moving toward a monistic egalitarianism.

CONTRIBUTIONS TO FREEDOM: POLITICAL, PERSONAL, AND ACADEMIC

The mere existence of independent schools in a nation is one of the crucial indicators of how that nation ought to be classified. As Brubacher points out:

---

[11] Joseph H. Fichter, *The Parochial School* (Notre Dame, Ind.: University of Notre Dame Press, 1958), p. 116.   [12] *Ibid.*, p. 24.

Those who hold that the state is but one among many competing forms of society hold to a pluralistic theory of society and the state. On the other hand those who regard the state as the all-inclusive category hold to a monistic or totalitarian theory.[13]

Basing his judgment on the decision of the United States Supreme Court in the *Pierce* case (1925), he states that "pluralism seems to be the educational philosophy of the United States Supreme Court."[14] If indeed this is the case, and if there is commitment to a pluralistic theory of society and state, then it is reasonable to expect the Court to nurture that pluralism in future decisions.

In his great treatise *On Liberty*, John Stuart Mill stated that:

> A general State education is a mere contrivance for molding people to be exactly like one another: and as the mold in which it casts them is that which pleases the predominant power in the government, whether this be a monarch, a priesthood, an aristocracy, or the majority of the existing generation, in proportion as it is efficient and successful, it establishes a despotism over the mind, leading by natural tendency to one over the body. An education established and controlled by the State should only exist, if it exist at all, as one among many competing experiments, carried on for the purpose of example and stimulus, to keep the others up to a certain standard of excellence.[15]

Independent schools represent a built-in safeguard for democracy against a day when "the majority of the existing generation . . . establishes a despotism over the mind." Although American public education has a long and effective tradition of local autonomy, the fact that they are government schools already has had consequences which render Mill's warning not irrelevant. A recent issue of the *National Elementary Principal* featured the topic, "Politics, Pressure Groups, and Education." In a penetrating analysis, Mary Ann Raywid stated that it would appear that the first thing public school leaders must do is:

> to concede what American educators have never been willing to concede: that public schooling is an intensely political question. All the way from what is taught and why, to the various circumstances

---

[13] John S. Brubacher, *Modern Philosophies of Education* (New York: McGraw-Hill Book Company, Inc., 1950), p. 148.

[14] *Ibid.*, p. 149.

[15] John Stuart Mill, *On Liberty* (New York: Appleton-Century-Crofts, Inc., 1947), p. 108.

and conditions under which public schools operate, the issues are political in nature.[16]

Miss Raywid gives two reasons for facing up to this fact. First, honesty demands it. Second, the problems which beset public education must be dealt with as are *all* political questions:

> . . . the problem is one of marshaling the majority. It is not nearly so much a matter . . . of encouraging the public to form a particular point of view as it is of organizing and facilitating the expression of views already held.[17]

This is an honest recognition of the loss, albeit unwillful, on the part of the educators, of the state schools' role of leadership, and of judgment on existing political and social institutions. All of educational theory is politicized, and autonomy is gone. Brubacher's analysis is to the point: a pluralistic system of education, "separating ethical sovereignty from the state and lodging it in the individual or the church will assure the state of a more honest estimate of its own vices and virtues when studied in the schools."[18]

Evidence that independent schools do in fact function more freely in this capacity is found in Fichter's study. He reports that the pupils in the independent school demonstrated more favorable attitudes than did the public school children on practically all of the statements made concerning concrete social problems of the adult world. He concludes by stating that it appears that the teachers in the independent school:

> are in a better position to express broader and more liberal views in these matters than are the teachers in the public school. . . . There appears to be little question of fact, so far as these tests extend, that the parochial school children receive a broader social education than the public school children.[19]

The issue may be stated in another way, namely, that for some people there is not academic freedom. This is true with respect to social, political, and economic issues. There are schools where the teaching of attitudes favorable to the United Nations is practically forbidden. There are other schools where the same holds true for

---

[16] Mary Ann Raywid, "Political Extremism and the Public Schools," *National Elementary Principal*, XLIII (January, 1964), p. 31.

[17] *Ibid.*

[18] Brubacher, *op. cit.*, p. 149.

[19] Fichter, *op. cit.*, pp. 130–131.

teaching equality of races. In such cases the teacher is free to seek a community where he will be allowed to teach according to his convictions. But for the teacher who has strong religious convictions which he feels must permeate all of his teaching, academic freedom is not to be found within the developing legal framework of the public elementary and secondary schools.

The author, as a college supervisor of student teachers for a Christian college, has had, in more than one state, the experience of having student teachers report back the instructions they received with respect to how they should exercise their religious convictions. They were told to take care that they did not transmit their religious beliefs, or explicitly impose on their teaching the implications of those beliefs. In such cases it was necessary to inform the student teachers that if they wished to be free from such thought control they would have to find a position in an independent school. And it should be added that the administrators who gave such instructions were more law-abiding than those administrators who seek ways to circumvent the increasingly clear legal implications of the secular commitment of public education.

An independent school does not necessarily have more academic freedom than does a public school. In some ways, it may have less. It too has its commitments and its standards for hiring teachers. The point is that a pluralistic system of education adds up to increased academic freedom for all — parents, pupils, and teachers. The spirit and mind of man are more free when there are clear-cut choices in the kind of education available, and when those choices may be made without penalty, financial or otherwise.

The academic freedom of the public school teachers, pupils, and patrons also is enhanced by the presence of independent schools. So long as every teacher, parent, and pupil has a live option available to him, so long as every subject in the curriculum can be taught somewhere independently of the "official orthodoxy,"[20] there is always a judgment in the land on the public institutions and on the "official orthodoxy."

Likewise, the academic freedom of the independent school teacher is enhanced by the presence of public schools. The independent school,

---

[20] It seems to me that there is only one teaching which is always forbidden in a true democracy, and that is any teaching which advocates destroying the pluralistic system itself.

too, is constantly under judgment. Independent school teachers, pupils, and patrons, too, have options available to them. With respect to academic freedom the independent school is no more a boon to the public school than the latter is to the former. The benefits flow from the pluralistic character of the situation.

In summary, the independent school represents a built-in safeguard for democracy against a despotism over the mind, whether that despotism be of a political party, a priesthood, or of the majority of the electorate. Not being a state school, and being relatively free from politicizing, it tends to assure a more honest estimate of the vices and virtues of the state. Academic freedom for all is enhanced by the presence of a pluralistic system of education.

CONTRIBUTIONS TO THE INCULCATION
OF MORAL AND SPIRITUAL VALUES

In a speech delivered at the national convention of the American Association of School Administrators, Dr. Louis Evans, minister of the First Presbyterian Church of Hollywood, California, reported the following conversation:

Secretary of the National Education Association: "Louie, if we don't get more religion into our college people, they're going to have college minds in science and third-grade minds in religion. We put a three-year-old kid spiritually at the wheel of a twelve-cylinder scientific motorcar and it's going to wreck us if something doesn't happen."

Dr. Evans: "Doctor, what can we do? Take the car away?"

N.E.A. Secretary: "Evans, you know you can't do that. We've just got to make that kid grow up spiritually, and if we don't, he'll wreck us in the atomic age as sure as you're living."

Dr. Evans went on to say:

> Separation of church and state? All right, but they have let that deteriorate into a separation of God and education. Our fathers never dreamed of that. George Washington said, "To expect morality in our citizens without inculcating in them the principle of our holy religion is absurd and impossible." Thomas Jefferson once said, "Let's not have religion on the campus," but he changed his mind because the thing didn't work. Horace Mann ended up as professor on the faculty of a Christian college, and Thomas Jefferson was loud in his declaration and he ended up by saying, "Whenever you have a theological seminary and a university in close proximity, you had better mix faculties, because we need God in education." Now here

it is. How are we going to get God back to us so the soul catches up with the brain?[21]

All segments of American education are deeply concerned about the teaching of morals and values. Spiritual and moral questions have always been the most important ones in education. More important than a new scientific discovery is what man does with the discovery. There has never been a time in the history of man when he held so much power in his hands. It is also doubtful that there has even been a time when forces alien to free human institutions were organized on such a massive scale, determined to wipe out those free institutions. Repeatedly our national leaders remind us that the road ahead is going to require of us a moral and spiritual toughness in the face of unrelenting demands for sacrifice and courage. Profound understanding and commitment is the necessary prerequisite for expecting the sacrifice and courage from our future citizens. But there is considerable evidence to indicate that our past manner of:

handling problems of moral conduct and civic behavior has tended to develop individuals who are unable to give justifications for their behavior, except, of course, those derived from common sense. Youth . . . believe democracy to be the best way of life, but are unable to defend it effectively when challenged by those who hold contrary views. Indeed, they are often unable to tell whether or not another view affirms or denies democracy.[22]

We live in a day in which education must tap all the roots which have nourished the growth of Western democracy. It did not spring full-bloom into being. The oldest major root — considered by many to be the taproot — is the Hebraic-Christian tradition. Nietzsche, the Nihilist German philosopher, perceived this when he characterized it contemptuously as:

The equality of souls before God, this lie . . . this anarchistic bomb of a conceit, which has become the last revolution, the modern idea and the principle of the destruction of the whole social order — this Christian dynamite.[23]

[21] Louis Evans, "Religious Stewardship for Today's Children," *Leadership for American Education* (Washington, D. C.: American Association of School Administrators, 1952), pp. 31–32.

[22] Harry S. Broudy, B. Othanel Smith, and Joe R. Burnett, *Democracy and Excellence in American Secondary Education* (Chicago: Rand McNally & Co., 1964), p. 140.

[23] James Keller, *All God's Children* (New York: Christopher Books, 1953), p. 62.

This is the root that was tapped by the authors of the Declaration of Independence when they wrote:

> We hold these truths to be self-evident, that all men are created equal, that they are endowed by their Creator with certain unalienable Rights, that among these are Life, Liberty, and the pursuit of Happiness.

The independent school can tap the religious roots of our culture, not merely through objective study, but more vitally as a source of an imperative to work for our free, democratic institutions. In addition to humanitarian, rational, pragmatic arguments, the independent school roots devotion to the democratic way of life in such imperatives as, "Thou shalt love thy neighbor as thyself," and, "What doth Jehovah require of thee but to do justly, and to love mercy, and to walk humbly with thy God." As Episcopalian Bishop Pike says:

> Furthermore, since the public schools have not yet solved this problem of giving a religious basis to citizenship, I think we are going to have to rely for a long time upon the church schools for that leaven within the culture which can keep a culture alive and which can keep these flowers still growing because the roots are being nourished.[24]

The problem of teaching morals and values exists also in relation to questions of a more ethical nature, questions of right and wrong. The assertion that morality is a serious problem in American society needs little documenting. One can turn to the police blotters and find there the names of juveniles from suburbia as well as from the slums.

Just as serious to thinking Americans ought to be the phenomenon of over 50 percent of our young people being guided by a nonrational conformism rather than by a rational, personal conviction of what is right and what is wrong. Most characteristic of our age, according to David Riesman, is the "other-directed individual" who has his private radar system well developed to pick up the signals of approval or disapproval from his social peers.

Disappearing is the "inner-directed" individual who has within him a strongly internalized system of morals and values, a built-in gyroscope to guide him through the maze of living in a rapidly changing world. J. Edgar Hoover, who has studied the problem for a long time, has said repeatedly that our schools fail seriously when they neglect to

---

[24] James A. Pike, "The Protestant Dilemma in Education," address given before the Advisory Council of Christian Schools, Los Angeles, Calif., January 29, 1953.

teach a proper observance of law and moral government, when we forget that what we need today is an inculcation of "the immortal lessons of the Ten Commandments and the Sermon on the Mount. . . . This is the surest antidote to stem the rising tide of lawlessness."

Moral education needs a "fixed point" of reference and support. Robert Browning said, "You take out of this world a moral God to whom a moral debt is due, and you lose all sense of dueness, and there is no one to whom to pay the debt." No system of education can avoid this requirement. In providing the "fixed point" of any educational system it is difficult to bypass a religious commitment. That is the ultimate court of appeal in questions of right and wrong, of good and evil. If education does not have this, then it offers a form of ethical and moral relativism. If, on the other hand, it does have such a fixed point, then it does have a religious commitment. Philip Phenix has made the same point:

> There is no teacher, no school, which can escape the problem of life orientation, the ultimate commitments by which every person must live. Every analysis of life and culture must take account, either implicitly or explicitly, of those fundamental commitments which underlie every human action. This is precisely the domain of religion. Democracy, communism, and the various economic systems cannot be analyzed in their most profound dimensions without getting into the question of ultimate values. This is, finally, a religious question.[25]

A secular state educational system committed to nonsectarianism is thus faced with an exceedingly complex problem as it seeks to teach moral and spiritual values. The Educational Policies Commission of the National Education Association has issued an excellent report and analysis of the status of this problem for American public education. In commenting about the importance of sanctions for our behavior and our values, the committee stated that:

> *from the point of view of educational policy and program,* sanctions are of primary importance. Children and young people typically, and sometimes annoyingly, want to know *why.*[26]

---

[25] National Education Association, *The Scholars Look at the Schools* (Washington, D. C.: Association for Supervision and Curriculum Development, N.E.A., 1962), p. 18.

[26] National Education Association and the American Association of School Administrators, Educational Policies Commission, *Moral and Spiritual Values in the Public Schools* (Washington, D. C.: The Commission, 1951), p. 38.

The analysis in the report goes on to illustrate the sanctions which can be invoked to correct the behavior of a child who has received and kept overchange from a store clerk. The teacher may refer to the concept of justice, to the civil law, to the principle of property rights, and to other principles. But "the powerful sanctions of religious creeds and doctrines . . . may not be explicitly invoked in the public school classroom. . . ."[27]

Considering the nature of the world in which we live, many people judge it hazardous to assume that morality in a culture can be sustained through appeals to reasoned principles — though reason we all should — apart from sanctions as powerful as those which come from religious creeds and doctrines. Twentieth-century man has somewhat lost confidence in the power of reason to guide men's behavior. The furnaces of Dachau were built in the most rational and educated of nations. The current effort of a playwright to indict a powerful religious leader for allegedly not invoking religious sanctions against the incredible inhumanity of Dachau and Buchenwald is a clear testimony to the conviction that religious sanctions are indeed crucial.

It therefore appears once again, as in the case of full citizenship education, that if we are going to give a religious basis for the teaching of morality, we shall have to rely on the independent schools.

Speaking now as a Protestant Christian and as an educator, I have deep sympathy for my fellow evangelical Protestant friends who are disturbed by the United States Supreme Court decision removing the Bible from the public schools. I could wish with them that state schools and all men were evangelical Protestant. I can share their nostalgia for the nineteenth-century public school which in most communities was a quasi-Protestant public school. But history has moved on. We have been growing into a pluralistic society. Although, as has already been clearly stated, I believe that our free institutions are rooted in Christian principles, I do not believe that I have a right, by force of government, to impose my Bible beliefs on all citizens. In the eyes of my Jewish friends, the Gospel according to St. John is a sectarian book.

If my Protestant friends are sincere in their convictions that morals and values should be taught in the light of the Holy Bible, and in their conviction that all men ought to enjoy freedom of religion, then they ought not to work so much for a constitutional amendment which would put the Bible in the public schools, as to work for schools where the

---

[27] *Ibid.*, p. 46.

Bible can be the authoritative rule of faith and life. But these would have to be independent schools. That is Bishop Pike's point. Independent schools offer the best solution to our quandary in regard to teaching of moral and spiritual values.

RETROSPECT AND PROSPECT

1. Independent schools are performing a public function for the state, no less than the schools which are called "public." They both achieve the same secular purpose the state has in mind when it requires a formal education for all youth.

2. One seventh of the nation's educational investment is made by independent schools and represents an annual saving to the American taxpayers of $3.5 billion.

3. Historically and currently the independent school has made significant contributions to American education. It provides healthy competition, fruits of experimentation, and the benefits of cross-fertilization.

4. The independent school nurtures a much-needed diversity in American culture, yet her graduates are deeply committed to the core of democratic values which hold us together as a people.

5. The independent school represents a built-in safeguard for democracy against any potential tyranny of the mind resulting from a monistic state educational system. Existence of independent schools increases academic freedom for all — parents, pupils, and teachers. The spirit and mind of man are more free when there are clear-cut, free choices in the kinds of education available.

6. The independent school can tap the religious roots of our free democratic institutions, providing the powerful sanctions of religion to the maintenance of national and individual morality.

This chapter is a response to the "standing invitation" of the open but tough-minded empirical temper of the democratic process. The contributions of the independent school have been stated because, in the words of Franklin Hamlin Littell, "What is needed is less myth-building and more attention to the realities before the Republic."[28]

Independent schools are partners with public schools in the great task of educating the youth of America for intelligent citizenship in democracy. Each partner offers distinct and vital contributions. This

---

[28] Franklin Hamlin Littell, *From State Church to Pluralism* (Garden City, N. Y.: Anchor Books, 1962), p. 101.

partnership is an expression, within the genius of Western democracy, of unity in diversity, of the historic shift in the role of the state:

> from that of an agency actively promoting a separate interest greater than the sum of the interests of society towards the position of a neutral regulator and arbiter of equally legitimate and conflicting social influences. . . . It most directly involves education. One of its main elements is the emergence as distinct categories of "public" and "private" education. . . .[29]

The implications of this aspect of Western democracy await fuller expression in the United States. Our government has not yet assumed the role of "neutral regulator and arbiter of equally legitimate and conflicting social interests."

---

[29] Bernard Bailyn, *Education in the Forming of American Society* (New York: Vintage Books, 1960), p. 108.

CHAPTER VIII

Economy of Government Aid to Independent Education: A Taxpayers' Savings Plan

John J. McDonough*

I. THE AMERICAN WAY OF LIFE

Americans are "partners in pluralism" . . . each encouraging the others to make, and to have, the ability to carry out their own individual and personal decisions, in their own particular ways. This is the essence of free society in a democracy, which supposes personal choices, with the ability to act on one's own initiative.

We know that in communist states, such as Cuba and East Germany, there is little opportunity for carrying out significant personal decisions independently of the group. With education, for example, there can only be government schools in totalitarian nations, because those in power want it that way so they can fashion the lives and destinies of their fellow human beings, through controlling the institutions which people must utilize. But in our free society we want individuals to be able to decide each day on the schools they will attend, the religions, if any, they will embrace, the goods and services they will select. In the American way, the emphasis is on individuals deciding for themselves, whereas in totalitarianism the government decides what is best, and everyone must conform.

The "free market" naturally develops in our American way of life, with millions of Americans each day freely selecting their goods and services on the basis of each individual's personal preferences. This provides many choices, responding to the needs and desires of individuals, and gives us prompt recourse against inefficiency, unsatis-

---

* District Manager, Southwestern Bell Telephone Co., Kansas City, Missouri.

factory goods and services, or ones that do not fill our desires and needs. In the free market, multitudes of individual decisions are ceaselessly taking place on thousands of fronts. Under this system human satisfaction and human dignity are maximized. Freedom permits a consistent movement away from inferior values toward what is more congenial and agreeable to each individual.

The key to the greatness of America has been personal freedom in most areas of our American way of life — freedom of choice and freedom of action. Individual freedom means competition, and competition brings progress. Abraham Lincoln said, "The Government should do only those things the people cannot do for themselves or cannot do so well." Almost everyone would agree that the philosophy behind this expression from Mr. Lincoln, is, and ought to be, a vital part of our American way of life.

Free exchange and self-determination are at the heart of our free society. The greatest threat to freedom is any unnecessary concentration of authority and power. Such power can be concentrated in the hands of a businessman, a labor leader, a state education office, or a school board. The preservation of freedom requires the distribution of power, a system of checks and balances. Some who desire maximum authority and concentration of power label as "fragmentation" anything which would not give them all children to educate, with the connotation that it is also "un-American." A competitive free system, however, tends to maximize nonconformity by catering, as far as practicable, to the enormous diversities of human nature, tastes, and desires. A most effective persuasive power of the government is its taxing function. Government tax policies can encourage or discourage certain industries or segments of society. With education a discriminatory tax policy is already in effect, and it is gradually stifling independent schools. Our educational tax policy withdraws from many of our citizens the *ability* to provide an independent school education for their children by appropriating that part of the family budget which would be used for education. Often this situation forces parents to send their children to the public schools whether these citizens like it or not.

An often-heard question is: "What extra tax costs would result if independent schools closed?" But a seldom-heard question is: "What percent of our children would be enrolled in independent schools, if we had a free market in education?" This latter is an important question because it suggests that the liberty of a great many citizens is being curtailed, and that the vast tax cost on *all* our pocketbooks could be reduced if substantial numbers of students were voluntarily to shift enrollments to independent schools, where the taxpayers would not be carrying the full expense load. At present, about 15 percent of our grade and high school students attend independent schools, and about 40 percent of our college-level students are enrolled in independent colleges. It is entirely possible that, given some fraction of tax assistance for use by the recipient at the school of his choice, the percentage of independent students would quickly rise to about 50 percent in the grade, high, and college levels, with potential tax savings of from 30 to 50 percent for taxpayers.

The objective of our nation's founders was the formation of a central political establishment which would foster free choice and the free market in all aspects of life. This was to be a government, "of the *people,* by the *people,* and *for* the *people"* — *not* for the *institutions.* Today, the one-sided protectionism granted public schools, through permitting state institutions a total monopoly on money collected from and for all citizens, has resulted in a situation where our children are effectively compelled to attend these institutions whether or not we agree with their view of life, and even though this results in vastly increased taxation for *all* citizens. Our nation's founders had no intention that the free market should be included in *all* forms of American life, *except* education.

II. THE TAXPAYERS' SAVINGS PLAN

A premise of the Taxpayers' Savings Plan is that many students in public schools would be enrolled in nonpublic schools if it were financially possible. Dr. James B. Conant, on "CBS Reports," February 5, 1964, said, "If you had state or federal money now being available to anybody who wanted to set up a private school in such a city, you would have them multiplied. Instead of having most of your children, 80 or 90 percent going to one or two schools, you would have them distributed among a dozen or so."

This estimate seems excessive. While many citizens might choose nonpublic schools, given tax benefits for use at the schools of choice, it would be a disservice to our fine public schools to accept Dr. Conant's statement completely. Most of our public schools are excellent, and most of our fellow citizens are satisfied with these schools, which fully meet their needs as they see them.

But the needs of many other citizens as *they* see them are not fulfilled by this particular type of excellence. These people have different preferences and want something more. Many of these people want religious training for their offspring as part of the daily routine at their schools as well as in their homes and on Sunday. Some of them want different training standards and/or methods. Some of them need boarding schools, because of their type of life. Some of them just want to be different. And it is the essence of freedom, in our American way of life, to let people do what they want to do — and not to take away their ability to exercise their right through a monopolistic tax-distribution policy.

The Taxpayers' Savings Plan, occasionally referred to as the "TSP," is aimed at minimizing the tax load generally for *all* citizens whether or not they have children; whether or not they prefer independent schools, whether or not they choose to embrace a theistic philosophy of life. The Taxpayers' Savings Plan is designed to provide in education at least some degree of the free market that we now have in other facets of the American way of life.

The TSP is primarily an economy measure for governmental operations, based upon an economic estimate of supply and demand in education, for the purpose of determining at what point tax aid to independent school students *is most profitable for taxpayers generally;* at what point profitability is maximized, and where the point of diminishing return is located. Thus the TSP does not merely represent student aid, or aid to schools, but it is also a plan to give *aid to taxpayers.*

Education is our most basic industry. And we must recognize that it is in danger of becoming pure socialism. Webster defines socialism as "A political and economic theory of social organization based on collective or governmental ownership and democratic management of the essential means for the production and distribution of goods and services." With our public schools, the governments literally own the means of educating our children; the teachers are the government's employees and agents. And financially we will soon have to attend these schools, unless we are *very* well off.

Public school attendance is all right for those who freely choose these schools. But for those who would have to attend these schools against their judgment, although they would prefer to spend their tax share elsewhere, these schools would become enforced collectives.

More and more parents are finding themselves financially strapped down by rapidly rising public school costs, and therefore are denied the ability to exercise their constitutionally guaranteed right to select nonpublic education for their offspring. Their education money is collected from them in taxes amounting to about 6 percent of each household's yearly personal income, and it is monopolistically distributed *only* to government educational institutions, which must employ value systems that do not fully meet the needs of many of our fellow citizens.

Many enrollment shifts from independent to public schools are resulting, because of this totalitarian plan for education tax distribution. For example, half or more of the increase in enrollments in Missouri's public schools in 1963–1964 resulted from the financial crisis of independent schools and their "would be" users. And every shift put another student fully onto the tax dole of over $600 per year at the public grade and high schools, and over $1,200 a year at the university level.

Here is the way the problem was put by Mrs. Garth Courtois of Royal Oak, Michigan, as interviewed on "CBS Reports," in a television presentation of February 5, 1964:

> As a mother of ten young children, who I consider potential American citizens and who are American citizens, I am very much concerned about the kind of education they receive. I feel furthermore that without religious training according to my own beliefs, this cannot be achieved fully. A school bond election comes along — we own a home — my husband and I both go over to cast our vote. I have the feeling of being against the wall and holding the gun myself. I want my neighbor's children to have what they need in the way of education. But I have reached the point of feeling that there should be some fairness in this. He asks me for help in helping him to pay for what his child very really needs. I know he needs it. I know he needs money to educate his child; someone must pay the teachers; someone must build that building; someone must take care of the facilities; someone evidently should buy textbooks, transportation. I'm willing to help my neighbor. But I wonder if he is willing to help me.

For those whose first reaction to Mrs. Courtois comment might be something like "Well, Mr. and Mrs. Courtois' decision to have ten children was not a community decision, why should the community be involved?" — it should be pointed out that should Mr. and Mrs. Courtois decide to send these children to public schools, the community would certainly be *very* heavily involved, something in the order of $198,000 of projected estimated* education taxes being required as follows:

---

* See Charts 2 and 3, under 1970.

	Grade school	High school	College	Tax cost total
Children	10	10	10	
Years of schooling	x 8	x 4	x 4	
Cost per year	x 850*	x 850*	x 2400*	
Total cost	$68,000	$34,000	$96,000	$198,000

The decisions of Mr. and Mrs. Courtois, like those of all parents, are of concern to the community. If Mr. and Mrs. Courtois, and many other parents, can be encouraged to pay most of the educational expenses of their children themselves, and still have the children receive highest-quality education, taxpayers generally would stand greatly to benefit.

The Taxpayers' Savings Plan is designed to give general relief to all citizens by making available to those parents who desire nonpublic schooling for their children a portion of the tax funds which would be spent on their children if they attended public schools. The result would be many voluntary enrollment shifts from public to independent schools in the course of time. It is possible that the number of independent school students would rise from 15 percent of the total students to 50 percent within ten years. Under such a plan the amount of government aid would average about one fourth of the amount which would be spent on the average student in public schools. Thus about three fourths of the taxes that would otherwise have been required would be saved for each child not attending public schools. Tax savings would accrue amounting to something in the order of $15 to $25 per family per month, month after month.

Even if the percentage were to rise to only 25 percent, well below Dr. Conant's figure, savings to taxpayers would still be substantial. In 1970, there would be about 120,000 children in the independent schools of Missouri who would, without state aid, have been in the public schools. With the estimated annual cost per pupil at $850, the state would pay only $200 per pupil to have these children educated in non-public schools. This net saving of $650 per child would result in a gross tax savings of $78,000,000. From this we must deduct the $200 per child aid to be paid to the 175,000 children already attending independent schools. The net savings from the taxpayers of Missouri would thus be $43,000,000 for the year 1970.

However, we believe that there is good reason to suppose that 25 percent is a rather conservative figure and that 50 percent is a much more realistic estimate. Dr. Eugene Carson Blake, along with Dr. Conant,

---

* *Ibid.*

both of whom are nationally known educators, has said that given tax aid, enrollment shifts from public to independent schools would be substantial.

Charts 1, 2, and 3 demonstrate the workings of the plan. Using Chart 2, we see that in one state (Missouri), for example, for 1970, the total estimated tax cost per child in public grade and high schools will be about $850 (line *f*). If under the TSP, however, $200 (line *g*) were allowed at any accredited school, $650 would be saved for each "transferee." Multiplying this $650 saving per child by the number of expected enrollment shifts out of the public schools (line *e* — 412,500 students) we develop a gross tax savings potential of $268,125,000 per year. Subtracting the cost of $200 tuition vouchers for the students now independent (line *c* — 175,000 students) we find net taxpayers' savings of $233,125,000 per year — rising to $317,500,000 per year by 1975 for the grade and high schools alone, and another $44,100,000 per year savings at the college level (Chart 3). This totals over $361,000,000 (line *C 9* on Chart 1) tax savings per year by 1975 for Missouri alone, and perhaps much more than this if we suppose that the independent schools would otherwise collapse.

Thus tax aid for students to use at independent schools could vastly lower taxes by $15 to $25 per month or $180 to $300 per year per family (line *E 16* on Chart 1), rather than increasing taxes generally. Chart 4 graphically portrays the estimated shifts and related dollar savings possible through adoption of the TSP approach.

CHART 1

Taxpayers' Saving Plan — "TSP"
Summary of Annual Tax Savings Potential*
Grade and High Schools (Chart 2) and Higher Education Level (Chart 3)

	Column a 1965	Column b 1970	Column c 1975	Column d 1975 "X"
A. 1. Lines "1" (Charts 2 and 3) Total P.S. Taxes, No TSP:				
2. Grade and High (2)	$540,000,000	$ 850,000,000	$1,210,000,000	$1,320,000,000
3. College (3)	90,000,000	184,800,000	271,000,000	309,400,000
4. Total Taxes, No TSP	630,000,000	1,034,800,000	1,481,600,000	1,629,400,000
B. 5. Lines "M" Total P.S. Taxes With TSP:				

* Uses state of Missouri as an example. In many other states the costs are higher.

6. Grade and High (2)	403,125,000	616,875,000	892,500,000	
7. College (3)	90,000,000	165,000,000	227,500,000	
8. Total Taxes With TSP	493,125,000	781,875,000	1,120,000,000	1,120,000,000
C. 9. Tax Savings Potential With TSP (L. 4 — L. 8)	136,875,000	252,925,000	361,600,000	509,400,000
D. 10. Number of Major Mo. Taxpayers (MMT)	2,500,000	2,500,000	2,500,000	2,500,000
11. Taxes per Year per MMT				
12. No. TSP (L. 4 ÷ L. 10)	252	414	592	650
13. With TSP (L. 8 ÷ L. 10)	197	312	444	444
E. 14. Tax Saving Potential per MMT (L. 12 — L. 13)	55	102	148	206
15. Per Month (L. 14 ÷ L. 12)	5	9	12	17
16. Per Family per Month (L. 15 x 2)	10	18	24	34

CHART 2

Taxpayers' Savings Plan
Grade and High School Levels
Projected Annual Tax Savings*

If 50 percent of the students attend independent schools (because of state aid tuition voucher introduction)

	Column a 1965	Column b 1970	Column c 1975	Column d 1975 "X"**
a) Total Children	1,075,000	1,175,000	1,275,000	1,275,000
b) In Public Schools	900,000	1,000,000	1,100,000	1,200,000
c) At Independents	175,000	175,000	175,000	75,000
d) 50% of (a) above	537,500	587,500	637,500	
e) P.S. Reduction (d — c)	362,500	412,500	462,500	
ee) Stay in P.S. (b — e)	537,500	587,500	637,500	
f) Taxes per P.S. Student	$600	$850	$1,100	$1,100
g) Value of Tuition Voucher	$150	$200	$300	
h) Net Saving per Transferee	$450	$650	$800	
i) Gross Saving (e x h)	$163,125,000	0268,125,000	$ 370,000,000	
j) Tuition Vouchers for Independents (g x c)	$ 26,250,000	$ 35,000,000	$ 52,500,000	
k) Net Tax Savings (i — j)	$136,875,000	$233,125,000	$ 317,500,000	
l) Total P.S. Taxes, No Plan (b x f)	$540,000,000	$850,000,000	$1,210,000,000	$1,320,000,000
m) Total Tax Cost With Plan (l — k)	$430,125,000	$616,875,000	$ 892,500,000	
n) % Increase Without Plan (k ÷ m)	34%	38%	36%	48%

---

* Uses state of Missouri as an example.

** Estimate only about 75,000 grade and high school students could remain financially independent if most independent schools were (economically) constrained to close.

CHART 3
Taxpayers' Savings Plan
Higher Education Level
Projected Annual Tax Savings*

If 50 percent of the students attend independent colleges (because of state aid tuition voucher)

	Column a 1965		Column b 1970		Column c 1975		Column d 1975 "X"
a) Total Students (a — l)	72,000	(b)	110,000	(c)	130,000	(d)	130,000
b) State University and State Colleges (a)	45,000	70%	77,000	75%	97,000	85%	110,500
c) Independents (a — l)	27,000	30%	33,000	25%	33,000	15%	19,500
d) 50% of (a) above	36,000		55,000		65,000		
e) Leave State Schools (d — c)	9,000		22,000		32,000		
f) Annual Tax Cost Per State Student (e)	$2,000		$2,400		$2,800		$2,800
g) Tuition Voucher (¼ of f)	$500		$600		$700		
h) Net Saved/Transferee	$1,500		$1,800		$2,100		
i) Gross Tax Saving (e x h)	$13,500,000		$39,600,000		$67,200,000		
j) Tuition Voucher Cost (g x c)	$13,500,000		$19,800,000		$23,100,000		
k) Net Taxpayer Saving (i — j)	. . .		$19,800,000		$44,100,000		
l) Total P.S. Taxes, no TSP	$90,000,000		$184,800,000		$271,600,000		$309,400,000
m) Total P.S. Taxes, with TSP	$90,000,000		$165,000,000		$227,500,000		

* Uses state of Missouri as an example.

CHART 4

Estimated Shift in Enrollments From Public to Independent Schools and the Resulting Taxpayers' Savings Potential Resulting From Introduction of State Aid Plan of Limited Tuition Vouchers for Independent School Students
(Key to graph on p. 131.)
POSITION:

Point		Number of Students	Total Cost per Student	Tax Cost Total at the Public and Independent Schools	Total Tax Cost at Various Levels of Tuition Vouchers for Independent School Students	Tuition Voucher Allowance
a	P.S.	1,000,000	X $850	= $850,000,000 ⎫	= $850,000,000	. . .
	I.S.	175,000	. . .	. . . ⎭		
b	P.S.	587,500	X $850	= $499,375,000 ⎫	= $616,875,000	$200
	I.S.	587,500	200	117,500,000 ⎭		
c	P.S.	480,000	X $850	= $408,000,000 ⎫	= $616,500,000	$300
	I.S.	695,000	300	208,500,000 ⎭		
d	P.S.	400,000	X $850	= $340,000,000 ⎫	= $650,000,000	$400
	I.S.	775,000	400	310,000,000 ⎭		
e	P.S.	265,000	X $850	= $225,250,000 ⎫	= $771,250,000	$600
	I.S.	910,000	600	546,000,000 ⎭		

P.S.: Public Schools   I.S. Independent Schools

Heretofore, the lack of careful pricing out of numerous possibilities has obscured the fact that for the first part of the route (from zero to about $200 aid per child) almost all points of view have common interests . . . although for the last part of the route (from $200 to $850 aid per child) interests may be divergent. Chart 4 portrays the whole route, from zero dollars government aid to full and equal numbers of dollars of such aid. But note that Part 1 of the "route" is of common interest to the whole body of taxpayers, because taxation can be minimized, thus saving the average family perhaps $15 to $25

(Chart 4: Graph)

General Assumptions:

1. Many public school students would enroll elsewhere, granted some tax help.
2. With $200 tuition voucher about half the students would eventually be enrolled in independent schools.

(See Key, p. 130)

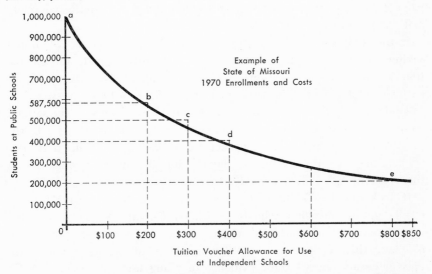

Tuition Voucher Allowance for Use
at Independent Schools

per month, month after month. This is the only part with which we are here concerned. Part 2 of the route may be the area of divergency, in that some taxpayers may feel that they don't want to stand the full tab for education. This is the tax aid amount per child above $200 and on up to what the taxpayers spend for each child in the public schools. This is not our present concern. But even in this second part of the route, if and when it were reached, there would be substantial savings, as compared with the otherwise growing possibility that more independent school students would be forced into the public schools. Furthermore, healthy competition would keep prices down and quality up in *both* public and private schools.

Part 1 of the route is an attempt to estimate and portray the cost area which independent school parents might have to make up from private and nontax-aided resources. In this private-enterprise approach, independent school patrons would be motivated to keep down costs at their schools through economies in curriculum and operation. In this perspective, we have a standard against which to allow tax aid, without the concern for going the whole route. The standard then is that there is clear reason for nearly everyone to get together and agree to allowing Part 1 of tax aid. All can agree on this since everybody will benefit in tax savings. This standard we might call *aid to taxpayers*. But to permit participation in tax funds beyond Part 1 is another matter, to be considered separately, since tax savings are not present and divergent views may override. This standard we might call *aid to students*.

If the TSP were applied on a national level, potential TSP dollar savings would be phenomenal. Illustrative of this estimate for the nation is the fact that Missouri accounts for about 2.3 percent of the nation's total personal income. Thus if $361,500,000 can be saved in Missouri each year (column *c*, line *C*, Chart I) for the nation the savings would approximate $18 billion annually in taxpayers' savings. If the savings for Missouri should in fact be $509,400,000 (column *d*, line *C* 9, Chart 1) the savings extended for the nation would be in the order of $25 billion annually by 1975.

It took about $550 tax dollars to educate each child in Missouri's public grade and high schools in 1963–1964, and Missouri is rather representative of the national average of all the states on costs. Here is where this tax money comes from, and what the figures for 1975 (just a decade away) show evidence of rising to:

ESTIMATES

	1963–1964	1975
Local	$358	$450
County	30	35
State	150	415
Federal	12	200
	$550*	$1100*

* Estimates based on annual reports of the Missouri State Education Office and on conversations with public school officials.

We Americans are facing a very modern educational tax problem, different from what we have known in the past. Research on these matters has uncovered this very important, largely overlooked point. The massively increasing enrollments at the public schools are partly due to the extremely serious financial problems at the independent schools — such problems as: many of their would-be students being priced out of the ability to attend, the doors closing to many, and teacher quality declining relatively, because of the pay differential as compared to public school teachers.

Over 5000 students were turned away from the independent schools of St. Louis, for example, in the year 1963–1964, according to the published statement. However, it is no doubt true that actually more than 10,000 were denied access to the schools of their choice in Missouri that year if we count in also the rest of the state and include also those who, for financial reasons, could not enter the independent schools. With public school enrollments mounting by about 20,000 per year, we can see that the population growth is only about half the cause, the other half being the forced curtailment of independent schools.

Illustrating the national scope of the problem, Reginald A. Neuwein, who is heading up a three-year study financed by the Carnegie Corporation, disclosed, in February of 1964, that Catholic independent schools alone turned down 188,000 students last year *for lack of space.* He did not attempt to estimate how many students did not even *try* to enter Catholic schools because of *financial* problems, particularly at the high school and college levels. Nor did he try to estimate the number of non-Catholic students who would prefer nonpublic and non-Catholic schools, but who cannot attend such because they do not exist in sufficient quantity to accommodate the demand.

III. THE AMERICAN BUSINESS COMMUNITY'S STAKE

Unquestioning acceptance of the "public schools overall" concept by American business leaders and the business community in general would not bode well for free market and private enterprise prospects for our nation's economy. Assumption that only government can really "run a school right" and that "it is better to have the government in complete control" is dangerous from more than one point of view. Don't we hear similar claims for having the government run the railroads, the steel industry, public utilities, etc.? Why do the world's finest businessmen, who know best the necessity of the free market, stand mute in the face of the increasing socialization of our schools, our most basic industry?

It would also behoove taxpayers and the business community to look into the potential tax savings outlined above. Heads of large and small businesses might have detailed studies made of the taxes their firms pay for public education (income tax, sales tax, property taxes, and other taxes), and have spelled out in these cost studies what dollar savings could be made through encouraging families that so wish to move off the total tax support of public schools onto comparative self-sufficiency at independent schools, if this is their choice. If, for example, only one fourth of the public school dollar entitlement were made available for use at the school of choice through tuition vouchers issued to parents, then about $400 to $800 per child attending the independent school would be saved taxpayers as compared with what it would cost them if that child attended the public school.

In conclusion, we may list some of the groups that would be helped by the Taxpayers' Savings Plan:

1. *Public schools and their teachers* would have available more operational and paycheck dollars, since fewer dollars would be required for bricks and mortar, and for additional teachers every year, partly to handle artificially induced enrollment shifts from the independent schools.

2. *All taxpayers,* including childless people, small families, and families without children in school, through lower taxes generally; and through more parents voluntarily paying more of their own bills, instead of being forced to have other citizens carry their full educational expenses.

3. *Consumers* would find somewhat lower prices, since businessmen would not have to pay such high business taxes for public education, thus not having to increase prices to cover these tax costs.

4. *Business people and their employees* would be assisted by being granted significant tax relief, thus enlarging business profits and workers' opportunities.

5. *All real-estate owners,* including homeowners, would be helped by having public educational costs cut, since their property taxes would be lessened or kept at present levels.

6. *Many parents* would have financial relief and greater satisfaction

by being able to make a less penalized choice in the education of their children.

7. *Education* would profit. Independent schools would be encouraged and revitalized. Both public and independent educators would set higher and higher standards for each other to match, moving forward in the competitive partnership of pluralism.

8. *Citizens in general* would be assured a continuation of freedom of choice in education (whether they use it or not) for both themselves and their descendents.

9. *The United States* would no longer stand apart from most of the world's democracies by refusing to allow at least *some* of the educational tax dollars to follow the child to the school of his choice.

IV. QUESTIONS AND ANSWERS ABOUT THE TAXPAYERS' SAVINGS PLAN

1. *Won't this original aid of $200 eventually lead to much greater state support for students in independent schools?*

The TSP is, as its name suggests, a means to effect tax savings for all Americans. It is intended to unite the common interests of our people in the matter of educational costs. The TSP is an economic instrument to estimate supply and demand in education and to indicate at what point the profitability to American taxpayers is maximized, and, consequently, where the point of diminishing return exists. Whether the aid should exceed the point of diminishing return, i.e., cover even more of the costs of students in independent schools, is entirely another matter, which must be left to the judgment of the American public as expressed in the acts of the various lawmaking bodies of our country.

2. *Where would the independent schools, which are overcrowded now, put these additional students?*

The initial financial aid of $200 per pupil will permit the undertaking of capital expenditures. Secondly, this aid will stimulate organizations and parishes which previously were hesitant about starting schools to begin such educational programs. Encouraged by the psychological impact of at least partial tax aid, private, possibly interdenominational schools will grow in number. These schools will answer the needs of those parents who choose to have their children receive instruction in religious and ethical matters beyond what is presently permitted in secularist public schools. Thirdly, the added competition of a larger nonpublic school system will, by the pressures of a free market system, lead to increased efficiency in both public and independent schools, thus reducing per pupil costs.

3. *Will there not be chaos in education, resulting from a proliferation of competing school systems?*

Chaos can result from any legislation which is not carefully planned and discretely implemented. When laws are passed regarding such automobile safety measures as seat belts or sealed-beam headlights, a reasonable amount of time is allowed to make the transition smooth and painless. This same approach would have to be taken with the TSP. We would need surveys, studies, and carefully made projections of the total impact of any legislation. Furthermore, reasonable standards of safety and academic excellence can be established by public and private agencies to assure a practical interworking of the various schools. This is, in fact, already being done today. Estimates as to the pace of the shift to private schools will determine the scheduling and means necessary to effect a smooth period of transition. It should be noted, furthermore, that chaos is not the product of a free-market system. For example, medical doctors and other professions operate in a free market, and certainly chaos is not at all a result. Moreover, by means of limited government control and stringent professional standards, the public interest is very well served.

4. *Who would make up the difference between the dollar amount of the tuition voucher and the full cost of educating the child at an independent school?*

This burden would fall mainly upon the parents who felt that the advantages of an independent school education, for religious or other motives, were worth the additional expense. However, churches and other organizations will also assume part of the cost.

5. *Why should I pay to have your child taught a religion I don't agree with?*

Under the TSP, education taxes would go down, not up. Not even the full cost of the nonreligious subjects would be covered by the state aid suggested, much less pay for the religion courses. So under these circumstances, i.e., reduced taxes, there could be no legitimate claim that one's religion is being paid for by another.

It might be noted too, that some of the government aid money received by individuals through social security, unemployment compensation, farm subsidies, etc., finds its way into stores that others do not patronize. We do not try to prevent these government aid programs because some prefer another supplier of goods or services. Some of the public money from these government sources even finds its way into independent schools, into various churches. But we do not want to discontinue these programs for this reason.

6. *What about "Separation of Church and State"?*

The Taxpayers' Savings Plan would not provide a preferred position to one religion, nor would it prefer religion over nonreligion. Nor would the TSP pay for religious training, as it would equate to only about 25 percent of the total public education cost — not even enough to cover the cost of the three R's at independent schools, much less the proportionate cost of the fourth R, religion, should a church school be the individual's choice.

The Taxpayers' Savings Plan is not designed to give public funds to religions any more than is Social Security or the dozens of other federal and state programs which provide public funds to individuals. The TSP is designed to aid individuals, not institutions. The TSP would provide a piece of paper which could be used somewhat like a social security check. No public funds would go directly to any church school. These educational entitlements would go to individuals who would use them in the free market for education wherever their judgment might lead them.

CHAPTER IX

Our Federal Constitution and Equal Justice in Education

Virgil C. Blum, S.J.*

The first part of this study will discuss the constitutionality of public aid for the education of church-related school children. The second part will discuss the civil rights of parents, particularly freedom of religion, in the education of their children.

I. THE CONSTITUTIONALITY OF PUBLIC AID FOR THE EDUCATION OF STUDENTS IN CHURCH-RELATED SCHOOLS

The principle or rule of law which must guide our discussion of the constitutional question of tax funds for the education of church-related school children was set down by the United States Supreme Court scores of years ago; but it was most recently restated in the *Schempp* Bible-reading case of 1963. The Court therein reasserted the rule of law which guides courts in deciding constitutional questions in church-state cases. It said, "The test may be stated as follows: What are the purpose and the primary effect of the enactment? If either is the advancement or inhibition of religion, then the enactment exceeds the scope of legislative power as circumscribed by the Constitution. That is to say that to withstand the strictures of the Establishment Clause there must be a secular legislative purpose and a primary effect that neither advances nor inhibits religion."

THE PRIMACY OF SECULAR EFFECTS IN PUBLIC LEGISLATION

This is the doctrine of the primacy of secular effects. The question

---

* Chairman of the Department of Political Science, Marquette University, Milwaukee, Wisconsin.

we must ask when discussing legislation which provides tax funds for the education of church-related school children is: What are the *purpose* and *primary effect* of such legislation? If either the legislative purpose or the *primary* effect of the legislation is to advance religion, the law is unconstitutional.* On the other hand, if the purpose and the *primary* effect of the legislation is the education of children in *secular* subjects, the law is constitutional.

In other words, if the legislative purpose in providing equal educational benefits to our nation's seven million church-related school children were to support the teaching of the Protestant, Catholic, Jewish, or Secularist[1] religion, the legislation would be unconstitutional. Or if the *primary* effect of the legislation were to aid the teaching of religion, the legislation would be invalid.

But if, on the other hand, the legislative purpose in providing equal education benefits to church-related school children were to aid their education in *secular* subjects, and if in fact the *primary* effect of such legislation were these children's better secular education, the legislation would be constitutional.

There can be no doubt, therefore, that government aid for the better education of church-related school children in sciences, mathematics, history, grammar, geography, and all the other secular subjects is constitutional. On the other hand, government aid which has as its purpose or *primary* effect the education of children in religion is unconstitutional.**

In other words, government can legislate for a *public* purpose; it can spend public funds for a public purpose which is achieved through the agency of a church-related school. To put it another way, the government's sovereign power to promote proper *secular* objectives is not paralyzed by incidental benefits which may accrue to religion as a by-product of its enactments. Such benefits are not the *primary* effect of legislation for a public purpose; they are incidental to the government's purpose, and irrelevant to the constitutional question.

Some opposing the use of public funds for the education of church-related school children maintain, however, that the education of such children does not serve a public purpose. They look upon these schools

---

[1] Secularism *is* a religion in both the theological and legal context, as I shall point out in the second part of this essay.

* Editor's note: According to the existing Schempp doctrine.

** Editor's note: Again, according to the existing Schempp doctrine.

as little more than Sunday schools, engaged for the most part in the teaching of religion. Such unawareness of the curricular content of church-related schools is hardly excusable in view of the demonstrated performance of the graduates of these schools. The graduates of church-related high schools perform as well as public school graduates in state and private competitive examinations in secular subjects. Moreover, they are readily admitted to both private and public colleges and universities.

The United States Supreme Court has repeatedly stated, moreover, that education of children in church-related schools serves a public purpose. In the *Cochran* textbook case of 1930, the Court, in upholding the validity of a law which provided secular textbooks for church-related school children, declared: "We cannot doubt that the taxing power of the State is exerted for a public purpose." Hence, even though the Court recognized that such welfare legislation resulted in incidental benefits to religion, it maintained that the benefits were irrelevant to the law's primary secular purpose. Of the textbook law the Court said: "Its interest is education, broadly; its method, comprehensive. Individual interests are aided only as the common interest is safeguarded."

When the state promotes the "common interest," for example, the secular education of *all* children, the fact that "individual interests are aided," such as the religious interests of parents, is immaterial because it is incidental to the primary secular purpose of the law. The Court made this point emphatically clear in the *Cochran* case when it insisted that, as far as the primary effect of the law was concerned, "the school-children and the state alone are the beneficiaries." This, said the Court, is the expenditure of public funds for a public purpose.

The Court again had occasion to underscore the fact that the education of children in church-related schools serves a public purpose in the *Everson* bus-ride case of 1947. Opponents of equal welfare benefits for church-related school children had charged that the education of those children did not serve a public purpose and that giving them bus rides was like giving Sunday school children bus rides. "It is much too late," the Court said, "to argue that legislation intended to facilitate the opportunity of [church-related school] children to get a *secular* education serves no *public* purpose." (Emphasis added.)

The doctrine of the primacy of secular effects was applied by the Supreme Court in the Connecticut *Snyder* bus-ride case of 1961. By dismissing the case for lack of substantial federal question, it upheld, seven to two, the constitutionality of bus rides for church-related school children against the contention that such rides aid religion. Since the primary effect of bus rides for schoolchildren is secular — their health, safety, and convenience — any benefit accruing to religion from this welfare legislation is incidental, and irrelevant to the purpose of the law.

Basing its decision on the doctrine of the primacy of secular effects, the Court declared in the *Everson* case, "the legislation, as applied, does no more than provide a general program to help parents get their children, regardless of their religion, safely and expeditiously to and from accredited schools." In *Everson*, as in the *Snyder* case, the legislative purpose and the primary secular effect of the law were the controlling factors in the Court's decision, and not simply by-products of the law.

It is significant that the Court adhered to the doctrine of the primacy of secular effects in the *Everson* case, since it was there that it declared the new doctrine that neither the state nor federal government may aid religion. What the Court meant, of course, was that aid to religion could be neither the purpose nor the primary effect of a state or federal law. The Court did in fact recognize that, while the legislative purpose and the primary effect of bus rides were secular, an incidental benefit did accrue to religion. Again, in the *McGowan* Sunday closing law case of 1961, the Court, summarizing the *Everson* reasoning, mentioned the incidental benefits to religion:

"The Court, speaking through Mr. Justice Black, recognized that 'it is undoubtedly true that children are helped to get to church schools,' and 'there is even a possibility that some of the children might not be sent to the church schools if the parents were compelled to pay their children's bus fares out of their own pockets when transportation to a public school would have been paid for by the State.'"

The Court then alluded directly to the *purpose* and *secular effect* of the bus law, saying: "But the Court found that the purpose and effect of the statute in question was general 'public welfare legislation,' that it was to protect all school children from the 'very real hazards of traffic,' that the expenditure of public funds for school transportation, to religious schools or to others, was like the expenditure of public funds to provide policemen to safeguard these same children or to provide 'such general government services as ordinary police and fire protection, connections for sewage disposal, public highways and sidewalks.'"

The fact that a program of tax-provided bus rides to church-related schools makes it possible for some parents to send their children to these schools — thus incidentally aiding religion — is irrelevant to the secular purpose of the law. The purpose and the primary secular effect of the bus-ride law — the health, safety, welfare, and convenience of school-children — are relevant and central to the question of its constitutionality. Incidental benefits to religion, on the other hand, are irrelevant to the constitutional question.

The doctrine of the primacy of secular effects has general application, and is limited only by constitutional guarantees of personal rights and freedoms. For example, rights of freedom of conscience prohibit the state from making the flag salute compulsory in public schools as a means of fostering national unity and cohesion, since this regulation would violate the religious conscience of Jehovah's Witnesses.

The Court applied the doctrine of the primacy of secular effects in the *McGowan* Sunday closing law case. It found that the legislative purpose and primary effects of Sunday closing laws were secular — rest, repose, relaxation, and recreation for the people of a highly industrialized nation. Hence, the Court held that these laws were constitutional, despite the fact that, as it recognized, the laws benefit Christian religions. It declared: "The fact that this day is Sunday, a day of particular significance for the dominant Christian sects, does not bar the State from achieving its secular goals."

In other words, incidental benefits which accrue to religion as a by-product of laws enacted for a secular purpose do not bar the state from achieving its proper secular goals. The sovereign power of the state to provide for the general welfare cannot be stifled by legislative by-products that aid religion.

Nor does the state have to use alternative means to achieve secular goals that would not incidentally aid religion. In the *Gallagher* Sunday law case, the Court said, "we reject appellees' request to hold these statutes invalid on the ground that the State may accomplish its purpose by alternative means that would not even remotely or incidentally aid religion." Provided it does not violate the constitutional rights of citizens, the state is free to use any means to achieve its secular goals, including means which result in incidental benefits to religion.

The secular character of a governmental action is not changed by its incidental effects. A law does not cease to be secular, enacted for a secular purpose and having a primary secular effect, by an incidental effect benefitting religion. The essential secular nature of a law is not changed by its accidental characteristics — its incidental effects. The Supreme Court underscored this truism in the *Two Guys* Sunday law case when, referring to the benefits such a law provides for the Christian religions, it said: *"Yet this does not change the character of the enactment. It is still, essentially, but a civil regulation made for the government of man as a member of civil society. . . ."*

SECULAR EFFECTS IN CHURCH-RELATED EDUCATION —
LEGISLATION AND PRACTICE

The application of the doctrine of the primacy of secular effects to a law providing tax funds for the education of church-related school children in secular subjects is clear and beyond reasonable challenge. The purpose and primary effect of such an expenditure of public funds are the education of these children in *secular* subjects — an unassailable secular purpose aimed at an unassailable secular effect. Benefits which may accrue to religion from such legislation are secondary, incidental, and irrelevant to the secular purpose of law.

A $3 billion federal-aid-to-education program designed to help the nation's 47 million youngsters in the study of *secular* subjects, for example, would clearly have a legislative purpose and primary effect which are secular. The congressional purpose of such a program would not be the aid of religion. Nor would the primary effect of such a program be the aid of the Protestant, Catholic, Jewish, or Secularist religions. In the language of the Supreme Court, there would be "a secular legislative purpose and a primary effect that neither advances nor inhibits religion."

The doctrine of the primacy of secular effects is not new in education legislation. It has been applied more or less consistently and more or less purely by Congress and the federal courts, while it has at times been neglected by state legislatures, and particularly by state courts. Starting more than 170 years ago, there have been literally thousands of grants of money and land to church-related schools. These grants demonstrate that our state and federal governments have, in fact, frequently aided church-related schools in the education of students in secular subjects (and sometimes even in religious subjects). Our policy makers have always looked upon such programs as an expenditure of public funds for a public purpose.

A few examples of government aid to church-related schools will indicate how old is the doctrine of the primacy of secular effects:

1. During the first three decades of our national history, the states more or less regularly made direct grants to Baptist, Episcopalian, Unitarian, Lutheran, Presbyterian, Catholic, Jewish, and Christian Reformed elementary schools. (The extent of such grants are revealed in the monumental work *Public Funds for Church and Private Schools*, by Richard J. Gabel.)

2. In 1789 Congress reenacted the Northwest Ordinance under which land grants were made to church-related elementary schools.

3. The state of New York gave Union (Presbyterian) College over $350,000 from 1795 to 1815.

4. The federal government gave generous land grants to Columbia (Baptist) College, now George Washington University, in 1832, and to Georgetown (Catholic) College in 1833.

5. The federal government gave $5 million to church-related schools for the education of Negro children from 1865 to 1871.

6. The federal government gave a grant of $26,000 to Wilberforce (Methodist) University in 1870, and the Ohio legislature supported the university's teacher-training and industrial departments with grants totaling $77,000 in 1913–1914, $279,160 in 1927–1928, and $529,100 in 1929–1930, and has continued to do so.

7. The state of Rhode Island gave Brown (Baptist) University $1,000 in 1854, and in 1862 the federal government gave a generous land grant to that university under the Morrill Act and, moreover, gave it the income from the land until 1893.

8. The federal government granted $29,500 in 1888 and $29,980 in 1892 to Presbyterian, Episcopalian, Catholic, and other mission schools in Alaska.

9. Local governments granted $62,000 to McPherson (Lutheran Baptist) College in 1909; $13,000 to St. Olaf (Lutheran) College in 1909; $3,000 to Bethany (Lutheran) College in 1905; $2,440 to Fairmount (Congregational) College in 1912; $1,000 to Highland (Presbyterian) College in 1914; $8,000 to Campbell (Unitarian Presbyterian) College in 1916; and between $21,500 and $50,000 to Western (Methodist) University from 1913 to 1917.

10. The state of Maine gave public funds to Baptist, Catholic, Methodist, Quaker, and other church-related schools until 1937.

While these grants are not large by today's standards, some were by yesterday's, and they do establish the fact that, despite the denials of the absolute church-state separationists, the use of tax funds in aid of church-related schools has a long history in America.

SECULAR EFFECTS IN CHURCH-RELATED HOSPITALS: LEGISLATION AND INTERPRETATION

Congress has also applied the doctrine of the primacy of secular effects in making grants to church-related hospitals. And the Supreme Court has upheld such grants on the ground that they serve a public purpose.

In 1897 Congress provided funds which the commissioners of the District of Columbia allocated for the construction of Providence Hospital. This institution was and is operated by a group of Catholic hospital Sisters. The purpose and primary effect of such an aid program are the care and cure of the sick — a proper secular purpose.

The Supreme Court upheld the expenditure of these federal funds for a Catholic hospital in the *Bradfield* case of 1899. It held that the federal law which provided funds for the construction of Providence Hospital was not a violation of separation of church and state. The Court reasoned that the hospital was a secular corporation, incorporated "for the purposes for which such an institution is generally conducted," that is, "the care of sick and invalid persons." This is the secular purpose of a hospital. The actual care of sick persons is the primary secular effect of the federal law.

Providence Hospital was and is run by a Catholic Sisterhood, and it is conducted under the auspices of the Catholic Church. But these factors, said the Court, are "wholly immaterial," since they do not change the purely secular character and function of the hospital. These conditions, reasoned the Court, "do not in the least change the legal character of the hospital, or make a religious corporation out of a purely secular one as constituted by the law of its being."

The hospital is a legal institution serving a public purpose, and the religious belief of its incorporators, said the Court, "is of not the slightest consequence." A hospital is a hospital; the religious beliefs of its operators do not change it into a religious institution. The Court in fact emphatically rejected the contention that the religious beliefs of hospital operators change a secular institution into a religious institution. It said: "That the influence of any particular church may be powerful over the members of a nonsectarian and secular corporation, incorporated for a certain defined purpose and with clearly stated powers, is surely not sufficient to convert such a corporation into a religious or sectarian body."

This is simply to say that the religious orientation of a secular institution does not change the secular character of its function. In providing funds to such an institution to perform a public service, government is legislating for a public purpose, and incidental benefits accruing to religion are irrelevant.

SECULAR EFFECTS IN CHURCH-RELATED EDUCATION — TODAY'S LEGISLATION AND PRACTICE

In 1963 Congress enacted and President Lyndon B. Johnson signed into law the Higher Education Facilities Act which authorized $1.2 billion for the construction of college and university classrooms, libraries, and laboratories. The Act provides $835 million in grants and $360 million in low-interest loans over three years. Church-related colleges and universities are eligible for grants and loans under the provisions of this law.

The question of church-state relations was sharply raised, and Congress expressly limited the use of federal funds to the construction of classrooms to be used exclusively for the teaching of certain secular subjects — mathematics, engineering, the natural and physical sciences, and the modern foreign languages. These classrooms may not be used for the teaching of religion or theology.

Congress there adhered to the doctrine of the primacy of secular effects. The legislative purpose and primary effects of the law are secular — providing facilities for the teaching of secular subjects. In the *Schempp* case the Supreme Court declared, as indicated above, that for a law "to withstand the strictures of the Establishment Clause there must be a secular legislative purpose and a primary effect that neither advances nor inhibits religion." No one, presumably, would maintain, for example, that the congressional purpose or *primary* effect of the Higher Education Facilities Act of 1963 is to aid religion.

In this College Facilities Act, the legislative purpose is the construction of classrooms for the teaching of students in *secular* subjects. The *primary* effect of the law is the education of more students in *secular* subjects — a secular effect, with an incidental benefit accruing to the Protestant, Catholic, Jewish, and Secularist religions. Consistently with the rule set down by the Court, the primary effect of the law neither advances nor inhibits religion.

Nearly all congressmen accept the doctrine of the primacy of secular effects, as indicated by their vote on the College Facilities Bill. The House passed this bill by an overwhelming majority, 258 to 92, and the Senate passed it by a vote of 54 to 27. Many of those voting against the federal aid bill, moreover, did so, not because they reject the doctrine of the primacy of secular effects, but because they are opposed to federal support of education.

From the earliest days of our history, Congress has provided funds to church-related schools for scientific research or for the education of students in secular subjects. Some of the more important research and educational programs in which Congress has in recent years supported the secular researches of faculty members and/or the secular education of students are the: (1) G.I. Bill of Rights, (2) National Youth Administration, (3) National Defense Education Act, (4) Public Health Service Act, (5) War Orphans' Educational Assistance Act, (6) National Science Foundation Act, (7) College Housing Loan Program, (8) Atomic Energy Act, (9) National Aeronatics and Space Act, (10) Health Professions Educational Assistance Act, and (11) Higher Education Facilities Act.

Faculty and students of church-related colleges and universities are eligible to participate in these federal research and education programs on an equal basis with the faculty and students of state institutions. So may church-related schools themselves. The fact that their participation in such programs may result in incidental benefits to religion is irrelevant to the legislative purpose of the program.

The federal government has never, to be sure, entertained the notion that its sovereign power to legislate for the general welfare or national defense is paralyzed when, as a by-product of its legislation for a secular purpose, an incidental benefit may accrue to religion.

The significance for church-related higher education of the congressional application of the doctrine of the primacy of secular effects can be easily demonstrated. For example, under the National Defense Education Act, graduate fellows receive a stipend of from $2,000 to $2,400 a year, with an allowance of $400 a year for each dependent. Moreover, the federal government gives a cost-of-education grant of $2,500 a year to the school attended by the NDEA fellow.

Among the institutions participating in this program are Methodist, Catholic, Jewish, Latter-Day Saints, Baptist, Disciples of Christ, and Congregational universities.

During 1962–1964, Methodist universities were awarded a total of 264 NDEA graduate fellowships. This was more than all other church-related universities combined. If each fellow received an average of $2,400 a year, the federal government made NDEA grants to Methodist university students in the range of $633,600 in this period. Furthermore, the government made additional NDEA cost-of-education grants to Methodist universities for the education of 264 fellows in the range of $660,000 over the same period.

The state of New York, to give another example, has several programs which aid students to get an education in church-related and other colleges and universities. As of 1963–1964, its Regents Scholarship program provided a total of 17,400 scholarship awards of from $250 to $700 a year to each year's high school graduates. In 1963–1964, over 50,000 such awards were in effect. In 1964–1965, the total was over 70,000. The maximum scholarship was increased to $1,000 in 1965. Moreover, under its Scholar Incentive program, the state of New York in 1963–1964 provided direct tuition grants (scholar incentive awards) of $100, $200, or $300 a year to about 125,000 college students. In 1964–1965 the total grants numbered about 143,000. In 1965, the maximum grant was increased to $500.

Since New York gives both scholarship and scholar incentive students freedom of choice in education, a large proportion of these subsidized students attend church-related schools. It may be noted in passing that several other states now have general scholarship programs which give freedom of choice in education. Included are California, Kansas, Illinois, Michigan, Rhode Island, Maryland, New Jersey, and Massachusetts.

New York has applied the doctrine of the primacy of secular effects in other educational programs as well. The state and city of New York, for example, turned over, without charge, two public hospitals to Yeshiva University, a Jewish institution, for teaching and research purposes. The Bronx Municipal Hospital Center, which cost $45 million in public funds, was the first to be affiliated with Yeshiva by contract in 1953. The second hospital, a state mental institution costing $70 million, was affiliated with Yeshiva by contract five years later.

According to the terms of the contracts, the city and state gave to Yeshiva University the *exclusive jurisdiction* and *supervision* over staffing, medical services, laboratory experiments, analysis, operations, and research projects. Thus, at no capital cost to it, Yeshiva has complete control over the essential operations of this $115 million complex of public hospitals. Moreover, the state and city agreed to supply and maintain all equipment and laboratories, and to provide all services, thus assuming for the university most of the high operating costs of the hospitals.

Finally, for clinical services rendered to the community, the city of New York agreed to pay the university the sum of $750,000 a year for ten years.

The purpose and primary effect of these extremely valuable contracts with Yeshiva University are, of course, secular — medical teaching and research. But these arrangements result in valuable incidental benefits for the Jewish religion. Such benefits, however, are the by-products of the contract, and are irrelevant to the secular purpose of the contracting parties.

The State of Maryland during 1962–1963 made four separate grants totaling $2.5 million to four church-related colleges for the construction of classroom and science buildings and dormitories. These grants were challenged by The Horace Mann League as in violation of the First Amendment and the Maryland Constitution.

Judge O. Bowie Duckett of the Circuit Court for Anne Arundel County, however, ruled in 1965 that the grants violated neither the First Amendment nor the Maryland Constitution. His ruling was based on the *Schempp* doctrine of the primacy of secular effects. Referring to the *Schempp* doctrine, the court said: "To me, the test laid down by the Supreme Court in the 'Prayer' case means that if either the legislative purpose or the primary effect of the enactment advances or suppresses religion, the legislation is invalid, otherwise, it is valid."

Applying this doctrine, the court said, as to the legislative purpose, "it seems crystal clear that the Maryland Legislature was in no way concerned with religion in making the appropriation." As to the primary effect of these enactments, the court said, "the grants to these Colleges are for the construction of secular college buildings in no way connected with religion." On the basis of this rationale, the court held that "all the appropriations are valid and constitutional."

In reaching this conclusion the court quoted, interestingly, a statement by Mr. Leo Pfeffer in *Church, State and Freedom*, p. 476: "When the *Everson* decision is coupled with the *Cochran* decision, they lead logically to the conclusion that a state may, notwithstanding the First Amendment, finance practically every aspect of parochial education, with the exception of such comparatively minor items as the proportionate salaries of teachers while they teach the catechism."

This is nothing more or less than the application of the doctrine of the primacy of secular effects to the question of the use of tax funds for the education of church-related school children and students in secular subjects.

SECULAR EFFECTS IN CHURCH-RELATED HOSPITALS —
TODAY'S LEGISLATION AND INTERPRETATION

Congress applied the doctrine of the primacy of secular effects when it enacted the Hill-Burton Act of 1946. Under the terms of this Act, the federal government has granted more than $1.1 billion for the construction and equipping of voluntary hospital and other health facilities. A large proportion of these grants were made to Protestant, Catholic, Jewish, and Secularist institutions. Such an expenditure of public funds results in incidental benefits to religion which are irrelevant to the secular purpose of the law. These incidental benefits to religion do not bar the federal government from cooperating with hospital groups to provide adequate facilities to care for the sick.

While the Yeshiva-New York agreement has not been challenged in the courts, a similar arrangement between Ketchikan, Alaska, and a group of Catholic hospital Sisters was challenged in the *Lien* case of 1963. The city of Ketchikan had erected a $2 million hospital under the Hill-Burton Act with a combination of federal, state, and local funds. Upon its completion, the city leased the hospital to a group of Catholic hospital Sisters for ten years at $1 a year. Lien, a taxpayer, charged among other things, that the lease violated the state constitution which provided that: "No tax shall be levied, or appropriation of public money made, or public property transferred . . . except for a public purpose."

Although the Alaksa court did not cast its reasoning in terms of the purpose and primary effect of the contract, it did apply the "use test" which, in effect, is the same thing. The court made a distinction between the character of the *use* to which public funds are put and the character of the *agency* expending the funds. If the *use* of the funds serves a public purpose — i.e., achieves a primary effect which is secular

— the expenditure is constitutional, and the character of the *agency* is irrelevant. In the words of the court: "The test is the character of the use to which the property is put and not the character of the agency operating the property."

The decisive constitutional question is not with whom is the contract made for the expenditure of public funds, but for what *purpose* and for what *use* are public funds expended. If the purpose and use are public, the character of the agency which spends the money is irrelevant. It may be private or church-related. On the basis of this doctrine, the Supreme Court of Alaska held constitutional the $1-a-year lease of the community hospital to the Catholic hospital Sisters.

DOCTRINAIRE ABSOLUTISM REJECTED

Absolute church-state separationists object to welfare legislation which incidentally benefits religion. They demand that the government be paralyzed in its efforts to provide for the secular needs of all the people if, in its efforts to do so, an unintended benefit accrues to the people's spiritual needs.

This "doctrinaire absolutism" has been repeatedly rejected by the Supreme Court. While "the constitutional standard is the separation of Church and State, the Court declared in the *Zorach* released-time case of 1952, "the First Amendment does not say that in every and all respect there shall be a separation of Church and State. Rather, it studiously defines the manner, the specific ways, in which there shall be no concert or union or dependency one on the other. That is the common sense of the matter."

The absolute church-state separationists would not only cripple the government in its efforts to achieve the common good, they would also force it to adopt policies that "would," in the words of the Court, "be preferring those who believe in no religion over those who do believe," which the Constitution forbids. Moreover, said the Court, "we find no constitutional requirement which makes it necessary for government to be hostile to religion and to throw its weight against efforts to widen the effective scope of religious influence."

In a free, democratic, pluralistic society, "accommodation" must be the constitutional standard of the state's relations to its citizens who have a spiritual life as well as a natural life. "Otherwise," said the Court, "the state and religion would be aliens to each other — hostile, suspicious, and even unfriendly." The state must, indeed, accommodate itself to the fact that citizens are members of two societies — civil and religious.

Attempts of any state to deal with the citizen as though he were *merely* a member of civil society are not only hostile to his nature, but destructive of the integrity of his personality. When the state refuses to accommodate its policies to man's spiritual nature, it treats him as though he were a merely material "thing," a mass of chemical compounds and physical reflexes with no relation to God. Such policies are in fact based on a Secularistic theology — they suppose that God is totally irrelevant to human affairs.

The state that is not wholly Secularistic recognizes the fact that many citizens have a spiritual allegiance to a Higher Being, and it will, to the extent of its commitment to liberty, assure their free exercise of religion without penalty — without conditioning a share in welfare benefits on the surrender of freedom of conscience. When such a state legislates for the secular needs of its citizens, it does not object if, incidentally, the legislation aids their religious development. This kind of accommodation to the citizens' total nature, freely permitting (and not obstructing) their spiritual growth, is demanded by the constitutional guarantees of freedom of conscience and equal justice under law.

When, in legislating, a state makes an accommodation to the total nature of man, incidental benefits may accrue to religion. But since such benefits are neither the purpose nor primary effect of the legislation, they are irrelevant to the purpose of the law and immaterial to the constitutional question. This doctrine of the primacy of secular effects was underscored by Dr. Robert M. Hutchins, former president of the University of Chicago, one time dean of the Yale School of Law, now president of the Fund for the Republic, when he wrote in *The Saturday Evening Post* in 1963: "The fact that a school is owned by a church, or that it gives some religious instruction, or that its teaching is 'permeated' by religion, or that federal aid to it is incidentally of some benefit to the church is immaterial."

RELIGIOUS "PERMEATION" DOES NOT CHANGE ESSENTIAL NATURE

It is of course Hutchins' contention that, as far as the First Amendment and the aid issue are concerned, the permeation of secular subjects by moral and religious values is immaterial. He holds that such permeation is irrelevant to the state's purpose in the secular education of children. That is to say, the state's primary purpose in subsidizing the education of church-related school children — their advance in secular knowledge — would be achieved, notwithstanding the religious permeation of secular subjects taught the children. The reason for this is apparent. The secular character of secular subjects is not changed by a moral or religious permeation.

A religious permeation of secular subjects no more changes their secular character than a dye changes the cotton fabric of a woman's blouse. Even a child knows there is no such thing as Protestant grammar, Catholic geography, Jewish chemistry, or Secularist algebra. The nature or character of secular subjects cannot be changed by religious colorations. No amount of Lutheran permeation can change grammar into Lutheran grammar, and make it essentially different from grammar taught in Catholic schools.

If there were in fact a Protestant grammar, a Catholic geography, a Jewish chemistry, and a Secularist algebra, how would high school seniors of church-related schools qualify for the National Merit Scholarship competition in which all students take the *same* tests? The Merit Scholarship competition is clear evidence that students who attend church-related schools receive a secular education as good as that received by students in our public schools.

All secular subjects are more or less permeated by moral and religious values. Since the humanities and social sciences deal more intimately with human activities than do the life and physical sciences, they are more value-impregnated. This does not mean, however, that the study and interpretation of man in his political, social, economic, and creative activities is the study of religion. It does mean, though, that it is impossible to study and interpret man and his activities apart from his moral and religious values. To maintain that man can be studied and his activities interpreted apart from these values is to fail to understand history, as well as the nature of man and the purpose of education.

Supreme Court Justice Robert Jackson took such religious permeation of secular subjects for granted. Even as he insisted, in the *McCollum* case (1948), that public schools must teach exclusively *secular* subjects, he wrote: "The fact is that, for good or ill, nearly everything in our culture worth transmitting, everything which gives meaning to life, is saturated with religious influences, derived from paganism, Judaism, Christianity — both Catholic and Protestant — and other faiths accepted by a large part of the world's peoples."

The opponents of public support for a secular education which supposes, for example, the existence of God, the creation of men, the Divine Law, and moral accountability for human action, are therefore really demanding that all tax-supported education revert to sheer Secularism. They demand the removal of every shred of moral and religious content, thus suppressing, in Justice Jackson's words, "nearly everything in our culture worth transmitting, everything which gives meaning to life."

The recognition of the moral and religious content in the various cultures of man, including our own, does not change the character of the humanities and social sciences into religious subjects. Nor does the Lutheran professor's interpretation of the Reformation change his course in modern history into a course in the Lutheran religion. The religious orientation of a secular subject does not change the basic secular character of the subject.

II. PARENTS' CIVIL RIGHTS IN EDUCATION UNDER THE CONSTITUTION

This essay has thus far attempted to show that equal tax funds for the education of church-related school children in secular subjects is constitutional. The second part of the essay will deal with the question of parents' freedom of religion in the education of their children under the Constitution.

In his statement on the education-aid issue at the University of Chicago Law School, Dr. Hutchins called attention not only to the doctrine of the primacy of secular effects, but also to the constitutional guarantee of religious freedom as applied to the education of children. "If it is objected that nonbelievers are thereby taxed to aid religion," he said in urging federal aid for *all* children, "the answer is that by hypothesis the aid to religion is *incidental* to the *over-riding public benefit* that cannot be obtained without including institutions under religious auspices, and that, since the object of the religion clauses of the First Amendment is to guarantee and promote *religious freedom*, such incidental benefits, which do not limit religious freedom, do not invalidate the legislation." (Emphasis added.)

RELIGIOUS FREEDOM IN EDUCATION AT STAKE

Hutchins first makes the point that if the government were to enact legislation to aid the secular education of church-related school children, their mental development — "the over-riding public benefit" — would be the primary secular effect of the law. Any incidental benefits which religion might receive would be irrelevant, and the law would be constitutional. Hutchins then introduces a second consideration, that of parents' religious freedom in the education of their children.

The religious freedom issue is vital. It cannot be ignored. In this connection, Hutchins reminded his listeners that "it is a violation of the First Amendment to apply pressure, direct or indirect, upon the conscience of any person." The denial of tax funds for the education of church-related school children in secular subjects is, for many parents, an irresistible coercion suppressing their religious freedom in educating their children. On the other hand, Hutchins insists, "aid to all educational institutions that meet federal standards would promote religious freedom as well as education." But, as of now, parents enjoy religious freedom in education neither on the state nor on the federal level. Both demand the surrender of rights of conscience as a condition for sharing in tax funds for educating children in secular subjects. Such a condition forces parents to choose between the dictates of their religious conscience on the one hand, and sharing in education tax funds on the other. This violates their rights of conscience.

In the important *Sherbert* case of 1963, the Supreme Court declared that the imposition of such conditions on sharing in welfare benefits is a violation of religious freedom. The Unemployment Security Commission of South Carolina had conditioned availability of unemployment benefits on Mrs. Sherbert's willingness to surrender her belief that, as a Seventh-Day Adventist, she should not work on Saturdays. By its ruling, South Carolina had placed Mrs. Sherbert in the conscience-wrenching position of having to choose between her religious beliefs and welfare benefits.

The Supreme Court, in a seven to two decision, declared of the Commission's requirement that "the ruling forced her to choose between following the precepts of her religion and forfeiting benefits, on the one hand, and abandoning one of the precepts of her religion in order to accept work, on the other hand." Such a policy penalizes religion; it denies welfare benefits to a citizen because of his religious beliefs; it demands the surrender of religious beliefs as a condition for sharing in welfare programs. In a society which respects the rights of conscience, such indirect suppression of religious freedom cannot be allowed. Hence, the decree was held invalid by the Supreme Court. "Governmental imposition of such a choice," said the Court, "puts the same kind of burden upon the free exercise of religion as would a fine imposed against appellant for her Saturday worship." This doctrine of religious freedom but underscores the doctrine enunciated by Thomas Jefferson in his "A Bill for Establishing Religious Freedom," where he wrote: "No man shall be compelled to . . . suffer on account of his religious opinions or belief; but . . . all men shall be free to profess . . . their opinion in matters of religion, and . . . the same shall in no wise diminish, enlarge or affect their civil capacities."

Yet, when parents exercise their religion in the choice of a church-related school for their children's education, they suffer the loss of tax funds for their instruction in secular subjects. Their children may share in such funds *only* if they surrender the constitutional right to the free exercise of religion in the choice of a school. What the Court said in the *Sherbert* case regarding the denial of welfare benefits on religious grounds has equal application to the denial of education benefits on religious grounds. "It is too late in the day," the Court declared, "to doubt that the liberties of religion and expression may be infringed by the denial or placing of conditions upon a benefit or privilege."

The conditions imposed by the several states upon a child's sharing in education tax funds, if we may transfer the language of the Court, puts the same kind of burden on the free exercise of religion as would a fine imposed against parents for the choice of a church-related school. Children are deprived of benefits because of their religious beliefs. Such a denial of benefits on religious grounds, said the Court in the *Everson* case, is a violation of the First Amendment. This fundamental doctrine of religious freedom was reaffirmed and strengthened in the *Sherbert* case. "This holding," the Supreme Court said, referring to and quoting *Everson*, "but reaffirms a principle that we announced a decade and a half ago, namely that no State may 'exclude individual Catholics, Lutherans, Mohammedans, Baptists, Jews, Methodists, Non-believers, Presbyterians, or the members of any other faith, *because of their faith or lack of it,* from receiving the benefits of public welfare legislation.'"

The Court here reiterates a fundamental doctrine of freedom, that in the distribution of its welfare benefits, the state may not discriminate against citizens because of their religious beliefs. A classification of citizens on religious grounds violates the First and Fourteenth Amendments. Equality of treatment for all citizens, on the other hand, is the best guarantee of freedom in a free society.

When the state or federal government denies fair and equitable education benefits to some seven million children *because of their religious beliefs*, it unwittingly violates constitutional guarantees of freedom of conscience and equal justice under the law. The right of choice of school, unanimously upheld by the Supreme Court in the *Pierce* case of 1925, then becomes, for many American parents, an empty phrase, since our governments penalize the choice by depriving children of any share in education tax funds. The mere fact that some parents can pay the penalty imposed by the state does not alter the fact that freedom of choice in education is as meaningless in America as was freedom of worship in Elizabethan England, where a heavy penalty was imposed on attendance at Mass.

Education legislation which denies tax funds to church-related school children, and thus imposes a burden on the exercise of religion in the choice of school, is clearly in conflict with constitutional guarantees of freedom of religion. This was indicated by the Supreme Court in the *Braunfeld* Sunday closing law case of 1961, wherein the Court said: "If the purpose or *effect* of a law is to impede the observance of one or all religions . . . that law is constitutionally invalid even though the burden may be characterized as being only indirect."

The fact that some parents are able to make up the fair share in education funds denied by the state does not mean that they enjoy freedom in education. They have a choice in education — a penalized choice — but they do not enjoy freedom of choice in education. Freedom penalized is not freedom, but repression of freedom. This doctrine of freedom was reaffirmed by the Supreme Court in the *Sherbert* case when it declared: "To condition the availability of benefits upon this appellant's willingness to violate a cardinal principle of her religious faith effectively penalizes the free exercise of her constitutional liberties." Education legislation which compels parents to surrender religious freedom in education effectively penalizes the free exercise of constitutional liberties.

If the federal government made voting in national elections mandatory, and emphasized the constitutional right of every citizen to vote either Democratic or Republican, yet provided a $10 voting grant to every citizen who voted the Democratic slate, withholding the same from any who voted otherwise, voters would indeed have a choice of parties. But would they have a free choice? Obviously not. While the choice of the Democratic slate of candidates would be heavily subsidized, the choice of the Republican slate would not be. Such legislation would deny equal benefits to citizens who wish to vote the Republican ticket, and would in fact put all citizens under pressure to vote the Democratic slate. It would not only destroy freedom of choice in politics, but would also create a state-controlled, one-party political system.*

COERCION IN OUR EARLIER PUBLIC SCHOOLS

Except for the fact that many Protestants, Catholics, and Jews are willing to pay the state-imposed penalty on the choice of an independent school, America would have a state-controlled monolithic educational system. The state would then be directly using its legal power (compulsory education laws) to enforce conformity to state-established orthodoxies, rather than the economic pressure it now uses.

Coercion in the field of education raises another important question under the First Amendment. When a child is coerced to conform to moral and religious values in conflict with his own, his freedom of conscience is seriously violated.

Parents have the civil right to send their children to a school whose moral and religious values are, according to the parents' choice, Protestant, Catholic, Jewish, or Secularist. But the state does not have the right to compel a Protestant child to attend a school whose moral and religious values are Catholic or Secularist. Such compulsory conformity violates freedom of conscience.

Until the early decades of the twentieth century, the public schools were mainly Protestant schools. Catholic, Jewish, and Secularist children were compelled to absorb Protestant moral and religious values and interpretations as a condition for sharing the education tax funds. Protestantism was really the "established religion" of the tax-supported schools. If parents objected to having their children indoctrinated with moral and religious values in conflict with their own, they had only one alternative. They could bear the burden of constructing and operating their own private schools. This is what Catholic and other parents did after protesting the indoctrination of their children.

Missouri University Professor Lloyd P. Jorgenson wrote in *Phi Delta Kappan* in 1963 that "The Common School Movement was, in its inception and development, a distinctly Protestant phenomenon. Many of the older denominations at first had serious misgivings about the movement. But the main body of Protestantism accepted it from the

---

* Editor's note: In 1965, the public grant to those attending public schools averaged about $600.

outset. This was particularly true of the most rapidly growing groups, the Methodists and Baptists."

Protestant groups not only recognized the public schools as Protestant, but claimed them as such. The leading Congregational journals, says Jorgenson, "repeatedly explained that the public school was essentially a Protestant institution. Methodist and Baptist spokesmen also identified the public schools with Protestantism."

When Catholic parents protested in the courts that the coercive indoctrination of their children in Protestantism was a violation of their civil rights, they received no relief. When a Catholic parent in Boston protested in court that a public school teacher had flogged his child across the hand for thirty minutes for refusing to read the Protestant Bible, the court ruled that the teacher had the right to use physical punishment to enforce this violation of conscience.

Catholics have never objected to religion in the public schools. While eager to support a system of teaching religion that respects the freedom of conscience of *all* children, they objected to the enforced indoctrination of their children in the Protestant religion. For many decades, however, their civil rights received no protection in the courts. When a Catholic child in Maine, for example, refused to read the Protestant Bible, she was expelled. The child's father sought protection in the courts. He received none. The highest court of Maine ruled, first, that the school regulation requiring the reading of the Protestant Bible was constitutional, and, second, that the regulation could be enforced on all the children, *even on those children who were of different religious faiths.*

THE RELIGION OF SECULARISM NOW "ESTABLISHED" IN THE SCHOOLS: COERCION CONTINUES

But the public schools are no longer Protestant. Neither are they Catholic or Jewish. They are Secularist. The Supreme Court spelled out removal of the last remnants of Protestantism from the public schools in 1963 when, in the *Murray* and *Schempp* cases, it held that it was illegal piously to read the Bible and say the Lord's Prayer in state schools. In so doing the Supreme Court also firmly established the religion of Secularism in our public schools.

The most discerning educators hold that there is no such thing as religious neutrality in the classroom. Omission of Bible reading and courses in religion does not make education neutral regarding belief in

God. When religion is omitted from the school curriculum, says Sir Walter Moberly in his scholarly book *The Crisis in the University*, you "insinuate . . . silently, insidiously, and all but irresistibly . . . that it is a matter of secondary importance."

Many academicians, moreover, will agree that when religion is omitted from the public school curriculum, the children naturally conclude that it is of no importance. When religion is ignored, says Dr. Luther A. Weigle, former dean of the Yale Divinity School, "it is natural for children to conclude that religion is negligible, or unimportant, or irrelevant to the main business of life." But this is the very doctrine of Secularism. Secularism is a man-centered religion; it believes that God is unimportant and irrelevant to human affairs, that man is an end in himself, and capable of creating for himself, without God, a paradise on earth.

Protestant theologians like Dr. Robert McAfee Brown of Stanford University and Dr. Martin Marty, assistant editor of *Christian Century*, agree that Secularism is a religion. Dr. Brown recently wrote: "Secularism is itself a 'faith.' The *object* and *content* of secularism's faith may be, and indeed are, very different from the object and content of the faith possessed by a Catholic or a Protestant or a Jew, but a faith it is and religion it is."

Secularism is considered a religion by the Supreme Court. In the *Torcaso* case of 1961, the Court maintained that there are "religions based on a belief in the existence of God and religions founded on different beliefs." One of the latter religions which "do not teach a belief in the existence of God," said the Court, is "Secular Humanism" or Secularism.

Secularism is not the religion of a small group of intellectuals who have rejected God. It is, as Dr. Martin Marty has pointed out, the fastest growing religious body in America, and it is making its major gains by inroads into the Protestant, Catholic, and Jewish religions. Secularism is a religion without God, although some Secularists may, superficially, call themselves Protestants, Catholics, or Jews. Whatever they call themselves, Secularists insist there is no real place for God in human affairs.

Secularists may actually proclaim belief in the existence of God, but they have lost faith in God; their faith is in man, and man's capacity to solve the problems which confront mankind. Man is self-sufficient; he is the measure of all things. Secularism is this-world-centered, and it teaches that man's fulfillment is found in his immersion in the things of this world.

Secularism obviously has no room for God, whether in business, labor, politics, the professions, or education. Secularism is "man in self-adoration," creating his own ideas of good and evil in moral and religious matters, and usually ending in amoral neutralism and indifferentism.

Objecting to the Supreme Court's removal of the Bible and the Lord's Prayer from the public schools, and seeing therein the establishment of Secularism as the religion of the schools, the Episcopal Reverend Walter M. Haushalter described the meaning of Secularism for our society. He wrote: "Secularism is society and culture without God, moral nihilism with no stable values to save us from equating good and evil. Secularism hopes for the peaceful coexistence of God and Satan where we may snuggle down into the softness of material joys. Its deepest antagonism to Christianity is a tolerant pacifism that takes no sides for roses against weeds, lambs against wolves, and ends up with frenzied hates against only their self-chosen enemies."

Secularism is the religion to which all children, whether Protestant, Catholic, or Jewish must today partly conform as a condition for sharing in education tax funds. American children, unlike children in virtually every other nation outside the iron curtain, do not actually enjoy freedom in education. If parents cannot bear the penalty imposed by the state on the choice of a church-related school, their children must, in violation of their conscience, conform to the moral and religious values of Secularism.

In assessing this national policy, so violative of freedom of religion, the late Dr. Bernard Iddings Bell, a noted Episcopalian clergyman and educator, wrote fifteen years ago: "As the American school system is now conducted, and more and more conducted, there is no such thing as religious liberty in American education. There is liberty only to be unreligious."

But today the American people are becoming increasingly concerned about "civil rights." As they come to know better the meaning of freedom of choice in education, they will incline more and more to giving *all* parents, regardless of religious belief and practice, a fair share of public funds for the education of their children in secular subjects. This will come to pass with reasonable speed only if the proponents of civil rights in education make positive efforts to inform and educate their fellow citizens about the lofty place that freedom of choice in education must occupy in a free and open society.

If they do so, there is every reason to believe that the dream expressed by President Lyndon B. Johnson as he opened the New York World Fair will be fulfilled. "If I am right," he said, "then at the next world fair people will see an America in which no man is handicapped by the color of his skin, or the nature of his belief — and no man will be discriminated against because of the church he attends or the country of his ancestors."

CHAPTER X

State Constitutions and Religion in Education

James R. Brown[*]

A reading of the bills of rights contained in the constitutions of the fifty states, establishes the fact that all state constitutions, in unmistakable terms, provide for freedom of religion, although they vary considerably in manner of expression.

A summary of what the states cannot do in the area of religion has been made by T. N. Cooley. State constitutions today contain provisions prohibiting:[1]

1) Any law respecting an establishment of religion.
2) Compulsory support of religious instruction.
3) Compulsory attendance upon religious worship.
4) Restraints upon the free exercise of religion.
5) Restraints upon the expression of religious belief.

Religious liberty, however, does not give any sect the right to oppose its views to the policy of government in order to frustrate that policy. Religious liberty is not construed to permit individuals or sects to engage in practices that would be opposed to the policy of "live and let live" intended by the state constitutions.[2] Religious liberty does not include "the right to introduce and carry out every scheme or purpose which persons see fit to claim as part of their religious system."[3]

It would be subversive of good government to subordinate the state's power to restrain acts prejudicial to the public welfare, and pro-

---

[*] Professor of Public Administration, University of Hartford, Hartford, Connecticut.
[1] T. N. Cooley, *Constitutional Limitations*, 6 ed., p. 575, in "Religious Liberty Juridically Defined," by Francis A. McCullough, *Notre Dame Lawyer*, XIII (May, 1938), 263.
[2] *State* v. *Powell*, 58 Ohio 324, 341; 50 N.E. 900, 901 (1898).
[3] *Mayor of Frazee's Case*, 63 Mich. 396, 405; 30 N.W. 72 (1886).

ductive of social injury, to the convictions of each individual as to acts which religious sentiments may demand.[4]

National constitutional documents, like the United States Constitution and the Declaration of Independence, recognize the Judaeo-Christian philosophy of life and government in explicit terms, acknowledging man's dependence on his Creator and relating the government of the nation and the people's participation in that government to God's providence.

The broad principles are often set down in the preambles to state constitutions. The preambles of thirty-seven of the state constitutions contain words of gratefulness to God as the Author of our freedom, and many of these invoke divine favor and guidance.[5] The constitutions of six states[6] proclaim that God permits the people to enjoy free government and civil and religious liberties. The preambles to the constitutions of Arkansas and Kansas thank God for the privilege of being able to form a free government. The constitution of Delaware states that the right of setting up government comes from God, and that of North Carolina thanks God for the preservation and the existence of the Union and of human liberties. The preamble to the Massachusetts state constitution thanks God for the opportunity to form a body politic. The constitutions of only five states, New Hampshire, Oregon, Tennessee, Vermont, and Virginia, either do not have a preamble or do not acknowledge God in their opening statements. Of these five, New Hampshire's constitution, in Article 6 of Part I, encourages the public worship of God, and that of Vermont, in Chapter I, Article 3, says that all denominations and sects should observe the Lord's Day and worship God.

These documents containing the fundamental principles and structure of the fifty state governments, with the few exceptions noted above, in various words recognize God as the Author of our being, the Creator and Ruler of the universe, the Source of our liberties and of the powers of government.

Chief Justice John Marshall wrote:

That the people have an original right to establish, for their future government, such principles as, in their opinion, shall most conduce

---

[4] *Frolickstein* v. *Mayor of Mobile*, 40 Ala. 725 (1867).

[5] For examples of acknowledgments of God, see *Constitutions of the United States National and State*, Published for Legislative Drafting Research Fund of Columbia University, 2 vols. (Dobbs Ferry, N. Y.: Oceana Publications, 1962).

[6] Delaware, Illinois, Maine, Massachusetts, New Jersey, and Rhode Island.

to their own happiness is the basis on which the whole American fabric has been erected. The exercise of this original right is a very great exertion; nor can it, nor ought it, to be frequently repeated. The principles, therefore, so established, are deemed fundamental.[7]

One must conclude that the people of the states were fundamentally religious and expected the governments set up under the state constitutions to create and maintain a political environment friendly to religion and to encourage the practice of religion and the teaching of religious and moral truths.

These sentiments appear in many judicial statements interpreting the fundamental law, the following being but a few examples:

> Christianity, general Christianity, is, and always has been, a part of the common law of Pennsylvania. . . .[8]

> The people of this state, in common with the people of this country, profess the general doctrines of Christianity, as the rule of their faith and practice; . . .[9]

> . . . there are many precepts of Christianity, of which the violation cannot be punished by human laws; and as obedience to them is beneficial to civil society, the state has wisely taken care that they should be taught, and also enforced by explaining their moral and religious sanctions, . . .[10]

Justice Brewer, of the United States Supreme Court, noted that God was invoked in the commission of Christopher Columbus, and that He has been invoked ever since, in colonial grants or charters, in the Mayflower Compact, the Fundamental Orders of Connecticut, the Pennsylvania Charter of Privileges of 1701, the Declaration of Independence, and the state constitutions. He concluded:

> There is no dissonance in these declarations. There is a universal language pervading them all having one meaning; they affirm and reaffirm that this is a religious nation. These are not individual sayings, declarations of private persons; they are organic utterances; they speak the voice of the entire people.[11]

---

[7] *Marbury* v. *Madison,* 1 Cranch 137, 176 (1803).

[8] *Updegraph* v. *The Commonwealth,* 11 S. & R. 394, 400 (1824).

[9] Chancellor Kent in *The People* v. *Ruggles,* 8 Johns 290, 292 (1811); "And in the case of *Rex* v. *Woolston* (Str. 834; Fitzg. 64) on a like conviction (blasphemy), the court said they would not suffer it to be debated whether defaming Christianity in general was not an offense at common law, for whatever strikes at the root of Christianity tends manifestly to the dissolution of civil government," p. 293.

[10] *Barnes* v. *First Parish,* 6 Mass. 401, 410 (1810).

[11] *Church of the Holy Trinity* v. *United States,* 143 U.S. 457, 470 (1892).

Some state constitutions recognize the importance of the public worship of God, and recommend this practice, but declare that it must be freely offered. Thus Delaware:

> Although it is the duty of all men frequently to assemble together for the public worship of Almighty God; and piety and morality, on which the prosperity of communities depends are hereby promoted; yet no man shall or ought to be compelled to attend any religious worship, to contribute to the erection or support of any place of worship, or to the maintenance of any ministry, against his own free will and consent. . . . (Article I, Section 1.)

The Massachusetts constitution states:

> It is the right as well as the duty of all men in society, publickly, and at stated seasons to worship the Supreme Being, the great Creator and preserver of the Universe. (Part I, Article III.)

Other state constitutions stress the fundamental necessity of religion and morality to the good order of the state. For example, Nebraska:

> Religion, morality and knowledge, however, being essential to good government, it shall be the duty of the Legislature to pass suitable laws to protect every religious denomination in the peaceable enjoyment of its own mode of public worship, and to encourage schools and the means of instruction. (Article I, Section 4.)

and North Dakota:

> In all schools instruction shall be given as far as practicable in those branches of knowledge that tend to impress upon the mind the vital importance of truthfulness, temperance, purity, public spirit, and respect for honest labor of every kind. (Article VII, Section 149.)

Other public documents and practices recognize God as the author of our being and acknowledge our dependence upon Him. Proclamations setting aside days of prayer and thanksgiving are issued every year, and the importance of religion and morality are often mentioned in the public messages of state and municipal officials. Legislatures and councils begin their deliberations with prayers, and the inauguration ceremonies of governors and mayors are preceded by invocations and followed by benedictions given by clergymen of various faiths.

PRIOR TO THE CIVIL WAR

Although many of the early colonists came to this continent to escape religious persecution and be rid of the restrictions placed upon religious expression by the established churches of Europe, most of them proceeded to erect commonwealths in which the closest ties existed between the Church and the civil government. In Virginia the Anglican Church was established, very much as it was in England and was granted state support. In Massachusetts, church and state were united; those who held office and exercised the franchise in the civil community were members of the Puritan Church. The meeting house served for the public worship of God, as well as the debate of public policy; the congregation of the church and the civic body were one and the same.

There was no church established, nor was there any union of church and state in the colonies of Pennsylvania[12] and Rhode Island.[13] In Maryland[14] and New York[15] there was no establishment either, while these colonies were governed by Catholics. In none of these colonies, however, was there any hostility toward religion. They could not be called secularist, or even the forerunners of secularist states. Whether a church was established or not, in all the colonies, at the time of their settlement and first growth, Christianity was fostered and recognized as the true source of the principles of freedom and government which the citizens enjoyed.

At the time of the break with Great Britain there were established churches in ten colonies; only Delaware, Pennsylvania, and Rhode Island had no established church.[16] All during the colonial period, and for a long time after the Revolution, religion and education were closely tied together.[17] The religious atmosphere in colonial America was very noticeable indeed and this was for a long period — almost 150 years. There were many colonists, especially in New England,

---

[12] See Pennsylvania's *Charter of Liberties* (1701) in Ray A. Billington, Bert J. Loewenberg, Samuel H. Brockunier, and David S. Sparks, *The Making of American Democracy*, rev. ed. (New York: Holt, Rinehart, and Winston, 1962), Vol. I, p. 56.

[13] See *Plantation Agreement at Providence* (1640) in Henry Steele Commager, *Documents of American History*, 7 ed. (New York: Appleton-Century-Crofts, 1963), p. 25.

[14] See *Maryland Act of Toleration* (1649) in Billington, Loewenberg, Brockunier, and Sparks, *op. cit.*, Vol. I, p. 56.

[15] See *New York's Grant of Religious Toleration* (1683), in John T. Ellis, ed., *Documents of American Catholic History* (Milwaukee: Bruce, 1956), p. 120.

[16] See Carl F. G. Zollman, *American Church Law* (St. Paul, Minn.: West Publishing Co., 1933), Chaps. II–V; William Warren Sweet, *Religion in Colonial America* (New York: Chas. Scribner's Sons, 1942); Sanford H. Cobb, *The Rise of Religious Liberty in America* (New York: Macmillan, 1902), Chaps. I–VIII.

[17] Alvin W. Johnson and Frank H. Yost, *Separation of Church and State in the United States* (Minneapolis: University of Minnesota Press, 1948), Chap. II.

who believed a new order had been born on these shores and that a theocracy — a "new Israel" had been established.

During the Revolution or immediately after it, the Anglican Church in five of the states was disestablished.[18] This was largely a political reaction because the Episcopal Church in the United States was closely identified with the British government, since the colonial church had been founded and fostered by the established Church of England. Disestablishment came more slowly in the states with Congregational Churches: Vermont, 1807; Connecticut, 1818; and Massachusetts, 1833. The principal motive behind these moves was in itself religious: the desire to secure religious liberty and freedom of religious expression for all. This was a modification of the traditional principle of the Protestant Churches of that era, but it was hardly materialistic or secularistic.

The founders of the states firmly believed that religion and morality were not only necessary for good civil government, but that they were the very basis of it. Since religion and morality, so necessary to the political and social order, were acquired through education, the first schools were established to teach these subjects as well as reading, writing, and arithmetic. The first American schools in every section of the country, in every state, and at every educational level, were private schools, some controlled by churches, some operated by individuals with or without public aid.

The type of education offered was primarily religious, and religion was given as much attention as the arts, as may be learned from *New England's First Fruits,* an account of the early days of Harvard College.[19]

The point is that in the states of this Union, while religious liberty was guaranteed, religion was fostered and considered to be of great importance. There was no establishment, but there was no neutrality about religion and certainly no hostility toward it. Religion and morality were taught in all schools, most of which were private, and many of which received public aid in the form of grants of land, rights to revenues from certain public utilities such as bridges or ferries, and appropriations or grants of money.[20]

---

[18] Cobb, *op. cit.,* Chap. IX.

[19] Samuel Eliot Morison, *The Founding of Harvard College* (Cambridge, Mass.: Harvard University Press, 1935), p. 421.

[20] See Reverend R. J. Gabel, *Public Funds for Church and Private Schools* (Washington, D. C.: Catholic University Press, 1937).

A combination of gradually evolving events caused a weakening of religious motives among the people of the states. With the decline of Puritanism in the northern colonies, the rise and fall of the movement known as "The Great Awakening," the proliferation of sects, and the increase in the number of people who were Universalists, or belonged to no church, or gave only formal allegiance to some ecclesiastical institution, the first champions of secular schools appeared.[21]

From 1820 through 1850, *elementary* education in New England, New Jersey, New York, Ohio, Pennsylvania, Michigan, and the Northern Middle West generally became public. In the beginning of this movement, societies like the Public School Society of New York City were formed to provide education for the children of the poor who could not afford to pay the fees charged by the private schools at the time. These organizations extended their educational activities to provide schools for all children, and in so doing they received direct support from town and city treasuries. Finally they became departments of municipal governments, maintaining "free" schools for all children and receiving practically all their financial support from those governments. As the schools became departments of government, attendance at them became compulsory.

In the South, elementary education during this same period (1820–1850) remained for the most part in the hands of private schools. In all parts of the country, secondary schools (or academies) and colleges, with few exceptions, continued under private auspices, usually church controlled or related.

POST-CIVIL WAR

After the Civil War, the tide of education rose rapidly and swept the country. Increased immigration was contemporaneous with the decline of the old Protestantism and the rise of many new sects. From 1840 onward, some hundreds of thousands of people came to these shores from Europe, most of them from countries where Catholicism was the predominant religion, and large numbers of whom did not speak English.

There is a great deal of evidence that the strongest unifying force behind the advance of "nonsectarian" public education was the large influx of Catholic immigrants. The growing Catholic population, disturbed by the Protestantism their children were taught in the common

[21] Gobel, *op. cit.*

schools, wanted Catholicism taught to Catholics. Failing to achieve that, they began to build their own schools.

A significant result of these alarms was that many state constitutions were amended and laws were passed to divorce religion from the public educational system. By the end of the nineteenth century there had come into existence a large array of constitutional provisions, statutes, court decisions, and administrative practices, the purpose of which was to ensure the secularization of the public schools and to deny public money to nonpublic schools.

It should be understood that the shift from private schools with a religious orientation to public schools with a secular orientation was favored also by a number of domestic events previously mentioned. One was the decline of Puritanism in the North and Anglicanism in the South. Another was the proliferation of the so-called evangelical sects who opposed not only the establishment of church-related schools but even the incorporation of churches.[22] Still another was the rise of new religious bodies like the Unitarians and the Universalists that taught ethical principles but eschewed any formal dogmatic theology.

It was people with this sort of background who furnished the leadership to secularize the public schools. The more orthodox, older Protestants and the newer evangelicals, all of whom believed deeply in religion and wanted it taught to the young, followed this leadership partly because they were fearful that one or the other of them would try to dominate the rest, and even more because they were concerned about the great influx of foreign-born Catholics. John Dewey says:

> If one inquires why the American tradition is so strong against any connection of State and Church, why it dreads even the rudiments of religious teaching in state-maintained schools, the immediate and superficial answer is not far to seek. The cause was not, mainly, religious indifference, much less hostility to Christianity, although the eighteenth century deism played an important role. The cause lay largely in the diversity and vitality of the various denominations, each fairly sure that, with a fair field and no favor, it could make its own way; and each animated by a jealous fear that, if any connection of State and Church were permitted, some rival denomination would get an unfair advantage.[23]

---

[22] See the "Presbyterian Protest Against the Incorporation of Churches" in *Cases on Church and State in the United States,* compiled by Mark de Wolfe Howe (Cambridge, Mass.: Harvard University Press, 1952), p. 13.
[23] John Dewey, *Intelligence in the Modern World,* Ratner ed. (New York: Modern Library, 1939), pp. 706–707.

Dewey goes on to say that the emergence of the United States was late enough in the history of the world to take full advantage of state consciousness, and this caused the people to believe the life of the state was more important than that of its ecclesiastical divisions and that it could maintain that life only aloof from them.

However, the secularization of the public schools did not mean that the inhabitants of the states had become irreligious or that they were indifferent to religion or thought religion of no importance. Far from it. They supported nonreligious public schools because their leadership convinced them there was no other way to keep the common schools from either being destroyed by strife or being dominated by one religious body. It need not be added that the immigrant Catholics had little leadership other than their bishops and no political power in the nineteenth century.[24]

Constitutional and statutory provisions were introduced in several states to support the secularization of public schools and to deny public support to nonpublic educational institutions. These provisions continue to the present time.

THE PRESENT CONDITION

State constitutional provisions relating to independent and especially church-related educational institutions may be grouped under the following headings:

1. Public school funds may be used only for the support of the common schools — fifteen states.[25]

2. No grant or appropriation of the money, property, or credit of the state may be made to schools not under the exclusive control of the state — seven states.[26]

---

[24] Such men as Alfred E. Smith, governor of New York, often graduates of parochial schools, spokesmen of the Roman Catholic minority, appeared in the next century.

[25] Connecticut, Art. VIII, sec. 2; Delaware, Art. X, sec. 4; Hawaii, Art. IX, sec. 1; Indiana, Art. VIII, sec. 3; Iowa, Art. IX, par. 2, sec. 3; Kansas, Art. VI, No. 3; Massachusetts, Amend. XLVI, sec. 2; Nebraska, Art. VII, sec. 9; New Jersey, Art. VIII, sec. IV, par. 2; North Carolina, Art. IX, sec. 4; Rhode Island, Art. XII, secs. 2 and 4; South Dakota, Art. VIII, sec. 3; Tennessee, Art. XI, sec. 12; Texas, Art. VII, sec. 5; West Virginia, Art. XII, sec. 4.

[26] Alabama, Art. IV, sec. 73 (unless voted by two thirds of all members of the legislature); California, Art. IV, sec. 22, Art. IX, sec. 8; Colorado, Art. V, sec. 34; Massachusetts, Amend. XLVI, sec. 2; Montana, Art. V, sec. 35; North Dakota, Art. VIII, sec. 152; Pennsylvania, Art. III, sec. 17 (unless voted by two thirds of all members of the legislature).

3. No appropriation of public funds may be made for any sectarian institution, purpose, or society — twenty-two states.[27]

4. No state aid may be extended to educational institutions controlled by a sectarian denomination — thirteen states.[28]

5. No state aid may be given to sectarian schools — fifteen states.[29]

6. No state aid may be given to private schools — four states.[30]

7. No appropriation of public money may be made to any school in which sectarian doctrine is taught — six states.[31]

A check of these lists reveals that some states whose constitutions limit the proceeds of school funds to common, free, or public schools do not prohibit *state aids* to nonpublic education. Maine requires towns to provide public schools and permits the state to endow "all academies, colleges, and seminaries within the state":[32] providing the right to exercise controls adjudged necessary is granted the state. Arkansas and Maryland limit the use of their school fund only to "the purposes of education."[33] Ohio and Kansas merely prohibit a religious sect, or sects, from controlling common or public school funds.[34] The Vermont constitution just states that:

. . . a competent number of schools ought to be maintained in

[27] Arizona, Art. II, sec. 12; California, Art. IV, sec. 30; Colorado, Art. V, sec. 34, Art. IX, sec. 7; Florida, Declar. of Rights, sec. 6; Georgia, Art. I, sec. I, par. XIV; Idaho, Art. IX, sec. 5; Illinois, Art. VIII, sec. 3; Indiana, Art. I, sec. 6; Louisiana, Art. IV, sec. 8; Michigan, Art. II, sec. 3; Minnesota, Art. I, sec. 16; Missouri, Art. I, sec. 7; Montana, Art. V, sec. 35; Nevada, Art. 11, sec. 10; Oklahoma, Art. II, sec. 5; Oregon, Art. I, sec. 5; South Dakota, Art. VI, sec. 3; Texas, Art. I, sec. 7; Utah, Art. 1, sec. 4; Washington, Art. I, sec. 11; Wisconsin, Art. I, sec. 18; Wyoming, Art. I, sec. 19.

[28] California, Colorado, Idaho, Illinois in footnote 27 above; Florida, Art. XII, sec. 13; Missouri, Art. X, sec. 8; Montana, Art. XI, sec. 8; New York, Art. XI, sec. 4; South Carolinia, Art. XI, sec. 9; Utah, Art. 10, sec. 13; Virginia, Art. IX, sec. 141; Washington, Art. IX, sec. 4; Wyoming, Art. VII, sec. 8.

[29] Alabama, Art. XIV, sec. 263; Alaska, Art. VII, sec. 1; Arizona, Art. IX, sec. 10; California, Art. IX, sec. 8; Delaware, Art. X, sec. 3; Florida, Art. XII, sec. 13; Kentucky, sec. 189; Louisiana, Art. XII, sec. 13 (an exception is made for higher education under certain conditions); Mississippi, Art. 8, sec. 208; New Hampshire, Part II, Art. 83; New Mexico, Art. XII, sec. 3; North Dakota, Art. VIII, sec. 152; Pennsylvania, Art. X, sec. 2; South Dakota, Art. VIII, sec. 16; Texas, Art. VII, sec. 5.

[30] Arizona, Art. IX, sec. 10; California, Art. IX, sec. 8; Louisiana, Art. XII, sec. 13 (an exception is made for higher education under certain conditions); New Mexico, Art. XII, sec. 3.

[31] Idaho, Art. IX, sec. 6; Massachusetts, Amend. XLVI, sec. 2; Minnesota, Art. VIII, sec. 3; Nebraska, Art. VII, sec. 11; New York, Art. XI, sec. 4; South Dakota, Art. VIII, sec. 16.

[32] Maine Constitution, Art. VIII.

[33] Arkansas Constitution, Art. XIV, sec. 2; Maryland Constitution, Art. VIII, sec. 3.

[34] Kansas Constitution, Art. 6, sec. 8; Ohio Constitution, Art. VI, sec. 2.

each town, or by towns jointly with the consent of the General Assembly, for the convenient instruction of youth.[35]

The constitutions of Arkansas, Connecticut, Iowa, New Jersey, North Carolina, Rhode Island, Tennessee, and West Virginia restrict the proceeds of the school fund, however constituted, to the support of common or free public schools. In these states there is no constitutional bar to public aid to independent schools, although court interpretations may raise such bars. The constitutions of the other thirty-seven states, as the survey above indicates, deter public support to independent, church-related schools in one way or another.[36] It is to be noted, however, that they do not specifically prohibit aid to individuals for their education.

JUDICIAL INTERPRETATIONS

Religion and education are so intimately connected that their relationship continues to be the subject of considerable litigation in the states. Robert F. Drinan, S.J., dean of the Boston College Law School, has written:

> The juridical status of the non-public school in America is at best anomalous; it is a public institution for the purpose of compulsory education while at the same time it is a private institution not meriting the tax support that is given to the public school . . . neither the statutory nor the decisional law of America have had adequate opportunity to define the role, the status, and the public rights and duties of the non-public school.[37]

Nevertheless, some question has been raised and decisions handed down which enable the inquirer to reach certain conclusions.

One conclusion is that especially in the late nineteenth century, direct tax aid by the states to nonpublic schools as such was generally disapproved as a violation of state constitutions.[38] In 1879 appli-

---

[35] Chapter II, sec. 64.

[36] See also: "Catholic Schools and Public Money." Notes (*State ex rel. Johnson v. Boyd*, 28 N.E. [2d] 256, Indiana 1940). *Yale Law Journal*, Vol. 50, No. 5, March, 1941, pp. 917–927. "Separation of Church and State in the United States: a Summary View," David Fellman, *Wisconsin Law Review*, Vol. 1950, No. 3, May 1950, pp. 427–478.

[37] Reverend Robert F. Drinan, S.J., "Should the State Aid Private Schools?" *Connecticut Bar Journal*, Vol. 37, No. 3, September, 1963, pp. 363–364.

[38] *In re Opinion of the Justices*, 214 Mass. 599; 102 N.E. 464 (1913). *State ex rel. Van Straten* v. *Milquet*, 180 Wisc. 109; 192 N.W. 392 (1923). *Judd* v. *Board of Education*, 278 N.Y. 200; 15 N.E. (2d) 576 (1938). *Gurney* v. *Ferguson*, 190 Okl. 254; 122 Pac. (2d) 1002 (1941). *Sherrard* v. *Jefferson County Board of Education*, 294 Ky. 469; 171 S.W. (2d) 963 (1942). *Mitchell* v. *Consol. School Dist. No. 201*, 17 Wash. (2d) 61; 135 Pac. (2d) 79 (1943). *Visser* v. *Nooksack Valley School*

174   EDUCATIONAL FREEDOM; CASE FOR AID TO INDEPENDENT SCHOOLS

cation for a pro rata share of public tax funds to be paid to students in private schools was disapproved as unconstitutional in Mississippi.[39] An attempt in 1892 to gain tax exemption for educational expenditures by parents whose children attended private schools was unsuccessful in Kentucky.[40] In Kansas in 1892, the courts decided that no state tax funds could be given to private colleges,[41] and in South Dakota in 1891 the courts ruled that the state may not make any payment of tuition to private colleges.[42]

Various state supreme courts have declared that aid may not be given to independent, church-related schools as part of the public school system.[43] In 1942 the Missouri court concluded that the inclusion of St. Cecilia's Parochial School in the public school system of Meta, Missouri, was unconstitutional, even though the practice had continued for ten years.[44] In Iowa, in 1918, the court decided that even though the time given to religious instruction was minimal, public funds could not be used to support any school which gave such sectarian instruction.[45] Whether changed circumstances and changed attitudes would lead to different interpretations today is questionable.

There are some signs of a gradual relaxation dictated by circumstances. On questions of almost all other forms of state aid to church-related institutions and schools, court decisions vary. Connecticut and Maine have sustained bus transportation laws on the basis of the *Everson* case.[46] In Alaska, New Mexico, Oklahoma, Oregon, Vermont, Washington, and Wisconsin, the highest courts have decided against allowing bus transportation or the benefits of similar public welfare laws to parochial school students, despite the *Everson* decision's state-

---

Dist. No. 506, 33 Wash. (2d) 699; 207 Pac. (2d) 198 (1949). *McVey* v. *Hawkins*, 364 Mo. 44; 258 S.W. (2d) 927 (1953).

[39] *Otken* v. *Lamkin*, 56 Miss. 758 (1879). Such aid was constitutionally provided for in North Carolina to avoid racial integration (Art. IX, sec. 12, adopted 1956), provided the school attended is nonsectarian.

[40] *Underwood* v. *Wood;* 93 Ky. 177; 19 S.W. 405 (1892).

[41] *Atchison, Topeka, and Santa Fe R.R.* v. *Atchison*, 47 Kan. 712; 28 Pac. 1000 (1892).

[42] *Synod of Dakota* v. *State*, 2 S.D. 366; 50 N.W. 632 (1891).

[43] *Williams* v. *Stanton School District*, 173 Ky. 708; 191 S.W. 507 (1917). *State ex rel. Public School No. 6* v. *Taylor*, 122 Neb. 454; 240 N.W. 573 (1932). *Richter* v. *Cordes*, 100 Mich. 278; 58 N.W. 1110 (1894). *Wright* v. *School District*, 151 Kan. 485; 99 Pac. (2d) 737 (1940).

[44] *Harfst* v. *Haegen*, 163 S.W. (2d) 609 (1942).

[45] *Knowlton* v. *Baumhover*, 182 Iowa 691; 166 N.W. 202 (1918).

[46] *Snyder* v. *Newton*, 147 Conn. 374; 161 A (2d) 770 (1960); cert. denied, 365 U.S. 299. *Squires* v. *Inhabitants of Augusta*, 155 Me. 151; 153 A (2d) 80 (1959). *Everson* v. *Board of Education*, 330 U.S. 1 (1947).

ment that benefits of public welfare legislation "shall be denied no one because of his faith or lack of it."[47] New York amended its constitution to permit bus rides for nonpublic school children in 1938 (Article XI, sec. 4), and New Jersey included this right in her new constitution of 1947 (Article VIII, sec. 4, par. 3).

It has been decided in Connecticut, Illinois, Indiana, and Kentucky that public school authorities may rent space in buildings owned and operated by churches as long as the boards of education retained the essential elements of control.[48] In the Indiana case, the public school board entered into arrangements with Catholic authorities to pay the salaries of nun-teachers in the Catholic schools to prevent them from closing and leaving over eight hundred children without educational facilities. In Illinois, a school board was permitted to allow the temporary use of public school buildings for religious meetings, the court having stated that:

. . . religion and religious worship are not so placed under the ban of the constitution that they may not be allowed to become the recipient of any incidental benefit whatever from the public bodies or authorities of the State.[49]

The wearing of religious garb by anyone teaching in public schools is forbidden by statute in Nebraska and Oregon, and it has been decreed unconstitutional in New York.[50] However, it has been upheld in Connecticut, Indiana, North Dakota, and Pennsylvania on the grounds that the laws do not prescribe the dress of teachers.[51]

The question of free textbooks has been litigated in several courts.

In 1922 the New York Supreme Court ruled that such a practice:

[47] *Matthews* v. *Quinton* (Alaska) 362 Pac. (2d) 932 (1961). *U. S. National Bank of Portland* v. *Snodgrass*, 275 Pac. (2d) 860 (1954). *Dickman* v. *School District No. 620* (Oregon) 366 Pac. (2d) 533 (1961). *Zellers* v. *Huff*, 55 N.M. 501, 236 Pac. (2d) 949 (1951). *Swart* v. *So. Burlington Town School District*, 167 A (2d) 514 (1961). *Holcombe* v. *Armstrong*, 39 Wash. (2d) 860; 239 Pac. (2d) 545 (1952). *Perry* v. *School District No. 81, Spokane*, (Wash.) 344 Pac. (2d) 1036 (1959). *State ex rel. Reynolds* v. *Nusbaum*, (Wis.) 115 N.W. (2d) 761 (1962).
[48] *New Haven* v. *Torrington*, 132 Conn. 194; 43 A. (2d) 455 (1945). *Millard* v. *Board of Education*, 121 Ill. 297; 10 N.E. 669 (1887). *State ex rel. Johnson* v. *Boyd*, 217 Ind. 348; 28 N.E. (2d) 256 (1940). *Crain* v. *Walker*, 222 Ky. 828, 2 S.W. (2d) 654 (1928).
[49] *Nichols* v. *School Directors*, 93 Ill. 61 (1879).
[50] *O'Connor* v. *Hendrick*, 184 N.Y. 421; 77 N.E. 612 (1906).
[51] *New Haven* v. *Torrington*, 132 Conn. 194; 43 A. (2d) 455 (1945). *State ex rel. Johnson* v. *Boyd*, 217 Ind. 348; 28 N.E. (2d) 256 (1940). *Gerhard* v. *Heid*, 66 N.D. 444; 267 N.W. 127 (1936). *Hysong* v. *School District*, 164 Pa. 629; 30 A. 482 (1894).

"plainly comes within the prohibition of the Constitution" forbidding direct or indirect aid to sectarian education. Even if the argument is conceded that the books are furnished to the pupils and not the school, still, the court maintained, this is certainly an indirect aid.[52]

In Mississippi the supreme court took a different view. In the words of Justice Alexander:

> There is no requirement that the church should be a liability to those of its citizenship who are at the same time citizens of the state, and entitled to privileges and benefits as such. Nor is there any requirement that the state should be godless or should ignore the privileges and benefits of the church. . . .

> The religion to which the children of school age adhere is not subject to control by the state; but the children themselves are subject to its control. If the pupil may fulfill his duty to the state by attending a parochial school it is difficult to see why the state may not fulfill its duty to the pupil by encouraging it "by all suitable means." The state is under duty to ignore the child's creed but not its need. It cannot control what the child may think, but it can and must do all it can to teach the child how to think. The state which allows the pupil to subscribe to any religious creed should not, because of his exercise of this right, proscribe him from benefits common to all.[53]

This view was upheld by the United States Supreme Court in a similar case, where it sustained a Louisiana textbook statute on the basis that the "school children and the state alone are the beneficiaries" of the supplying of books by the state.[54]

A review of the state constitutional provisions makes it clear that the people of the state have wished to support morality and religion generally in the schools. Such rules as those prescribing prayer or Bible reading as a voluntary practice were not intended to interfere with the free exercise of religion, nor were they intended to lay the groundwork for an establishment of a state church. Even court decisions stopping such practices were not supported by arguments that the state should oppose religion. State *neutrality* was the reason given by the nineteenth-century "liberals" for suspending these religious prac-

---

[52] Fellman, *op. cit.*, p. 448; *Smith* v. *Donohue,* 202 App. Div. 656, 195 N.Y. Supp. 715 (1922).

[53] *Chance* v. *Mississippi State Board,* 190 Miss. 453, 467; 200 So. 706, 710 (1941).

[54] *Borden* v. *Louisiana,* 168 La. 1005; 123 So. 655 (1929); *Cochran* v. *Board of Education,* 281 U.S. 370 (1930).

tices, along with arguments that religion as such could safely be taught only in the church and the home.

In the fifty-year period from 1870 to 1920, Protestantism was undergoing great changes, and there was a drift away from traditional Christian teachings on the part of intellectuals, many ministers, some congregations, and most of the older church-related schools, such as Harvard, Princeton, and Yale. The native population was concerned over the tremendous influx of foreigners, and worried about whether they could all be assimilated, particularly if they set up their own religious schools, which were largely Catholic — a religion deeply suspect in the United States at that time. It does not follow, however, that when the people tried to achieve neutrality, they intended to make their state governments or their schools irreligious or hostile to the churches.

STATE ATTITUDES FAVORABLE TO RELIGIOUS INSTITUTIONS

The states have continued to show their support of religion by granting churches and church-related institutions tax exemptions:

> Every state in the Union, either by statute or constitutional provision, exempts religious property from taxation; there are specific provisions to this effect in the constitutions of 32 states in 15 of which the exemption is mandatory.[55]

These exemptions gave indirect aid to the institutions to which they are granted. This aid has been acceptable because tax exemptions are considered from the standpoint of the services rendered to the community:

> The fundamental ground upon which all such exemptions are based is a benefit conferred on the public by such institutions, and a consequent relief, to some extent, of the burden upon the state to care for and advance the interests of its citizens.[56]

Since tax exemptions are granted by all states to schools, church oriented as well as nonsectarian, this amounts to a general recognition of the public benefits they bestow upon the community. Court decisions have taken the position that it is important for the public good in a Christian nation to foster moral and religious education,

---

[55] Fellman, op. cit., p. 454.
[56] M. E. Church South v. Hinton, 92 Tenn. 188; 21 S.W. 321, 322 (1893).

and one way of accomplishing this is to grant tax exemptions to schools maintained by churches. Nondiscriminatory tax exemption laws do not violate state constitutional provisions since such laws do not establish any church nor do they give preference to any sect.[57]

State governments have acted in a benign fashion toward churches in other respects. They have permitted them to incorporate and hold property and administer that property in accordance with their own ecclesiastical rules. Early laws, such as the New York statute of 1786 which vested church properties solely in the hands of lay trustees, were amended to permit the holding of property by bishops as corporations sole. Churches have been protected against civil interference in their internal affairs and the relations of ecclesiastics to their superiors and their congregations have been declared to be matters governed by the discipline and rules of the churches themselves.[58] Despite occasional deviations from this pattern, the states' laws as interpreted by state courts have generally favored the greatest freedom for the churches in a climate generally favorable to their work.

As Father Drinan has pointed out, the close liaison between government and religion in matters of social welfare has hardly ever been the subject of much litigation:

A long tradition of cooperation between voluntary sectarian agencies and public welfare officials has apparently been of such a harmonious nature that little disagreement seems to have occurred over church-state problems.[59]

The amount of cooperation is very large:

Something of the extent of the utilization of voluntary agencies can be seen from the following: All but four states (Arkansas, Mississippi, Nebraska, and Nevada) supplement public services in connection with foster family care by the use of voluntary agencies. In the forty-two states which reported for a survey issued in 1962 by the Children's Bureau of the U. S. Department of Health, Education, and Welfare, 66% of the children received services primarily from public agencies and 34% from voluntary agencies. In New York

---

[57] See *Trustees v. Iowa*, 46 Iowa 275 (1877). *YMCA v. Douglas County*, 60 Neb. 642; 83 N.W. 924 (1900). *Garrett Biblical Institute v. Elmhurst State Bank*, 331 Ill. 308; 163 N.E. 1 (1928).

[58] See *St. Casimir's Polish R.C. Church's Case*, 273 Pa. St. 494 (1922); *The Rector, Church Wardens and Vestrymen of the Church of Holy Trinity in the City of Brooklyn, et al. v. John H. Melish, et al.*, Supreme Court of New York, Kings County, 1949, 194 Misc. 1006.

[59] Drinan, *op. cit.*, p. 26.

City in February, 1962, there were a total of 18,756 children under care outside their homes as charges of the Department of Welfare. Of these 17,015 or 90.7% were being cared for under the auspices of voluntary agencies.[60]

On the somewhat analogous questions concerning state aid to sectarian hospitals and orphan asylums, courts of various states have differed. The courts of Nevada, New York, and Pennsylvania decided against such aid, even though orphans or patients were admitted and cared for without reference to their religions. Yet, in Illinois the state supreme court decided payments could be made to Catholic institutions for the education of delinquents, pointing out the cost was less than if the state maintained its own schools. Hence the state, not the church, was benefited.[61] An Illinois court also permitted the Catholic Church to construct a chapel on a poor farm, on the grounds that the poor are not prohibited religious worship by the Illinois constitution.[62] The supreme court of Kentucky allowed state aid to church hospitals in order that the state might secure certain benefits available under the federal Hospital Survey and Construction Act of 1946.[63]

The increasing area of the state's welfare activities brings it into close contact with the churches. Since welfare recipients have souls as well as bodies, welfare legislation which affects the individual's physical needs inevitably affect his spiritual condition. The attitude of most states still remains friendly, and the churches are helped rather than hindered in their ministrations to their members who are in state institutions or are receiving state welfare aids:

> The churches of America have *not* allowed the state to take over all those areas of health and welfare services in which the church has always been active; in fact, the abdication of the church to the state in the matter of the secular education of youth seems to be almost the one case in America where the non-Catholic churches have declined to insist upon the role of the voluntary agency.[64]

CONTEMPORARY SCENE

The state's friendliness or animosity toward religion is of great im-

---

[60] Drinan, *op. cit.*, p. 27.

[61] *St. Hedwig's Industrial School* v. *Cook County*, 289 Ill. 432, 124 N.E. 629 (1919).

[62] *Reichwald* v. *Catholic Bishop of Chicago*, 258 Ill. 44; 101 N.E. 266 (1913).

[63] *Kentucky Building Commission* v. *Effron*, 310 Ky. 355; 220 S.W. (2d) 836 (1949).

[64] Drinan, *op. cit.*, p. 31.

portance to the churches today. As far as the churches as legal entities are concerned, that friendliness is under attack. A self-proclaimed atheist, Mrs. Madalyn E. Murray, filed suit on October 16, 1963, in Maryland's superior court in Baltimore against state laws which permit tax exemption for church-owned property and announced that she would take that suit to the U. S. Supreme Court if necessary. Sitting on that Court is Justice William O. Douglas, who has written (in a concurring opinion):

> The point for decision is whether the government can constitutionally finance a religious exercise. Our system at the federal and state levels is presently honeycombed with such financing. Nevertheless, I think it is an unconstitutional undertaking whatever form it takes.[65]

As far as individuals are concerned, between the federal income tax, rising state and local taxes, and the tendency of the cost of living to creep up just a bit faster than the income of many, the portion of the disposable income of most people which can be used to support the church and its institutions such as schools has had to shrink. In no area is this as evident as in education. For both institutional and personal reasons, the historic friendliness of the state toward religion must be preserved.

A modern example of state friendliness toward church-related and other independent schools is the growth of scholarship programs which give financial aid to qualified college students allowing them to attend the college of their choice. California provided 4480 scholarships for 1963–1964, awards ranging from $300 to $900 in private institutions, and $100 to $180 in public institutions. Illinois grants 6000 scholarships annually in amounts up to $600 each. Maryland recently established a program of 2000 state scholarships. Massachusetts grants over 2700 general state scholarships, averaging about $250 each. New Jersey awards up to $400 for tuition to 10,000 students, and New York had over 50,000 state scholarships and fellowships in effect in 1962–1963, with awards ranging from $200 to $700 for undergraduates, and $200 to $800 for graduate students.[66]

---

[65] *Engel* v. *Vitale*, 370 U.S. 421, 437 (1962).
[66] "The New Look in Higher Education," Daniel D. McGarry, a reprint from *Social Justice Review*, 3835 Westminster Place, St. Louis, Mo. 63108, available from Citizens for Educational Freedom, 844 Washington Building, Washington, D. C. 20005.

The attitude of the Supreme Court of the United States as reflected in such cases as *Engel* v. *Vitale,* 370 U.S. 421 (1962), outlawing the voluntary use of a prayer proposed by the New York Board of Regents, and *School District of Abington Township, Pennsylvania* v. *Schempp,* and *Murray* v. *Curlett,* 374 U.S. 203 (1962), declaring unconstitutional a state law providing for the daily reading of ten verses of the Holy Bible without comment, does not seem to reflect the general attitude of the states toward the churches or the intended meaning of the First Amendment of the U. S. Constitution.

Concerning the opinion that the First Amendment prescribes a "wall of separation" between church and state, Judge Desmond wrote in the *Zorach* case:

> The basic fundamental here at hazard is not, it should be made clear, any so-called "principle" of complete separation of religion from government. Such a total separation has never existed in America, and none was ever planned or considered by the founders. The true and real principle that calls for assertion here is the right of parents to control the education of their children, so long as they provide them with the state-mandated minimum of secular learning, and the right of parents to raise and instruct their children in any religion chosen by the parents. . . . Those are true and absolute rights under natural law, antedating, and superior to, any human constitution or statute.[67]

When the strictures of state constitutions against public support of religious institutions and schools and the court decisions outlawing Bible readings and prayers in the public schools are placed in their historical context, it becomes clear that they were the result of nineteenth-century prejudices and conditions and that a provincial American judiciary was unable to envision the full implications of the pluralistic society the people were freely erecting under God.

It is still true that the states were not then, and are not now "neutral" regarding religion and the churches. This would be completely contrary to their heritage, and would be to say, in effect, that the states considered the growing membership and influences of the churches within their borders as of no importance or even harmful. On the contrary, generally the states in this country have always known and still know that there can be no complete neutrality about religion, in accordance with the maxim of Christ: "He who is not with me is

---

[67] *Zorach et al.* v. *Clauson et al.,* Court of Appeals of New York, 100 N.E. (2d) 463 (1951).

against me; and he who does not gather with me scatters" (Lk 11:23). Concerning "neutrality" the writer of the comment on the *Engel* v. *Vitale* case in the *Fordham Law Review* has said:

> Under the absolutist view, carried to its logical conclusion, any given law promulgated for the public good, can be subjected to a constitutional prohibition if it can also be shown to render "aid to religion." Hence we reach an area in which neutrality to religion is professed, but where the inevitable result is hostility.[68]

Hostility toward the churches and toward religion, although it is the mark of a few groups in our communities, is not the historical nor, we vouch, the present attitude of the great majority of the people in the states of the United States. That attitude has always been and is now one of cooperation and friendliness toward organized religion, which is recognized as one of the most important bases of our freedoms.

Today the major threat against morality and religion as the basis of free government arises from well-organized, vocal, and efficient groups, such as the Free Thought Society of America, who would destroy religion entirely, thereby undermining free government. For they would erect the atheistic state, which would inevitably bring with it all the instruments of physical coercion so familiar in communist countries.

The spread of the ecumenical spirit has reduced if not removed the old fears of religious conflict in America. The pluralism of American society is recognized as a fact. The great influx of foreigners has tapered off for forty years, and the immigrants have been assimilated. Church-related schools of all denominations have produced American citizens as loyal and progressive and dependable as those who have attended public schools.

It is time that the original intent of the people of the states should be reinstated, and the recent trend of the United States Supreme Court cases, lately taking up outdated theories of old-fashioned liberalism, be reversed. The reaffirmation of the true tradition of a God-centered, though pluralist society will restore that climate, favorable to the free exercise of religion, that has been our American heritage.

The traditional friendliness of the states toward churches and church-related institutions and schools can be expressed in ways that do not

---

[68] "Constitutional Law — Establishment of Religion — State Sanction of Prayer Violates Constitution" (Comment), *Fordham Law Review*, Vol. 31, 1962, pp. 202–203.

seem to be unconstitutional. For example, individual real-estate tax-payers could be permitted to retain a portion of their taxes levied to support schools, provided the money were used to maintain independent schools. State payments to local governments to aid them in operating their schools are usually made on a per-pupil basis. In the case of pupils attending independent schools, these grants could be made directly to parents, provided the full grant was used toward the education of children. State scholarships could be greatly increased in number and amount, and also made more attainable for larger numbers of pupils at all grade levels, for use by those who chose to attend independent schools. State grants for the partial payment of tuition in excess of a certain amount can also be made available, as in the New York State Scholar Incentive program. None of these involve payment of appropriated funds to religious institutions; all are much cheaper than expanding state school systems to educate all children; and all tax-credit, scholarship, or aid-to-parents plans preserve and encourage freedom of choice in education.

All reasonable efforts should be made to encourage the growth of religion and religious freedom by extending aids to individuals where necessary. In no other welfare activity of the community are there any blocks to religious freedom. If individuals desiring a religious-oriented education are deprived of their freedom of choice by financial restrictions, recipients of welfare may be next, and churches may find themselves taxed. If religious freedom cannot be advanced and protected by statutory law, then it may be necessary to remove restrictive clauses written into state constitutions during the nineteenth century, or to amend the federal Constitution so as to provide for freedom of choice in education and freedom of religion in state-supported schools. Whatever the remedies, there should be a strong reaffirmation of the traditional religious values in American society, since they are the origin of our liberties and the bulwarks of our freedom.

CHAPTER XI

Objections to Aid Answered

Vincent P. Corley*

Parents of students in independent schools are on the defensive as regards their right to direct and control the education of their children. Some of the major arguments encountered by these parents are briefly considered here.**

THE "NO TAX FUNDS FOR RELIGIOUS INDOCTRINATION" OBJECTION

A common opinion expressed by many Americans runs something like this excerpt from a recent letter to the editor of a metropolitan newspaper: *"I object to the use of my tax funds to indoctrinate other people's children in a religion which I cannot conscientiously support. This is unfair."* Supreme Court Justice Hugo Black phrased it thus: "No tax in any amount . . . can be levied to support any religious activities or institutions, whatever they may be called, or whatever form they may adopt to teach or practice religion."[1]

ANSWER

One might cite the U. S. Supreme Court decision in *Massachusetts v. Mellon* (1923),[2] which held inconsequential and undeterminable an individual taxpayer's interest in governmental expenditures (else chaos would result). Or one might dismiss Justice Black's remarks as irrelevant *dicta* in a court decision that, in fact, *approved* tax subsidy of bus transportation for students attending parochial and other independent schools.

---

* Editor, *Freedom in Education.*
** Editor's note: The objection that public assistance to students in independent schools is unconstitutional from a federal or state point of view is discussed in detail in the preceding chapters.
[1] *Everson* v. *Board of Education*, 330 U.S. 1 (1947).
[2] 262 U.S. 447 (1923).

But further considerations are necessary. To refute the argument against using tax funds to subsidize the education of children in nonstate schools we must consider the role of government in education, the role of the school in a free society, and the rights of parents and other citizens as regards education and their taxes for education.

In the United States the role of government in education has traditionally and legally been to serve as an agent of parents. "According to this conception," says Dr. Will Herberg, noted Jewish author and educator, "the governmental operation of schools is not something inherent in the very notion of democracy; it is rather a function assumed by the government to meet a great and urgent public need where non-governmental efforts obviously do not suffice. But the government has not preempted the field and was never intended to preempt it. On the contrary, the parents (or whatever agency they choose to represent them) retain their *prior* right to educate their children and to determine the kind of education they are to receive."[3]

In this connection, clear and cogent are the words of Supreme Court Justice James McReynolds in the landmark Oregon case, *Pierce* v. *Society of Sisters*, 268 U.S. 510 (1925): "the child is not the mere creature of the state; those who nurture him and direct his destiny have the right, coupled with the high duty, to recognize and prepare him for additional obligations." It was stated also by this same court that the religious schools in question "are engaged in a kind of undertaking long regarded as useful and meritorious" and that they "discharge their obligations to patrons, students, [and] the state."[4]

The accredited school, whether it be public or independent, secular or religious, serves primarily as an agent of parents to educate children in order to equip young citizens with the rudimentary academic tools which will enable them properly to live and serve in civil society. The controlling principle is that while government can properly make education compulsory, and simultaneously tax for education, it cannot in a free, pluralistic society compel parents to enroll their children in government schools. This negative restraint on government has a positive corollary: government must — or should — assist and cooperate with parent-citizens in their response to the dictates of law; and such participation in parental affairs by government cannot be from a position of uncompromising strength. The same "power and prestige

---

[3] In *Religion in America*, ed. John Cogley (New York: Meridian, 1958), p. 121.
[4] *Pierce* v. *Society of Sisters*, 268 U.S. 510 (1925).

of government" that the Supreme Court described in proscribing an official prayer for optional use in New York public schools[5] should not be the force, however subtly at work, that nullifies parental rights in education.

Therefore, *any* school which fulfills the public purpose of compulsory education laws by training student-citizens to serve the common good merits more than perfunctory, oblique recognition by government. Such recognition, to be meaningful, should be accorded to the individual student and his parents who choose independent, nongovernmental schools in response to the dictates of law and their own consciences. This can be achieved only by some kind of participation by these individuals in their education tax funds.

If citizens must render Caesar his tribute, Caesar should reciprocate by cooperating with parents in the exercise of inalienable and constitutional rights. The state exists to serve its citizens — not to dominate them, and tell them where and how they shall educate their children. And when government enters the field of education, it must serve all citizens on an equal basis; it should accommodate itself and adjust equitably to the situation which it has created by law.

To those individuals who object to the use of their tax funds (however commingled with other revenue) for the education of independent school children, it can be said: Your taxes would serve the purpose for which they are levied, namely, the education of student-citizens in prescribed secular subjects in qualified schools. To use tax funds to subsidize completely the education of students in state schools, and to assist in the education of students in secular subjects at accredited, independent schools is subsidizing education, not religion. Such a practice recognizes that equity requires Citizen X to assist Citizen Y to *educate* his children — *when reciprocity prevails*. And if Citizen X happens to be childless, or a mercantile proprietor, or a corporation stockholder, he benefits by the nondiscriminatory use of his tax funds for education, whether the educating agency is a public school or an independent school. An examination of the educational background of his associates, his employers, his employees, his customers, members of the Armed Forces who defend his interests in war and peace, and public officials who represent him in government will confirm that independent school graduates serve Citizen X and their country as do their public school counterparts.

---
[5] *Engel* v. *Vitale*, 370 U.S. 421 (1962).

Inquiry about the motives of parents in choosing an independent school offering God-centered *education* for their children is a form of thought control, especially when accompanied by the penalty of withholding tax benefits for nonconformity. "The Fathers of our Constitution," says U. S. Supreme Court Justice Wm. O. Douglas in *U. S. v. Ballard*, 322 U.S. 78 (1944), "fashioned a charter of government which envisaged the widest possible toleration of conflicting views. Man's relationship to his God was made no concern of the state." This toleration extends to subsidizing chaplains in the Armed Forces, tax exemptions for religious organizations, special concessions to clergymen and divinity students in war and peace, tax grants to religious groups for research and education, and tax relief for gifts to religious organizations. Church groups also benefit by postage concessions and even operate post offices.

The conscience of the individual parent is sacred. Whether he chooses for his children a God-centered education in an accredited independent school or a non-God-centered education in an accredited state school, his choice should not be subject to the approval or disapproval of his neighbors and the state. In a free society, his rights to freedom of mind and religion should be capable of exercise without penalty or abridgment.

THE "DIVISIVE AND UNDEMOCRATIC" OBJECTION

Another common objection to proposals for governmental aid to independent school students concerns the very nature of education and the democratic way of life. The objection is that public schools "are a fundamental of democracy" and that nonstate schools are devoted to a special private or religious purpose, not to the broad, general purposes of a democracy. It is said that the private schools create divisive groups in our society, and, while they may be tolerated, their influence is undesirable. Hence there should be no governmental subsidy of their students.

Basic to this argument is the assumption that a democracy, and specifically our North American variety, can thrive and perpetuate itself only if its junior citizens, or at least the overwhelming majority of them, are educated in state-controlled institutions. It is charged that a diversion of students from the state educational system would serve also to weaken democratic society.

Answer

It is agreed that the purpose of compulsory-education laws is to ensure a literate and informed citizenry, who will perpetuate the body politic and promote the common good. In his *Tenth Annual Report* (1846) Horace Mann stated that "the general intelligence which they (Free Schools) are capable of diffusing is indispensable to the continuance of a republican government." This is another way of saying that a nation cannot long remain ignorant and free. Yet the legal doctrine of *res ipsa loquitur*, the facts speak for themselves, might be cited to affirm the public-service nature of the education received at independent schools. Not only is it obvious, as we have seen, that independent school students upon graduation live and serve well in our democracy, but their education is *de facto* recognized by the individual states as serving the general purpose of compulsory-education laws. Independent school students benefit the entire community and the nation. But there is no reciprocation and little recognition of this service.

The assertion that "public schools are a fundamental of democracy" is only a half-truth. Essential in a democracy is *education*. Furthermore equally important is freedom and diversity in the pursuit of knowledge. Freedom of mind and religion are inherent in the nature of a pluralistic, democratic society and in the nature of man himself. If we are to take seriously Supreme Court Justice Jackson's admonition to "let man's mind alone" and Mr. Justice Douglas' assertion that "we are a religious people whose institutions presuppose a Supreme Being," we must reject any system which implicitly makes the state supreme in the education of children and which prohibits parents from giving their children full-time religious training.

That public schools are fundamental to democracy and that any participation by independent school students in their parents' tax funds would weaken our national unity are propositions contrary to our national history and to the existing situation in education. Public schools are comparative newcomers to our educational effort. It might be said that the development of public education in the United States along neighborhood and district lines, sometimes obviously gerrymandered, has often worked against real assimilation of races, cultures, and creeds, as well as different strata of society, in our nation. And if our suburban public schools are, in the main, "private schools run on public funds,"[6] as was stated by U. S. Commissioner of Education Francis Keppel, it should be noted that many independent schools, both urban and suburban, reflect in their enrollment a real pluralism of American cultures, creeds, racial origins, and economic status.

The unifying force peculiar to a democratic society is spiritual. It is generated by a national dedication — "under God" — to fundamental civil liberties for all citizens. "Stalin, Hitler, and Mussolini were vigorous opponents of divisiveness. But the national unity of the United States is not, thank God, the unity of dictatorship. It is not conformism by the bayonet or the concentration camp. Neither is it the amorphous homogeneity of the melting-pot. It is the harmonious coexistence and cooperation for the common good of a free people with theological, philosophical, political, and institutional differences. As Justice Jackson said in 1943 in the flag-salute case of *West Virginia Board of Education v. Barnette*: 'Compulsory unification of opinion achieves only the unanimity of the graveyard.'"[7]

THE "FREE-CHOICE" OBJECTION

One of the arguments against subsidizing independent education is the assertion that all parents have a choice of the public schools for their children's education. "The public schools are there to serve you. If you choose another school, don't ask the taxpayers to subsidize your private choice," the argument goes. Sometimes accompanying this are comparisons between public swimming pools, police and fire protection, roads, hospitals, and their private alternatives. Here, for example, is the way the Honorable Jennings Randolph, U. S. Senator from West Virginia, put the argument in a speech on federal aid to education: "It is, therefore, not discriminatory in any legal sense to deny Federal assistance to parochial schools. The public schools are available for all who desire to attend them."[8]

ANSWER

Can the Senator be saying that government has no interest or concern whatsoever in the education of children — its junior citizens — *unless*

[6] Quoted in Martin Mayer, *The Schools* (New York: Harper & Brothers, 1961), p. 40.

[7] William J. Kenealy, "Equal Justice Under Law: Tax Aid to Education," *The Catholic Lawyer*, XIV, No. 3 (Summer, 1961), p. 199.

[8] *Congressional Record*, January 23, 1962, p. A401.

they are deposited with the state for the educational process? This is a harsh philosophy of government, and is practiced in none of the more enlightened democracies of the Western world.

The fact is that the state created this impasse in education. With penal sanctions, the state compels parents to educate their children and to pay taxes for education. And no one is compelled to go swimming or recreate in parks, travel on roads, etc.; nor are these neutral activities matters of conscience, as is the case with education.

It is understandable, perhaps, that a totalitarian state offers parents no choice, no accommodation, no alternatives in the education of their children. But in a free, pluralistic society the denial of the means of exercising a free choice and the rejection of the petitions of concerned parents constitute an affront to human dignity and freedom.

The word "choice" implies acceptable alternatives. But for many Americans there exists no real choice in education, no alternative to the public school. To say that this is the "will of the people" is both naïve and cruel. Incidentally, if parents who now send their children to independent schools suddenly decided to accept the state's "choice," all would discover that public school facilities are *not* available to educate all.

In a democracy all citizens should be able to exercise their natural and constitutional rights and be able to choose on an equal basis. Parents should not have to "ask the taxpayers to subsidize" their choice in schools. Since it compels and taxes for education, the state should support their choice and make it truly a free choice. But, if on the one hand the state offers "free" education to one group of its citizens for their choice of Brand X education and on the other hand denies assistance to another group for their choice of Brand Y — although both educations serve the public purpose — the state is denying the equal protection of the law to the latter group for its "free" choice. The state is thereby penalizing the exercise of natural and constitutional rights to freedom in education.

Freedom with a price tag is an abridgment of freedom. Even this ransomed freedom, a kind of poll tax for nonconforming parents, is becoming economically impossible for increasing numbers of parents in the United States. The "choice" argument rings hollow in their ears. For these parents compulsory attendance at public schools, outlawed by the Supreme Court in the 1925 *Pierce* case, is being achieved indirectly by the force of economic coercion.

THE "FRAGMENTATION" OBJECTION

"But if government assisted the education of students in parochial and other independent schools, public education would be undermined, and a fragmentation of education among the various religious sects and diverse private organizations would result. One group — Catholics — would benefit immediately and substantially. Perhaps even the communists would obtain participation in the tax funds to start their own schools." So goes another argument.

ANSWER

It is probable that many parents, if given equal participation in education tax funds, would withdraw their children from state schools and enroll them in independent, including church-related, schools. To assert that this number would be excessive would be to postulate poor service by and little appreciation of the public schools; in short, a large "captive" enrollment in these schools. The argument is based on ungrounded apprehensions of secondary consequences. Any group of responsible citizens should be free, subject to well-defined and reasonable civil regulations, to establish, operate, and develop its own school system in an atmosphere that encourages freedom and academic excellence.

If we are indeed committed to the concept which holds sacred the individual person and the inalienable rights of parents and the family, then we must not only reject obstacles to our fellow citizens' freedom in education, but we must go beyond mere toleration of noncomformity and diversity: we must actually aid and encourage individual initiative in education.

Most Americans are satisfied with public education and would continue to enroll their children in state schools, even if given an unpenalized choice of independent schools. Affirmation of their commitment to public education has been given by numerous individuals and organizations, including religious groups, in public statements and in testimony before governmental bodies. It is unlikely that there would be wholesale abandonment of state education in favor of private systems demanding personal commitment in their initial stages and continuing, sacrificial efforts thereafter.

To the charge that Catholics would benefit substantially under a nondiscriminatory education-aid program, Dr. Edwin H. Palmer of Westminster Theological Seminary, Philadelphia, replies: "But the Roman Catholic has his constitutional rights, too. The principle of separation of family and state applies to him as well as to the secularists."[9]

It would seem that opposition to education aid based on a citizen's religion is a segregation as frightening and intolerable as that based on the color of a citizen's skin. Segregation by religion is a form of thought control, for it compels a person to conform either to the state, or the majority, or to pay an increasingly heavy burden to educate his children in nonstate schools acceptable to his conscience.

Americans enjoy a wide diversity and variety of freedoms in virtually every aspect of their lives except in that which is most sacred to parents — education. A healthy, scholarly competition for academic excellence among a diversity of state and independent schools, whose students are treated equally by government, should be welcome in a free society.

THE "PERMEATION" OBJECTION

The argument based on the "permeation" of nonstate education with religious values dates back at least to Supreme Court Justice Rutledge's dissent in the 1947 *Everson* case. Justice Rutledge asserted that "commingling the religious with the secular teaching does not divest the whole of its religious permeation and emphasis or make them of minor part." In essence, the permeation argument says that, while students in independent, church-related schools are receiving an education in secular subjects, they also get something beyond that through the permeation of the secular subjects with religious values. This permeation with religion, the argument asserts, precludes governmental aid to students in nonstate schools, since the government would be subsidizing religion.

ANSWER

Any educational system imparts a value system of one kind or another and is "permeated" with religion, even if this is only the least common denominator of humanitarian secularism. Among findings of a study of 120 social studies textbooks used in New York City's public schools were: (1) *The belief that nothing in the textbooks can violate the religious feelings of public school students is not true. Many of the public school textbooks present Protestantism in a more favorable light than Catholi-*

---

[9] Edwin H. Palmer, "Separation of Family and State," *Torch and Trumpet*, March, 1962.

cism and Christianity more favorably than Judaism. (2) There are definite sectarian tendencies in the textbooks. (3) The books portray present-day religion as no longer being a potent molding force in society. (4) The historical facts about religious conflicts and persecutions are being presented in an inadequate fashion by the elementary social studies textbooks.[10]

It would seem that the solution is not only to correct the textbooks but also to reform the system of financing education, so that parents can have real academic freedom in the pursuit of truth.

The "permeation" argument should be obnoxious to free men in a pluralistic society. First, its proponents — unconsciously, no doubt — advocate a kind of thought control in education. They look beyond the formal subjects, the planned curriculum, the printed word itself, and point to something which, to them, is odd or unorthodox or offensive or "queer." Why? Because it deviates from the current "establishment" in education.

The educational process should be carried on in an atmosphere that stimulates academic diversity and experimentation, one responsive to the challenge that excites young minds to their maximum potential. But this is not possible when the state, acting as tax collector and distributor in one capacity, serves also as the sole authority in determining what ideologies *cannot* "permeate" education.

"NO CONTROL AND ACCOUNTING"

It is argued that there should be no education-tax participation by independent school students because there is no public control of their education and no accounting could be made for the use of tax funds. Touching all bases, some proponents of this argument reverse themselves and suggest that state control of independent education might even result if all students were given a share in school taxes.

ANSWER

The fact that the education a student receives in an independent school fulfills the public-service purpose of education laws achieves the end result of both control and accounting; i.e., tax funds are used for the purpose for which they are levied: to educate the citizen. Otherwise the independent school in question would be disqualified.

---

[10] Judah J. Harris, *The Treatment of Religion in Elementary School Social Studies Textbooks* (New York: Anti-Defamation League of B'nai Brith, 1963), p. 51.

The control-and-accounting argument flies in the face of the frequently almost scandalous expenditures, with no real public control,
in public education for nonacademic and noneducative programs in
its curriculum.

Chancellor Thomas H. Eliot of Washington University, St. Louis,
writes:

> Laymen assume that local control means control by the people of
> the district, usually through elected representatives. Professional edu-
> cators however are less clear about this. Their books and journals are
> rife with intimations that the people and even the school board mem-
> bers should keep their hands off the schools. . . . Many educators are
> insistent in urging, in effect, that the schools are the special province
> of the professionals, the voters being a necessary evil who must be
> reckoned with because they provide the money.[11]

And a report by Mr. F. V. Corwing, chairman of the Citizens Advisory Commission to the Joint Interim Committee on the Public Education System (California) in 1959, included this remark: ". . . Public
schools are not truly under popular control but rather are tightly bound
up by an overhead system of central agency domination."[12]

Control of independent schools by the state is already exercised as
regards the academic curriculum, number and length of school days,
teacher accreditation, safety and health regulations. "What we have now,"
says the Reverend James J. Higgins, "is state or community control
over all, but very little community or state support for the actual work
of education done by the private or church related school."[13]

The essential control is the compulsion upon parents to educate their
children and to pay taxes for education. Tax extraction by the state of
the means (money) to exercise parental control in education through a
free, unpenalized choice of schools is forcing more and more children
to public education under direct *state control*. The ultimate result would
be a monopolistic state school system and a monolithic society. "When
it is no longer possible for a man to find a school for his boy except
within a universal [state] system, it will be too late to worry about
freedom as we have known it, for it will be gone.[14]

---

[11] Quoted in *Schools Weighed in the Balance*, a staff study for the Association
of Christian Schools (Houston, Tex.: St. Thomas Press [Episcopal], 1962), p. 32.

[12] *Ibid.*, p. 33.

[13] James T. Higgins, "Federal Aid to Education and Freedom of Conscience,"
pamphlet (Liguori, Mo.: Liguori Press, 1962), p. 55.

[14] Address given by Princeton University president, Harold W. Dodds, at Loomis
School Dinner in honor of Frank and Frances Gubbs, May 7, 1953.

As to the dollar cost of freedom in education, the terms are almost incompatible. Liberty has no price tag. There is no "X" amount of money that can be defined as the proper appropriation to mold a human mind. We have seen that the purpose of compulsory education laws is to produce literate citizens who can serve the common good and perpetuate our democratic way of life. We have seen, too, that this purpose is achieved by the education students receive in independent schools. The United States is committed to a policy of "free" education. In a free society why must this education be limited to state schools?

Advocates of educational freedom propose only a fair share of education tax funds for every child. If a parent wishes to secure something "extra" for his child he would add to his fair share of taxes and pay for the something "extra" himself. His civil rights to freedom of mind and religion and equality before the law would remain unimpaired.

Education in independent schools is usually more economical than in state schools. A modicum of justice by way of tuition grants from government to independent school students would produce benefits to our culture and society. And they would flow not merely from tax savings and economic factors. The spirit of man is often distracted by the oppression laid on his academic pursuits by the heavy hand of government. Any meaningful encouragement by government to all students on a more or less equal basis would promote freedom and quality in education.

CHAPTER XII

Fight for Freedom

Mae and Martin Duggan*

In the past century, during the development of the public schools, certain religious groups, such as Catholics, Lutherans, Jews, and others, in increasing numbers, could not, in conscience, accept either the wholly secularist or the Protestant-oriented teaching offered by the public schools. However, in spite of their protests against compulsory school laws which forced them either to send their children to such schools in violation of their consciences or to forfeit their share of taxes collected for education, all such taxes were used only for children in public schools.

Certain religious groups had built their own schools, supported by private resources, while carrying the additional burden of public school taxes. Such groups believed that religion must constitute an integral part of education. Nevertheless, because of fiscal disabilities, Catholics, for example, were never able to accommodate more than 50 percent of their children. In 1965, there were approximately seven million students in independent schools, but they were entirely excluded from any share of taxes collected for education.

The financial crisis which has been creeping up on the more than 15,000 independent schools is easily appreciated when it is realized that the cost of education rose from a national average of about $13 per public school pupil per year in 1898 to approximately $600 per pupil per year in 1964–1965. Nonetheless, independent school parents were generally unaware of the threat to the existence of their schools. The occasional outcries raised against new burdens of educational taxation without participation were spasmodic and unorganized. A

---

* Mrs. Mae Duggan is a housewife and columnist. Her husband, Martin, is news editor of the *St. Louis Globe-Democrat*. They are parents of five children.

really serious nationwide effort to secure a just share of education funds in behalf of independent school children had never been made.

The question of federal aid to public education only had at various times alarmed and aroused independent school administrators, especially those of church-related institutions. But their reaction had been mainly negative and ephemeral; and no organized, sustained effort was made to change the tax structure which was draining all the education money off to the state-controlled school system.

The Barden Bill, a massive federal aid-to-education program proposed to Congress in 1949, did arouse strong opposition. This bill would have provided for federal grants in aid to education counting *all* school-age children in the United States, but actually alloting money *only* to children in public schools.

The defense of parents' rights in education had been merely a matter of "hinting for a hundred years" until the time of the Barden Bill. The opposition against an additional nonparticipating burden on the federal level was led by Francis Cardinal Spellman of New York, who defended the right of the religious-minded parent to place his child in a church-related school without penalty. Many fair-minded Americans of various faiths sympathized with Cardinal Spellman in his defense of educational and religious freedom. There were many others, too, who opposed federal aid to public schools because they feared that it would eventually bring federal centralized control of all education. These two interests helped to prevent passage of the Barden school-aid bill.

The National Catholic Welfare Conference (NCWC) stated that federal aid to public education *only* would place an insufferable burden upon religious-oriented education and hence upon parents who desired such education for their children. But they spoke mainly for Catholic church schools, and not for all independent and other religiously connected schools. There existed no independent interdenominational citizens' group to press for the educational rights of all American parents and citizens entitled to equal protection and favor of the laws.

Yet one phase of federal aid to education, that on the college level, had already been legislated on an equal basis for students in both private and state institutions. The so-called "G.I. Bill," which granted tuition, book funds, and stipends to World War II veterans to continue their education, had been enacted on a basis of freedom of choice. The veteran was at liberty to choose any qualified school, including elementary and high schools, as well as colleges. Many veterans elected to enter theological seminaries and were granted government aid to be educated to serve as ministers, rabbis, and priests.

Other forms of federal assistance programs, such as hot lunch and health programs and special types of assistance for war orphans, congressional page boys, etc., have consistently allowed equal participation to independent school students as well as those in public schools. As far back as the National Youth Administration (1936) under the "New Deal," tax money was granted by the federal government directly to students to aid their education, and was enjoyed by independent school students as well as public school students without restriction as to the school attended.

Indicative of the wishes and choice of parents has been the growth of independent schools in the United States, despite overwhelming obstacles. In 1898, out of a total enrollment of 16,458,764 students in elementary and secondary schools, 15,103,874, or about 92 percent, were in public elementary and secondary schools, and 1,354,890, or eight percent, were in independent schools on the same levels. In 1964–1965, the estimated number of students in average daily attendance in public schools, from kindergarten through high school was 39,000,000, while there were an estimated 7,000,000 students in independent elementary and secondary schools. For the entire country about 15 percent of elementary and secondary school students were in independent schools in 1964–1965. In higher education, about 40 percent of our students were in independent institutions. Indeed, these institutions actually constituted about 64 percent of our colleges and universities in number (1319 out of 2040). A significant fact is that, while public school enrollments increased 42 percent between the years 1940 and 1960, independent elementary and secondary school enrollments jumped 147 percent in the same period.

As the school-age population was growing, so was the cost of education. In 1898, the total annual expenditure for our public schools was $197,281,603, or an average of about $13 per pupil per year. In 1964–1965, the total public school expenditure was $23.3 billion, or an average of about $600 per pupil per year.

On the other hand, the actual expenditure per pupil for independent school students in 1965 was estimated at approximately $250 per year. This was paid entirely from the pockets of their taxpaying parents. The saving to other taxpayers amounted to at least $4,200,000,000 a year (7,000,000 x $600).

The federal government estimates that enrollment in independent elementary and secondary schools in the United States will run between nine and fourteen million by 1980. The National Education Association advocates a 100 percent increase in average expenditures per public school pupil by 1970. At the present $600 average cost per pupil this would mean $1,200 in five more years. Limited help to keep independent education will thus save taxpayers billions of dollars.

In the United States, prior to 1959, the only organized group that defended parents' rights in education was the National Catholic Welfare Conference (NCWC). In 1955, in their annual statement from Washington, D. C., the American Catholic bishops insisted that "the students of these parochial schools have the right to benefit from those measures, grants, or aids, which are manifestly designed for the health, safety and welfare of American youth, irrespective of the school attended." The statement was reinforced with these words:

> The right of the parent to attend to the child's education is, moreover, antecedent to any human law or institution. . . . It is vested in his very nature and is demanded as a fulfillment of his actual parenthood. In this it reflects the inviolability of the human person and his freedom under God. It is a manifestation of the law of nature in concrete action. So it is that private and religious education in America rests upon the law of nature as well as upon the law of the land.

The Murray-Metcalf Bill of 1959 proposed federal grants for schoolchildren. All schoolchildren from five years through seventeen years of age would be "counted in" for each state's allotment, but those attending independent schools would be "counted out" in the distribution. They would thus be forced to give up their entire share for the exclusive benefit of students in public schools, who would be the act's sole beneficiaries. The proposed program called for an expenditure of a total of $4,000,000,000 in federal funds, but not one cent would have aided the education of over 6,000,000 American schoolchildren attending independent schools.

Most of the testimony on this bill was in support. Only a few groups opposed it. A letter signed by Albert Cardinal Meyer, Archbishop of Chicago, then chairman of the Department of Education of the NCWC, noted the rights of parents in these two sentences:

> The Department of Education (NCWC), however, calls to the attention of the Senate the heavy financial burdens of parents who choose to send their children to private, non-profit schools. If Congress

in its wisdom determines to aid the parents of public school children, by means of federal assistance, it cannot in justice be indifferent to the parents of these non-public school children.

At this point Citizens for Educational Freedom came upon the scene to speak for parents' rights. A letter-to-the-editor* initiated interest, and within a month the organization was formed.

The constitution of this new organization declared:

> The purpose of this corporation shall be to undertake and promote whatever activities shall contribute to the fair and just treatment of all citizens of the United States of America, including student citizens, in the distribution of governmental tax monies for the purpose of education, with a view to assuring freedom of choice in education, to the end that the civil liberties of our citizens shall be secured.

While an ultimate aim would be a system whereby parents would receive vouchers, good for tuition and other educational benefits, usable in accredited schools of their choice, CEF leaders realized that an important battle had to be fought first. This battle was a drive to amend the Murray-Metcalf Bill to provide for fairness to all children or to block its passage in its unfair form.

Speaking engagements and newspaper publicity in the St. Louis area helped arouse interest. An interview, printed in Catholic newspapers throughout the nation, brought many inquiries regarding CEF. A column in *Our Sunday Visitor*, which called attention to CEF's fight against the Murray-Metcalf Bill, elicited a flood of letters, including memberships and financial support.

CEF was on the road to becoming a *bona fide* national parents' rights organization. Congress was soon flooded with copies of a petition signed by parents from all over the nation. The petition, supplied in bulk to those who wrote to the CEF office, stated:

> Since the Murray-Metcalf Bill now pending in Congress provides for federal subsidies of $25, $50, $75 and $100 per child over a four-year period, counting every school child in the United States, but distributes the money only to tax-supported schools, and since this federal aid bill is so grossly unfair to independent school children,
> We urge that the Murray-Metcalf Bill be amended to provide the same amount of subsidy per child, except that it be given fairly to

---

* Editor's note: Written by Mrs. Mae Duggan. With her husband, she was joined by Mr. Vincent Corley and a score of other St. Louisans as well as Judge Anthony W. Daley of Alton, Illinois, in forming CEF.

all children, as in the case of the G.I. Bill of Rights, each child to receive a certificate to be used toward his tuition at the school of his parents' choice.

In time, the Murray-Metcalf Bill was bottled up in Congress, and the battle was suspended.

Meanwhile chapters of CEF were being organized across the nation. A simple mimeographed newsletter called *The Fair Share News* became a printed monthly, *Freedom in Education,* an authoritative source of information on the current status of parents' rights in education. Stories in various magazines, such as *Ave Maria, The St. Anthony Messenger, The Catholic World, The Liguorian, The Queen's Work, America, Marriage,* and *The Social Justice Review,* attracted growing attention to the young organization.

By November of 1960 CEF held its first national convention and its president was able to report that there were an estimated 7000 members.

In 1961 CEF took its case to Washington. In testimony before Congress, CEF spokesmen proposed a "Junior G.I. Bill" for fair assistance to all schoolchildren. Representative James Delaney of New York cast the deciding vote in the House rules committee to defeat a proposed bill which would have excluded children in nonpublic schools. Instead, he later proposed a bill modeled on the fair share ideas of CEF.

An intensive campaign on the theme "Get the Picture, Congressman?" and "Why Doesn't My Johnny Count?" flooded Congress with thousands of postcards bearing pictures of parochial school children. Meanwhile, through the efforts of housewives and fathers, chapters of CEF were growing. By the end of the year CEF had fifty chapters across the country and members in all fifty states.

The year 1962 gave CEF its chance to concentrate on the Delaney "Junior G.I. Bill" as something positive. The simple provision of granting $20 federal assistance for each schoolchild, to be applied by parents in the accredited school of their choice, had wide appeal and brought more cosponsors in Congress than any other education bill.

Meanwhile in the various states, CEF chapters turned their efforts to expansion and local issues, such as equal school-bus transportation, textbook programs, and scholarships.

In Wisconsin there was great CEF activity which succeeded in passing a fair school-bus bill, later nullified by the state supreme court.

The Congressional Quarterly, authoritative reference journal on Congress and national politics, devoted a feature article to CEF on December 5, 1962. A note explained:

A classic example of how citizens deeply interested in an issue resort to political action is found in this story about Citizens for Educational Freedom. It wants equal aid to private and public schools. It has already shown remarkable political heft in certain Congressional races and at the Statehouse level, such as in local school bus situations.

Among early gains won by CEF for students in independent schools were textbook assistance in Rhode Island and aid to the handicapped children of Oklahoma and Missouri.

Perhaps the greatest early impact was in the state of Michigan. In one whirlwind year, from May, 1962, to May, 1963, CEF succeeded in obtaining a fair school-bus bill, having obtained advance assurance from the rival candidates for governor that if the legislature passed such a bill, it would be signed. Here CEF chapters brought into full participation influential members of the Lutheran and Christian Reformed Churches.

All across the country, persons of all faiths worked vigorously through CEF to secure justice in educational taxation. At its 1963 convention in Detroit, CEF manifested its interdenominational character by electing clergymen of four faiths to its national board.

Proof that CEF was gradually having an impact came from various sources. As early as June, 1962, Abraham Ribicoff, then Secretary of Health, Education, and Welfare in the Kennedy cabinet, showed that the administration was seeking a way to soften its stand against aid to parochial school students. Appearing on a "Meet the Press" television program, Mr. Ribicoff advocated a tax-credit plan for parents of parochial school children. After becoming senator from Connecticut in 1963, Ribicoff advanced six ways in which independent school students could be aided without violating the Constitution. Senator Ribicoff proposed: (1) income-tax deductions for private school and college expenses; (2) public financing of shared time; (3) government supported teacher-training programs; (4) more complete assistance to private schools for special purposes such as the teaching of mathematics, sciences, and foreign languages; (5) government-supported auxiliary services such as school lunches, health services, and bus transportation; and (6) continued if not stepped-up nondiscriminatory aid to higher education.

In August, 1962, Dr. Daniel Poling, editor of *The Christian Herald,* declared himself in favor of tax deductions for the cost of private education. At the same time, the National Union of Christian Schools, at its national convention, adopted this position: "Government aid is historically and in principle sound. Our Christian School system has a right to government aid."

Prominent Jewish Orthodox leaders, such as Professor William W. Brickman of Pennsylvania University and Rabbi Immanuel Jacobovits of New York, took a similar stand concerning aid to all church-related schools, including Jewish day schools. Rabbi Morris Sherer also testified before congressional committees on behalf of fair federal aid.

In an address at the University of Chicago, January 9, 1963, Dr. Robert Hutchins said:

> The wall of separation has done what walls usually do; it has obscured the view. It has lent a simplistic air to the discussion of a very complicated matter. Far from helping to decide court cases, it has made opinions and decisions unintelligible. The wall is offered as a reason. It is not a reason; it is a figure of speech.

Justifying fair aid to all students, Dr. Hutchins went on:

> A school is an educational institution and not a church, if its object is intellectual development and it is engaged, *bona fide,* in this task. The fact that it is owned by a church, or that it gives some religious instruction, or that its teaching is permeated by religion, or that aid to it is incidentally of some benefit to the church, is immaterial.

Late in 1963 President Johnson signed an *equal* Higher Education Facilities Act, which he declared to be the most important education bill ever passed in Congress. This act made almost a billion dollars available over a three-year period for matching grants and loans for construction and improvement of academic facilities in both public and independent institutions of higher learning.

Another significant development in 1963 was the publication of a Gallup Poll which showed that 49 percent of those questioned favored federal aid to *all* students, with 7 percent undecided. Thus only 44 percent wanted aid to public schools alone. Whereas in 1961 only 36 percent had favored aid to all students, while 57 percent wanted aid to public schools only.

Meanwhile, various other groups arose to aid the cause of freedom in education. Among such were the Americans for Defense of Independent

Education, founded mainly to enlist the support of intellectuals; the National Association for Parents' Rights in Education; the Catholic Lawyers Committee; the Association for Tax Credits for Education; various local bus and scholarship committees; and the Citizens National Committee for Higher Education, which, along with the Association of American Colleges, has promoted equal treatment of independent and public institutions of higher learning in federal aid programs.

Newspapers, magazines, and other communications media took little, if any, note of the plight of independent school children until CEF began its crusade in 1959 and the American Catholic bishops took a firm stand in 1961. But by 1962 news items and magazine articles on this subject were so numerous that it was difficult to keep up with clipping chores. Introductory bibliographies of only *some* of the current publications on the subject prepared by Roy Lechtreck and Daniel McGarry ran into hundreds of entries.

The tide continued to run in favor of the idea which CEF espoused: freedom in education. By 1965, several types of fair Federal Higher Education Acts had passed. The Higher Education Facilities Act of 1963 has already been mentioned. The Higher Education Assistance Act of 1965 will provide several billion dollars over a period of years, including scholarships for needy students and grants for improved library facilities, better academic offerings in developing institutions, and increased community services, all shared by independent as well as public institutions.

Further achievements on the federal level by 1965 included amendments to the 1958 National Defense Education Act, as well as the Economic Opportunity Act of 1964, and the Elementary and Secondary Education Act of 1965.

The NDEA (National Defense Education Act) of 1958 had contained certain inequities. Although millions of dollars in loans were provided for public and private college students alike, loans to students had been "forgiven" up to 50 percent of the loan only *if* the student taught full-time in a public school, whereas those who chose to teach in private or parochial schools had been required to pay back the entire amount. This feature was amended so that all students and teachers were equally treated. Also by the NDEA, teachers from public schools had been favored over those who taught in private schools in provisions for assisting them to take special training and improvement courses as well as for longer-term fellowships. Tuition had been allowed the private school teachers for advanced studies, but no subsistence allowance had been given them, although for public school teachers, in addition to tuition, there was a subsistence allowance for both themselves and their dependents. This discrimination was amended to give equal assistance.

As of mid-1965, there was also pending a bill by Representative Zablocki, (Democrat, Wis.) to rectify the NDEA laws in the matter of grants for equipment. While outright grants of funds were given to public schools for special equipment, private schools were offered only loans at four percent interest. The amendment would place students in both public and independent schools on an equal basis as regards participation in NDEA benefits by extending the grants feature of Title III to independent education.

The Economic Opportunity Act of 1964 recognized private and religious schools as partners in the drive to provide equal educational opportunity for all Americans. Many of the programs outlined and financed under this Act included private school students and facilities on an equal basis with public institutions. Work-study programs were an important part of this joint participation, as were preschool education, adult and night school education, and enrichment programs. So this new legislation set another precedent for fair federal funds to independent students and institutions.

In 1965 the revolutionary, massive, $1.255 billion per year federal Elementary and Secondary Education Act of 1965 passed with some limited forms of aid to independent school students. While the bulk of the aid was directly available for those students who attended public schools, it was also stipulated that: "A local educational agency [public: such as a public school district] may receive a basic grant . . . upon its determination . . . that, to the extent consistent with the number of educationally deprived children in the school district of the local educational agency who attend nonpublic schools, such agency has made provision for including special educational services and arrangements [such as dual enrollment, educational radio and television, and mobile educational services] in which children can participate without full-time public school attendance."

The amount of the 1965 Federal Elementary and Secondary Education Act was almost the same as that of the Murray-Metcalf bill six years earlier. However, the 1965 law contained a "poverty" formula to channel the aid to public school districts and schools with students in lower economic brackets. The complicated formulae and provisions and interpretations of the new law made it difficult to correct those provisions which might exclude independent school students from its full benefits. However, CEF pledged a continued effort to bring about amendment and interpretation of the act to obtain equality and freedom for all without undue government control.

A brief outline of some provisions of the Act follows: *Title I:* The bulk of the aid (one billion dollars for fiscal 1966) comes under this title. All children aged 5 to 17 whose family income is less than $2,000 a year, or who are receiving ADC, are counted. One half the average amount per pupil spent on the education of students in its public schools each year is allowed for each such student. (Example: if the amount is $600, the allowance will be $300 per child). The funds are to go to the local public educational agency or school district. The "poverty" pupil's fellow students can benefit along with the pupil himself, especially with nonscheduled services. The allowance is made for the school or school district the student attends, rather than just for the use of individual students.

Some possible forms of assistance to independent school children under Title I include: Educational TV and radio equipment, even including the salaries of operators and instructors; "mobile" services, bookmobiles, educational exhibits and films, presentations of music, drama, and the arts, and the personnel and equipment involved; services of teachers, consultants, instructional secretaries, nurses, doctors, etc.; guidance services for both pupils and parents; supplemental health services and even food, shoes, and clothing if necessary; psychiatric and psychological advice and services; pupil transportation and bus service. "Dual enrollment," or "shared time," which is part-time attendance at public schools, is also suggested, though CEF does not encourage this arrangement, since it sets up a situation which effectively forces parents to send their children to public schools and to two different schools, whether or not they so wish.

Lesser forms of aid were provided under other titles. *Title II* provided for school, library and instructional materials, including textbooks, for the use of *all* children ($100 million per year for five years). *Title III* provided for supplemental educational centers and services to be available for *all* children, but with control and title vested solely in public school authorities ($100 million per year for five years). *Title IV* provided for educational research and training subsidization — open to all ($45 million per year, in addition to $25 million already allotted).

While the 1965 Federal Education act was a small beginning toward equal participation in federal tax funds for private school students, much still remains to be done.

The greatest contribution of the act was that it enunciated the principle of a fair share for all, and stimulated closer cooperation between public and private education on local levels.

Meanwhile substantial victories for educational freedom were obtained in several states. In Michigan, after the great accomplishments of securing a fair bus bill and a state scholarship program, CEF obtained passage of an extensive auxiliary services bill and a greatly expanded college scholarship measure. The latter, after being passed one year, was quadrupled the next.

Pennsylvania passed a fair bus bill in 1965 with the Governor's endorsement.

In New York, a $10 student textbook allowance was passed with a remarkable amount of interfaith support. The Orthodox Jewish community did a particularly enthusiastic job on behalf of the bill.

Wisconsin passed a college tuition grant bill which provided up to $500 per needy student for tuition in excess of $400.

Hawaii and Minnesota enacted fair bus laws. Minnesota also obtained drivers' training for all.

In Indiana and Iowa, fair bus measures were passed in one house but defeated in the other.

The Ohio State Federation of CEF made an amazing growth in chapters (300 in one year) and was victorious in the drive for a fair school bus bill.

As of mid-1965, 25 states had equal school bus rides for independent school children. At least six of these states were added since CEF was founded in 1959.

Many proposals had been made for tax relief for parents of private school students. Tax credits and income tax deductions were the most popular. A federal Higher Education Tax Credit bill failed of passage in the Senate in 1964 by only two votes, and that largely because of some higher echelon "arm-twisting" which changed Senator Humphrey's vote to a "no," in spite of the fact that he had been one of the bill's co-sponsors.

A unique proposal for fair aid for private students was initiated by Republican members of the House as an alternative to the Democratic administration's federal aid to education act. The Republican version would have allowed credits on income tax for parents of independent school children, and tuition grants of equal amounts for students whose parents were in such a low income bracket that they would not benefit from tax credits on income tax.

In the spirit of the goals of Citizens for Educational Freedom, a key to attainment of educational freedom in America would be tuition grants on state, local, and federal levels.

On the federal level, a bill embodying such a plan was introduced into Congress in 1962, by Representative James J. Delaney (Democrat, N. Y.). Subsequently, this bill was cosponsored by many other representatives. The Delaney "School Children's Assistance Act" (or, as it is sometimes called, the "Junior G.I. Bill") proposed, for a two-year period, "an annual grant for financial assistance for each child attending school, whether public or private. The grants would be for $20 a year. "In the case of children attending a public school, the grants would be issued to the local school agency. . . . In the case of a private school child, the grant would go to the parent or legal guardian, and would be honored for payment only when endorsed by the payee to the school of the pupil's attendance and then endorsed by an authorized official of that same institution."

As of mid-1965 CEF had 1010 chapters scattered across the country, with state federations in 13 states. It had some 150,000 members, distributed through all fifty states. Much more work was to be done to achieve the ideals expressed in the *United Nations Declaration of Human Rights:*

> The family is the natural and fundamental group unit of society and is entitled to protection by society and the state.
> Everyone has the right to education. Education shall be free, at least in the elementary and fundamental stages.
> Education shall be directed to the full development of the human personality and to the strengthening of respect for human rights and fundamental freedoms. It shall promote understanding, tolerance, friendship among all nations and racial or religious groups.
> Parents have a prior right to choose the kind of education that shall be given to their children.

Public Aid to Nonpublic Education in the United States: A Bibliography

Brother Edmond G. Drouin, F.I.C.*

The following list is selective. It is offered as an introductory reading guide to contemporary expressions of views on the fiscal relationship between government and nonpublic education in the United States and on the arguments of those who have been re-examining public policy regarding this matter.

Section "A" includes bibliographies and certain reference materials leading to a broad variety of sources. The materials in sections "B" and "C" represent a core of general reflections and legal considerations. (No absolute line of demarcation could be determined between the two categories.) Discussions of some specific issues are listed in "D," and a limited number of entries about applications in other countries are suggested in "E."

A. INTRODUCTORY REFERENCE MATERIAL

BEACH, FRED F., and WILL, ROBERT F. "State Constitutions and the Non-public School," in *The State and Nonpublic Schools* . . . (U. S. Office of Education, Misc., No. 28, 1958). Washington, D. C.: U. S. Government Printing Office, 1958. Pp. 15–21. Includes very concise summaries and tables.

BRICKMAN, WILLIAM W. "Chronological Outline of Church-State Relations in American Education," in William W. Brickman and Stanley Lehrer, eds. *Religion, Government and Education.* New York, N. Y.: Society for the Advancement of Education, 1961. Pp. 251–269.

---

* Brother Edmond G. Drouin is Librarian at Walsh College, Canton, Ohio, and the compiler of *The School Question; A Bibliography on Church-State Relationships in American Education: 1940–1960* (Washington, D. C.: Catholic University of America Press, 1963), 261 pages.

BURR, NELSON R. "Religion and Education," in James W. Smith and A. Leland Jamison, eds. *A Critical Bibliography of Religion in America* (Religion in American Life, Vol. 4). Princeton, N. J.: Princeton University Press, 1961. Pp. 654–677.

CONFREY, BURTON. *Secularism in American Education: Its History* (Catholic University of America, Educational Monographs, Vol. 6, No. 1). Washington, D. C.: Catholic University of America, 1931. 153 pp.

The reference tables on pages 124 and 125 provide a quick historical guide to state legislative material. The tables have been reprinted in William K. Dunn, *What Happened to Religious Education?* (Baltimore, Md.: John Hopkins Press, 1958). Pp. 6–9. N.B.: Column IV is entitled "Public Funds."

DROUIN, (BROTHER) EDMOND G., F.I.C. *The School Question; A Bibliography on Church-State Relationships in American Education: 1940–1960.* Washington, D. C.: Catholic University of America Press, 1963. 261 pp.

Includes over 1300 entries organized in twelve units and five appendices.

EMERSON, THOMAS I., and HABER, DAVID, eds. "Aid to Education," in *Political and Civil Rights in the United States; A Collection of Legal and Related Materials.* 2d Ed. Buffalo, N. Y.: Dennis & Co., 1958. Vol. II, pp. 1137–1157.

B. GENERAL REFLECTIONS

"ABC's of Fight Over Aid to Parochial Schools," *U. S. News & World Report,* 50:52–54 (April 3, 1961).

"Aid to Education," *Christianity and Crisis,* 22:78–95 (May 28, 1962).

A special issue. Includes articles by John C. Bennett, Maurice Rosenblatt, James E. McClellan, Robert W. Lynn, Thomas G. Sanders.

BARRETT, PATRICIA. "Public Funds for Catholic Schools," in *Religious Liberty and the American Presidency; A Study in Church-State Relations.* New York, N. Y.: Herder and Herder, 1963. Pp. 49–55.

Applications related to the presidential campaign and the election of President John F. Kennedy.

BENDINER, ROBERT, *Obstacle Course on Capitol Hill.* New York, N. Y.: McGraw-Hill, 1964. 231 pp.

Attempts to trace the fate of federal bills in Congress.

BENNETT, JOHN C. "Aid to Parochial Schools: Two Considerations," *Christianity and Crisis,* 21:61–62 (May 1, 1961).

———. "State Aid and the Church-Related College," *Christianity and Crisis,* 23:56–59 (April 15, 1962).

BLANSHARD, PAUL. "Tax Dollars for Church Schools?" in *Religion and the Schools, The Great Controversy.* Boston, Mass.: Beacon Press, 1963. Pp. 119–167.

Other expressions of the author's views were published in *American Freedom and Catholic Power* (2d Ed. Boston, Mass.: Beacon Press, 1958), *Communism, Democracy and Catholic Power* (Boston, Mass.: Beacon Press, 1951), and other works.

BLUM, VIRGIL C. *Freedom of Choice in Education.* New York, N. Y.: Macmillan, 1958. 230 pp. Revised edition (paper), New York: Paulist Press, 1963. 224 pp.

For other brief expressions, see "Educational Benefits Without Enforced Conformity," *Homiletic and Pastoral Review,* 58:27–33 (Oct., 1957). "Freedom of Choice in Schools," *U. S. News & World Report,* 43:109–112 (Oct. 25, 1957). Reply, G. L. Archer, 43:134 (Nov. 8, 1957).

BRICKMAN, WILLIAM W. "Public Aid to Jewish Day Schools," *Tradition, A Journal of Orthodox Jewish Thought,* 3:151–185 (Spring, 1961).

————. "Public Aid to Religious Schools?" *Religious Education,* 55:279–288 (July-Aug., 1960).

BRICKMAN, WILLIAM W., and LEHRER, STANLEY, eds. *Religion, Government and Education.* New York, N. Y.: Society for the Advancement of Education, Inc., 1961. 292 pp.

Ten essays written by nine contributors.

BURTON, PHILIP. "Public Funds for Public Schools Only," *Christian Century,* 78:415–417 (April 5, 1961).

BUTLER, PAUL. "Government Aid to the Private School," *Catholic Mind,* 59: 205–215 (May-June, 1961).

BUTTS, ROBERT F., and McCLUSKEY, NEIL, G., S.J. "Public Funds for Parochial Schools?" *Teachers College Record,* 62:49–62 (Oct., 1960).

CANAVAN, FRANCIS P., S.J. "Politics and Constitutional Law," *America,* 104: 804–805 (March 25, 1961).

CASS, JAMES. "Church, State, and School — 1961," *Saturday Review,* 44:50–51 (July 15, 1961). Letters to the Editor. 44:32–33 (Aug. 19, 1961).

"Church-related Schools," *The New Republic,* 148:4–5 (March 2, 1963). Continued in "Schools and Churches," 148:3–5 (March 23, 1963) and 148:4–6 (May 11, 1963). Discussion (correspondence). 148:31 (March 9, 1963); 30–31 (March 16, 1963); 28–31 (Apr. 6. 1963).

Note different view expressed earlier. "Parochial and Public," *The New Republic,* 144:3–5 (March 20, 1961). Correspondence. 144:23–24 (April 3, 1961).

"Church Schools Get Public Aid," *U. S. News & World Report,* 27:17–19 (Aug. 5, 1949).

"Control of Schools," *America,* 110:247–248 (Feb. 22, 1964).

CORNELL, FRANCIS G. "Federal Aid is a Religious Issue," *School Executive,* 72:47–49 (June, 1953). Comment. R. H. Schenk, S.J., 72:13 (Aug., 1953).

COSTANZO, JOSEPH F., S.J. "Ribicoff on Federal Aid to Education," *Thought, Fordham University Quarterly,* 36:485–536 (Winter, 1961).

See also "New York's Aid to Education Program," *Catholic World,* 193: 154–161 (June, 1961).

CREEGAN, ROBERT T. "Subsidized Pluralism," *School and Society,* 86:32–34 (Jan. 18, 1958).

CROSS, ROBERT D. "The Schools in Modern Society," *Catholic Mind,* 62:27–31 (Jan., 1964). Reprinted from *Columbia College Today* (Spring-Summer, 1963).

DEARSKIN, JAMES. "Very, Very Educational," *The New Republic,* 145:13–16 (Aug. 7, 1961).

DELANEY, JAMES J. "Interview With Congressman Delaney" (with Francis Canavan), *America,* 105:662–663 (Aug. 26, 1961).

DRINAN, ROBERT F., S.J., and HUNT, ROLFE LANIER. "Should Public Funds Aid Parochial Schools?" *Parents' Magazine,* 38:70, 71, 118, 120, 122 (Nov., 1963).

DUBUQUE, IOWA (Archdiocese). BUREAU OF EDUCATION. *Aid to Education and Parental Responsibility.* Dubuque, Iowa: Bureau of Education of the Archdiocese of Dubuque, 1963.

DUGGAN, MAE. "Shared Taxes — Not Shared Time," *Today's Family,* 39:4–11 (March, 1964). Same. *Social Justice Review,* 57:90–93 (June, 1964). Same, abridged. *Social Digest,* 7:102–104 (June-July, 1964).

EUSDEN, JOHN D. "Public Aid to What Schools? . . ." *Christian Century,* 78:872–874 (July 19, 1961).

EVANS, JOHN WHITNEY. "Catholics and the Blair Education Bill," *Catholic Historical Review,* 46:273–298 (Oct., 1960).

An historical study, 1880–1890.

"Federal Aid and Catholic Schools," *Commonweal,* 79:500–542 (Jan. 31, 1964).

Special issue. Includes articles by George N. Shuster, Neil G. McCluskey, S.J., Milton Himmelfarb, Martin Mayer, Virgin C. Blum, S.J., O'Neil C. D'Amour, Dean M. Kelley, John G. Deedy, Jr., Philip Scharper, Robert T. Francoeur.

Federal Aid for All the Schools. New York, N. Y.: America Press, 1962. 64 pp. Bibliography: pp. 62–64.

Editorials, articles, and opinions previously published in *America.*

"Federal Aid to Education: A Call to Action," *Christianity and Crisis,* 23: 189–191 (Oct. 28, 1963).

Statement signed by the Editorial Board of *Christianity and Crisis.* For an earlier declaration, see "Statement on Church and State," *Christianity and Crisis,* 8:90 (July 5, 1948).

FISHMAN, JOSHUA, compiler; BRICKMAN, WILLIAM W., and LEHRER, STANLEY, eds. "Subsidized Pluralism in American Education," *School and Society,* 87:245–268 (May 23, 1959).

A special supplement. Articles by Robert T. Creegan, Richard L. Plaut, Charles Donahue, Martin P. Schworowsky, Marshall Sklare.

FOUNTAIN, WINFIELD S. "A Plea for Public Support of Pluralism in America," *Phi Delta Kappan,* 44:415–418 (June, 1963). Reply. Robert P. Smawley, same issue, pp. 419–421.

FREEMAN, ROGER A. "Tax Credits and the School Aid Deadlock," *Catholic World*, 194:201–208 (Jan., 1962).

FRIEDMAN, MILTON. "The Role of Government in Education," in Robert A. Solo, ed. *Economics and the Public Interest*. New Brunswick, N. J.: Rutgers University Press, 1955. Pp. 123–144.

FUND FOR THE REPUBLIC. *Religion and the Schools* (Fund for the Republic Pamphlets). New York, N. Y.: The Fund, 1959. 96 pp.
   Essays by Robert Gordis, William Gorman, Frederick Ernest Johnson, Robert Lekachman.

GABEL, RICHARD J. *Public Funds for Church and Private Schools*. Washington, D. C.: Catholic University of America, 1937. xiv, 858 pp. Also issued as a private edition, Toledo, Ohio, 1937.

"Good Cause, Bad Argument" (Editorial), *Commonweal*, 78:35–36 (April 5, 1963). Discussion. 78:166–169 (May 3, 1963); 329–330 (June 14, 1963).
   A plea for careful argumentation.

HAGAN, JOHN R. "A Plea for Conciliation," *National Catholic Educational Association Bulletin* (Proceedings Issue), 36:56–75 (Aug., 1939).

HANDLIN, OSCAR, and MILLER, WILLIAM L. "Two Views on Aid to Catholic Schools," *Catholic World*, 193:216–224 (July, 1961). Discussion. 193:338–339 (Sept., 1961); 194:130–131 (Nov., 1961).

HARDIMAN, EDWARD J. "Federal Aid to Education — For some or For All?" *Temple Law Quarterly*, 23:227–231 (Jan., 1950).

HARVARD LAW SCHOOL FORUM. *Public Aid to Parochial Education; A Transcript of a Discussion on a Vital Issue*. Cambridge, Mass.: Harvard Law School Forum, Hastings Hall, 1951. 56 pp.

HEFFRON, EDWARD J. "The Protestant, the Catholic, and School Taxes," *Catholic Digest*, 13:6–9 (April, 1949).

HERBERG, WILL. "Justice for Religious Schools," *America*, 98:190–193 (Nov. 16, 1957). Discussion. Nathan A. Perilman and W. Herberg, 98:426–428 (Jan. 11, 1958).

———. "Religion and Education in America," in James W. Smith and A. Leland Jamison, eds., *Religious Perspectives in American Culture* (Religion in American Life, Vol. 2). Princeton, N. J.: Princeton University Press, 1961. Pp. 11–15.

HOLEBROOK, CLYDE A. "Sectarianism, Pluralism and Tax-supported Institutions," *Christian Scholar*, 45:290–300 (Winter, 1962).

HUTCHINS, ROBERT M. "The Future of the Wall," *America*, 108: 146–148 (Jan. 26, 1963).
   Address delivered at a Conference on Church-State questions at the University of Chicago. (Conference papers published in Dallin H. Oaks, ed. *The Wall Between Church and State*. Chicago, Ill.: Chicago University Press, 1963.)

————. "A Liberal Calls for Aid to Church Schools" (Speaking Out), *Saturday Evening Post,* 236:6, 8 (June 8, 1963). Discussion. *Christian Century,* 80:819–820 (June 26, 1963); 1141 (Sept. 18, 1963). *America,* 108:874–875 (June 22, 1963).

JOHNSON, ALVIN W., and YOST, FRANK H. "Public Aid to Sectarian Schools," in *Separation of Church and State in the United States.* Minneapolis, Minn.: University of Minnesota Press, 1948. Pp. 100–114.

JOHNSON, FREDERICK ERNEST. "Federal Aid to Education," *Christianity and Crisis,* 21:46, 47 (April 3, 1961).

JORGENSON, LLOYD P. "The Birth of a Tradition," *Phi Delta Kappan,* 44:407–414 (June, 1963).

KAUPER, PAUL G. "Limited Federal Aid For Religious Schools," *School and Society,* 90:251–252 (Summer, 1962).

KERWIN, JEROME G. "A Political Scientist Looks at the Relationship of Government and Religious Education," *National Catholic Educational Association Bulletin,* 45:6–14 (May, 1949).

KLINKHAMER, (SISTER) MARIE CAROLYN. "The Blaine Amendment of 1875: Private Motives for Political Action," *Catholic Historical Review,* 42: 15–49 (April, 1956).

LA NOUE, GEORGE R. *Public Funds for Parochial Schools? A Resource Document* (Studies of Church and State). New York, N. Y.: National Council of the Churches of Christ in the U. S. A., 1963. 47 pp. Comment. *Christian Century,* 80:899 (July 17, 1963). *Commonweal,* 78:184 (May 10, 1963).

————. "Religious Schools and 'Secular' Subjects," *Harvard Educational Review,* 32:255–291 (Summer, 1962). Same, condensed, with title "The National Defense Education Act and 'Secular' Subjects," *Phi Delta Kappan,* 43:380–387 (June, 1962).

    Replies and Discussion. George E. Reed, *The Catholic Lawyer,* 8:197–205 (Summer, 1962). Edward P. McCarren, *Catholic Mind,* 61:20–22 (Oct., 1963). Charles M. Whelan, *America,* 107:399–401 (June 16, 1962). *America,* 107: 443–444 (June 30, 1962); 972 (Nov. 3, 1962): 1198, 1201 (Dec. 8, 1962).

LAWLER, JUSTUS G. "Federal Aid and Freedom: Role of the Religious School," *Commonweal,* 75:451–454 (Jan. 26, 1962).

LEVINE, DANIEL U. "Federal Aid for Nonpublic Education: Design for Decimating Public Schools," *Phi Delta Kappan,* 43:388–389 (June, 1962).

LIEBSON, BERNARD, and SHUSTER, GEORGE N. "Public and Private Education," *The American Scholar,* 19:217–226 (April, 1950).

LIPPMANN, WALTER. "Walter Lippmann Interviewed by Charles Collingwood," *The New Republic,* 148:15–18 (May 11, 1963).

    Text of part of a television conversation over "CBS Reports," May 1, 1963. Includes remarks about church-related schools and federal aid, pp. 17–18.

McCLUSKEY, NEIL G., S.J. "How Much State Support?" *America,* 101:722–728 (Sept. 19, 1959).

McCluskey, Neil G., S.J., and Pfeffer, Leo. "Federal Aid for Private and Parochial Schools?" *Current History,* 41:70–81 (Aug., 1961).

McDowell, John B. "Federal Aid" (Editorial), *Catholic Educator,* 32:537–539, 576 (Feb., 1962).

McGarry, Daniel D. "The Case for Governmental Aid to Independent Schools," *Social Justice Review,* 54:112–115, 123 (July-Aug., 1961); "Objections to Government Aid to Parochial Schools Answered," 54:155–157 (Sept., 1961); "Independent School Aid and the Constitutional Issue," 54:189–193 (Oct., 1961).

McManus, William E. "Federal Aid for All School Children," *Catholic Educational Review,* 43:193–202 (April, 1945).

Malloy, John F. "How to Talk About Federal Aid" (with editorial comment), *America,* 105:421–423 (June 10, 1961).

Moehlman, Conrad H. "Federal Aid to Education?" *Christian Century,* 64:106–108 (Jan. 22, 1947).

Murray, John C., S.J. "Is It Justice? The School Question Today," in *We Hold These Truths, Catholic Reflections on the American Proposition.* New York, N. Y.: Sheed and Ward, 1960, Pp. 143–154.

National Catholic Welfare Conference. "Federal Aid in Education; Statement Before a Subcommittee of the House Committee in Education and Labor, June 3, 1949," *Catholic Mind,* 47:630–640 (Oct., 1949).
Statement made by Father William E. McManus for NCWC.

Nelson, Claud D. "Proposal on the School-Aid Impasse," *Christian Century,* 78:448–450 (April 12, 1961).

O'Neill, James Milton. "Federal Aid to Religion is Legal," *The Sign,* 41:20–22 (Nov., 1961).

———. *Religion and Education Under the Constitution.* New York, N. Y.: Harper, 1949. 388 pp.

O'Toole, Thomas J. "School Aid — A Catholic View," *The New Republic,* 144:13–15 (April 10, 1961).

"Public Aid to Private Schools? Catholic and Protestant Views," *U. S. News & World Report,* 32:102–105 (Dec. 2, 1955). "More on Aid to Schools," 39:121–122 (Dec. 16, 1955).

Regan, Richard J., S.J. "Public Support and the Parochial Schools," in *American Pluralism and the Catholic Conscience.* New York, N. Y.: Macmillan, 1963. Pp. 104–132.

Ribicoff, Abraham. "A Senator's Plan to End Religious Issue in School Aid," *U. S. News & World Report,* 54:100–102 (June 3, 1963).
From an address in the *Congressional Record* (daily ed.), 109:8500–8504 (May 20, 1963).

"Roadblock to Federal Aid," *National Education Association Journal,* 38: 494–495 (Oct., 1949). Reply. William E. McManus, "Roadblock to Federal Aid," *America,* 82:95–97 (Oct. 29, 1949).

"School Aid and Religion" (Editorial), *Life,* 50:46 (March 17, 1961).

STOKES, ANSON PHELPS. *Church and State in the United States.* New York, N. Y.: Harper, 1950. 3 vols.

THAYER, VIVIAN TROW. *The Attack Upon the American Secular School* (Beacon Studies in Freedom and Power). Boston, Mass.: Beacon Press, 1951. Especially pp. 100–141.

THEISEN, SYLVESTER P. "Religion and the Free Society," *Social Order,* 13: 5–17 (March); 25–37 (April, 1963).

THOMAS, MAURICE J., and BLUM, VIRGIL C., S.J. "Voluntary Religious Isolation — Another School Segregation Story" (Thomas); "Academic Freedom and Tax Support for Independent Education" (Blum), *Phi Delta Kappan,* 40:347–358 (June, 1959).

"Three Thoughtful Opinions on Aid to Schools" (Virgil C. Blum, Kenneth B. Keating, C. W. Kiewiet), *America,* 105:193–194 (April 22, 1961). "Opinion Worth Noting," *America,* 105:333–335 (May 20, 1961).

WARD, LEO R. *Federal Aid to Private Schools.* Westminster, Md.: Newman Press, 1964.

WIDEN, IRWIN. "Federal Aid and the Church School Issue," *Phi Delta Kappan,* 36:271–276 (April, 1955).

WILLIAMS, JOSEPH C., and CARR, JAMES. "Forum: Should the Federal Government Aid Parochial Schools?" *Forum,* 111:100–106 (Feb., 1949).

C. LEGAL-CONSIDERATIONS

"Catholic Schools and Public Money," *Yale Law Journal,* 50:917–927 (March, 1941).

CORWIN, EDWARD S. "The Supreme Court as the National School Board," *Law and Contemporary Problems,* 14:3–22 (Winter, 1949). Revised from *Thought,* 23:665–683 (Dec., 1948).

COSTANZO, JOSEPH F., S.J. "Federal Aid to Education and Religious Liberty," *University of Detroit Law Journal,* 36:1–46 (Oct., 1958).

———. *This Nation Under God. Church, State and Schools in America.* New York, N. Y.: Herder & Herder, 1964. 448 pp.

CUSHMAN, ROBERT F. "Public Support of Religious Education in American Constitutional Law," *Illinois Law Review,* 45:333–356 (July-Aug., 1950).

DRINAN, ROBERT F., S.J. "Can Public Funds be Constitutionally Granted to Private Schools?" *Social Order,* 13:18–31, 48 (March, 1963); Discussion. 13:44 (May, 1963).

————. *Religion, the Courts and Public Policy*. New York, N. Y.: McGraw-Hill Book Co., 1963. 261 pp. (see especially pp. 116–201).

"Federal Aid to Religious Schools," *Notre Dame Lawyer*, 37:285–322 (March, 1962).
   Articles by James O'Meara, Paul M. Butler, Alfred L. Scanlan, Leo Pfeffer.

GRISWOLD, ERWIN N. "Absolute is in the Dark — A Discussion of the Approach of the Supreme Court to Constitutional Questions," *Utah Law Review*, 8:167–182 (Summer, 1963).

HAYES, JOHN C. "The Constitutional Permissibility of the Participation of Church-related Schools in the Administration's Proposed Program of Massive Federal Aid to Education," *De Paul Law Review*, 11:161–182 (Spring-Summer, 1962).

HENLE, ROBERT J., S.J. "American Principles and Religious Schools," *Saint Louis University Law Journal*, 3:237–251 (Spring, 1955).

KATZ, WILBER G. *Religion and American Constitutions*. Evanston, Ill.: Northwestern University Press, 1964. 124 pp.

————. "Religion and Law in America," in James W. Smith and A. Leland Jameson, eds., *Religious Perspectives in American Culture* (Religion in American Life, Vol. 2). Princeton, N. J.: Princeton University Press, 1961. Pp. 53–80 (especially pp. 54–68).

————. "Freedom of Religion and State Neutrality," *University of Chicago Law Review*, 20:426–440 (Spring, 1953).

KAUPER, PAUL G. "Church and State: Cooperative Separatism," in *Civil Liberties and the Constitution*. Ann Arbor, Mich.: University of Michigan Press, 1962. Pp. 3–51 (especially pp. 39–51). Previously published in *Michigan Law Review*, 60:1–40 (Nov., 1961).

————. "The Constitutionality of Aid to Parochial Schools," *Phi Delta Kappan*, 43:331–336 (May, 1962). Followed by an opposing opinion by C. Stanley Lowell, 43:338–343 (May, 1962).

KENEALLY, WILLIAM J., S.J. "Equal Justice Under the Law — Tax Aid to Education," *Catholic Lawyer*, 7:183–202, 242 (Summer, 1961).

KLINK, VAL R. "Governmental Aid to Non-profit Religious Schools and to the Children Attending Them," *Rocky Mountain Law Review*, 33:355–363 (April, 1961).

MCMAHON, PAUL B. "State Aid to Education and the Doctrine of Separation of Church and State," *Georgetown Law Journal*, 36:631–647 (May, 1948).

MANNING, LEONARD F. "Aid to Education — Federal Fashion," *Fordham Law Review*, 29:495–524 (February, 1961).

MITCHELL, WILLIAM A. "Religion and Federal Aid to Education," *Law and Contemporary Problems*, 14:113–143 (Winter, 1949).

MURRAY, JOHN C., S.J. "Law or Prepossession," *Law and Contemporary Problems*, 14:23–43 (Winter, 1949).

NATIONAL CATHOLIC WELFARE CONFERENCE, LEGAL DEPARTMENT. "The Constitutionality of the Inclusion of Church-related Schools in Federal Aid to Education," *Georgetown Law Journal*, 50:397–455 (Winter, 1961). Also issued as a reprint.

Summaries: "Latest in the Fight Over Aid to Schools, A Catholic Report on School Subsidy and the Law," *U. S. News & World Report*, 51:67–69 (Dec. 25, 1961). Reynolds C. Seitz, "Federal Aid Is Constitutional. An Analysis of the NCWC Study," *Catholic School Journal*, 62:23–25 (March, 1962).

NORTH, ARTHUR A., S.J. "An Exposition and Analysis of Policy Arguments Against Federal Aid to Parochial Schools," *Catholic Lawyer*, 9:43–56 (Winter, 1963).

OAKS, DALLIN H., ed. *The Wall Between Church and State*. Chicago, Ill.: Chicago University Press, 1963. 179 pp.

Articles by Robert F. Drinan, S.J., Harold E. Fey, Murray A. Gordon, Robert M. Hutchins, Paul G. Kauper, Philip B. Kurland, Monrad G. Paulsen.

PFEFFER, LEO. *Church, State and Freedom*. Boston, Mass.: Beacon Press, 1953. 675 pp. (especially pp. 424–494).

REED, GEORGE E. "The 'Permeation' Issue in Federal Aid to Education," *The Catholic Lawyer*, 8:197–205 (Summer, 1962).

SLOUGH, M. C., and MCANANY, PATRICK D. "Government Aid to Church-related Schools: An Analysis," *Kansas Law Review*, 11:35–75 (Oct., 1962).

STOUT, WILLIAM D. "The Establishment of Religion Under the Constitution," *Kentucky Law Review*, 37:220–239 (March, 1949).

SUTHERLAND, ARTHUR E. "Does the Constitution Really Ban U. S. Aid to Parochial Schools? A Harvard Law Professor Gives Congress an Answer," *U. S. News & World Report*, 50:109–112 (April 3, 1961).

Excerpts from a letter to Representative John W. McCormack, *Congressional Record* (daily edition), 107:A2026–A2029 (March 22, 1961); Errata correction (daily edition), 107:6243 (April 25, 1961).
A letter to Senator Wayne Morse was published in *Constitutionality of Federal Aid to Education in Its Various Aspects* (87th Congress, 1st Session, Senate Document No. 29). Pp. 52–62.

U. S. DEPARTMENT OF HEALTH, EDUCATION, AND WELFARE. "Memorandums Submitted by the Secretary of Health, Education and Welfare" (March 28, 1961), in *Constitutionality of Federal Aid to Education in Its Various Aspects* (87th Congress, 1st Session, Senate Document No. 29). Washington, D. C.: U. S. Government Printing Office, 1961. Pp. 1–48.

Text also published in *Congressional Record* (permanent edition), 107:5282–5397 (March 30, 1961), and (in part) in *Georgetown Law Journal*, 50:349–396 (Winter, 1961). Summary. *U. S. News & World Report*, 50:100–101 (April 10, 1961).
For other views, see Charles M. Whelan, "The President's Brief on Federal Aid," *America*, 105:140–141 (April 15, 1961). National Catholic Welfare Conference, *Georgetown Law Journal*, 50:397–455 (Winter, 1961).

VAN ALSTYNE, WILLIAM W. "Constitutional Separation of Church and State: The Quest for a Coherent Position," *American Political Science Review*, 57:865–882 (Dec., 1963).

D. SOME SPECIAL ISSUES

"And Now, School Buses; Transportation to Parochial Schools," *Commonweal*, 65:651–653 (March 29, 1957). Discussion. 66:129 (May 3); 66: 233–235 (May 31, 1957).

BENNETT, JOHN C. "The School Bus Issue," *Christianity and Crisis*, 17:49–50 (April 29, 1957). Comment. *Catholic Mind*, 55:356–357 (July-Aug., 1957). Reprinted from *The Pilot*, Boston, Mass.

BLUM, VIRGIL C., S.J. "Religious Liberty and the Religious Garb," *University of Chicago Law Review*, 22:875–888 (Summer, 1955). Followed by "Religious Garb in the Public Schools: A Study in Conflicting Liberties," 22:888–895 (Summer, 1955).

BOYER, WILLIAM W. "Public Transportation of Parochial-school Pupils," *Wisconsin Law Review*, 1952:64–90 (Jan., 1952).

BRYSON, JOSEPH R. "Mending the Breach," *Christian Century*, 65:649–651 (June 30, 1948). About school buses.

CARY, KENNETH W. "Protestant Strategy in California," *Christianity Today*, 3:6–8 (Oct. 27, 1958). On tax exemption.

"Catholicism and Public Schools in New Mexico," *Utah Law Review*, 3:467–480 (Fall, 1953). On the religious garb in Tax-supported schools.

CHAMBERS, MERRITT M. "Textbooks in Nonpublic Schools," *Nation's Schools*, 29:53–54 (Jan., 1942).

COSGROVE, JOHN E., and FLATTERY, EDWARD J. "Constitutional Law — Transportation of Parochial-school Pupils," *Notre Dame Lawyer*, 22:192–200 (Jan., 1947).

DECKER, GEORGE C. "NDEA Loans to Private Schools," *School Life*, 45: 19–21 (April, 1963).

DUGGAN, MAY, and DUGGAN, MARTIN. "Must We Miss the Bus?" *Ave Maria*, 86:8–11 (Sept. 14, 1957).

"Exception of Educational, Philanthropic and Religious Institutions from State Real Property Taxes," *Harvard Law Review*, 64:288–299 (Dec., 1950).

GARBER, LEE O. "If Nuns Teach in Public Schools, Kentucky Court Ruling Permits them to Wear Religious Garb," *Nation's Schools*, 59:81–82 (March, 1957). See earlier articles. *Nation's Schools*, 49:69–71 (Feb., 1952); 53:61–62 (June, 1954).

HARTNETT, ROBERT C., S.J. "Why the Furor About Buses?" *America*, 82: 466–468 (Jan. 21, 1950).

HEFFRON, EDWARD J. "Supreme Court Oversight," *Commonweal*, 46:9–11 (Apr. 18, 1947). The school-bus question.

KILLOUGH, LUCY W. "Exemptions to Educational, Philanthropic and Religious Organizations," in Tax Institute, *Tax Exemptions* (Tax Policy League Symposium), by James W. Martin, Lucy W. Killough, and others. New York, N. Y.: Tax Policy League, 1939. Pp. 23–38.

KING, LAWRENCE T. "Bigotry in California," *Commonweal*, 69:514–516 (Feb. 13, 1959). Tax exemption.

McEACHERN, MARGARET. "Nuns Carry on in North Dakota," *Catholic Digest*, 13:93–96 (March, 1949). Religious garb in tax-supported schools.

McGARRY, DANIEL D. "Scholarships in Seven States: The New Look in Higher Education," *Social Justice Review*, 56:19–21 (April, 1963).

―――. "State Scholarships for Higher Education?", *College and University Journal*, Vol. 4, No. 2: 33–37 (Spring, 1955).

McLEAN, W. MAURICE. "Public School Buses for Private and Parochial School Pupils?" *School and Society*, 74:181–182 (Sept. 22, 1951).

McMANUS, WILLIAM E. "School Lunch Legislation," *Catholic Educational Review*, 44:200–205 (April, 1946). See also *Catholic School Journal*, 46:226–227; 231–232 (Sept. 1946).

―――. "Non-Sectarian Bus," *Columbia*, 26:5, 17, 18 (April, 1947). Also published separately. Washington, D. C.: National Catholic Welfare Conference, 1947. 13 pp.

"Now Will Protestants Awake?" *Christian Century*, 64:262–264 (Feb. 26, 1947). Abridged. *Time*, 49:94 (March 3, 1947). The school-bus question.

O'BRIEN, JOHN A. "Equal Rights for All Children," *Christian Century*, 65:473–476 (May 19, 1948). Discussion. 65:655 (June 30, 1948). The school-bus question.

"The Opposition to the Oregon Free Textbook Bill," *The Jurist*, 2:363–370 (Oct., 1942). Concerning court action on this issue, see "Textbooks for Parochial Schools; The Dickman Decision," *Catholic Lawyer*, 8:70–73 (Winter, 1962). *Christian Century*, 79:1281 (Oct. 24, 1962).

PAULSEN, MONRAD G. "Preferment of Religious Institutions in Tax and Labor Legislation," *Law and Contemporary Problems*, 14:144–159 (Winter, 1949).

PAWLOWSKY, JOSEPH T. "Validity of Salary Payments to Teachers Wearing Religious Garb While Teaching," *Notre Dame Lawyer*, 16:148–150 (Jan., 1941).

POWELL, THOMAS R. "Public Rides to Private Schools," *Harvard Educational Review*, 7:73–84 (Spring, 1947).

POWELL, THEODORE. *The School Bus Law; A Case Study in Education, Religion and Politics.* Middletown, Conn.: Wesleyan University Press, 1960. xi, 334 pp.

"Public Funds for Sectarian Schools," *Harvard Law Review,* 60:793–800 (May, 1947). The school-bus question.

REED, GEORGE E. "The School Bus Challenge," *The Catholic Lawyer,* 5:99–105 (Spring, 1959).

"Relation of Freedom of Religion to Loan of Textbooks to Private Schools," *Bill of Rights Review,* 1:307–310 (Summer, 1941).

SHANAHAN, PATRICK E. "Guides for School Bus Legislation," *Catholic School Journal,* 61:85–88 (Feb., 1961).

E. APPLICATIONS IN OTHER COUNTRIES

BENABARRE, BENIGNO, O.S.B. *Public Funds for Private Schools in a Democracy; Theory and Practice in Fifty-one Countries.* Manila, Philippine Islands: M.C.S. Enterprises, 1958. 325 pp.

BRICKMAN, WILLIAM W. "Church, State and School in International Perspective," in William W. Brickman and Stanley Lehrer, eds. *Religion, Government and Education.* New York, N. Y.: Society for the Advancement of Education, 1961. Pp. 144–251.

DRINAN, ROBERT F., S.J. "Ten Nations Discuss Freedom of Education," *America,* 93:526–528, 530 (Sept. 3, 1955).

DUNNE, GEORGE H. "The School Question Viewed From Abroad," *Commonweal,* 74:247–250 (June 2, 1961).

HARTNETT, ROBERT C., S.J., ed. *The Right to Educate; Democracy and Religious Education — A Symposium.* New York, N. Y.: America Press, 1949. 48 pp.

KUEHNELT-LEDDIHN, ERIC M. VON. "A European View: Church-State Relations . . . ," *Commonweal,* 71:255–258 (Nov. 27, 1959).

MAUD, SIR JOHN P. R. "Freedom and Authority in Education," *Teachers College Record,* 53:150–167 (Dec., 1951). The situation in Great Britain.)

RYAN, EDMUND G., S.J. "France Supports Catholic Schools," *Catholic Educational Review,* 60:163–173 (March, 1962).

SISSONS, CHARLES B. *Church and State in Canadian Education; An Historical Study.* Toronto, Ont., Can.: The Ryerson Press, 1959. x, 414 pp.

VAN DER VELDT, JAMES H. "The Educational System in the Netherlands," *Catholic Educational Review,* 48:455–470 (Sept., 530–545; Oct., 1950).

Index